The
Imaginary Research Algorithm

A Formula for Success in Research

Second Edition

Kevin L. Potter

Potter Analytics LLC　　　　Los Angeles

The Imaginary Research Algorithm
A Formula for Success in Research
Kevin L. Potter

Potter Analytics LLC
400 Continental Blvd.
6th Floor
El Segundo, CA 90245
www.potteranalytics.com

ISBN: 978-0-9843412-2-1

Table of Contents

Introduction..v

Chapter 1...1

Chapter 2..29

Chapter 3..43

Chapter 4..63

Chapter 5..73

Chapter 6..87

Chapter 7...109

Chapter 8...121

Chapter 9...143

Chapter 10..165

Appendix A..187

Appendix B..209

Introduction

The Imaginary Research Algorithm is a human solution for the process of locating data in informational databases. Whether the database is at a local library or through a popular website, *The Imaginary Research Algorithm* will assist in an efficient and effective manner to ultimately create better researchers in an information age where information overload is a reality. Sifting through information is a critical skill that must be sharpened and polished through cognitive (mental) effort. Certain technologies are leading people down a challenging path that are making them more and more dependent on technology and less dependent on their mental capabilities. Not to paint technology with a broad negative brush, but the need for balance between cognition and technology is very necessary.

The Imaginary Research Algorithm is dedicated to students of all ages, but especially to future secondary students who are potentially growing up with the Internet as research option number one. There is nothing wrong in general about the "Internet Age", but specifically, students are beginning to allow databases and search engines to think for them. This is one of the negative aspects of the Internet. *The Imaginary Research Algorithm* was developed to cure some of the challenges created by an information-oriented society.

A.) Information Overload
B.) Commercial Media Filtering (Internet Specific issue)
C.) Lack of Thought or Reflection
D.) No Digestion Just Regurgitation

A.) Information Overload—is the availability of too much information where it can become extremely difficult to sort through the number of possibilities. For example, an internet search result page can easily list over 20,000 results. It is very time consuming and energy draining to look through every page and link. This would be considered overload.

B.)   Commercial Media Filtering is an internet specific issue. If you are using the Internet to research, commercials are hard to avoid completely. The Internet is filled with ecommerce web sites. Since I first started working on *The Imaginary Research Algorithm*, search engines have become more and more skillful at finding information over the years. You don't necessarily have to sift through unnecessary links as much. (In other words, access to more instant answers.) Major search engines will almost always be tied to advertising and marketing whether directly or indirectly. Ecommerce is a part of the Internet. Therefore, avoiding commercials during research is the issue.

C.)   Lack of Thought and Reflection—is the missing link of the pre-research process. For example, here are four different initial research paths. The topic is "deforestation".

1.) A person can guide the research for information by being prepared to search for specific terms related on the topic. This method can save time and energy. For example, if a person needs to know about the "effects of deforestation", then this person can save time by being specific. The more specific, the more time you can potentially save. This is a more assertive approach that integrates with *The Imaginary Research Algorithm*.
2.) A person can be led by the search results (database results). In this scenario, a person can find information on "deforestation", then eventually narrow down to "effects of deforestation". Please note, this could be effective when people do not know anything about the topic.
3.) A person can guide the search initially with keywords. Then, he or she can gather additional keywords from his or her initial research. For instance, as the person initially reads about the "effects of deforestation"; other search keywords can be used in databases to find additional results.
4.) A person can be led by search results, initially. Then, he or she would gather additional keywords. For example, the student needs information on the "effects of deforestation". He or she notices that the word "rainforest" could be used as a keyword in the next search.

D.)   No digestion Just Regurgitation—is the aftereffect of research and the digital information age. With so much information out there, the world's junior researchers (students) are drowning in the world wide waters. In many instances, there is not enough time to gain mastery or fluency. Modern students use the Internet as a supplemental brain because the Internet provides instant answers. On an unconscious level or subconscious level, why should a student place importance on remembering certain facts and figures if the Internet will play the role of their auxiliary memory system? The reason, teachers assign research assignments, is to have students build mental structures upon mental structures until students gain fluency or mastery in a subject. Furthermore, research includes the thinking process that involves connecting the dots between gathered information. Technological progress creates positive benefits and negative challenges. It is imperative to establish new methods and devices to counteract the negative aspects of web research.

With the challenges of the Internet for research identified, it is time to identify the goals of *The Imaginary Research Algorithm*
    a.) To stimulate cognitive processes for research
    b.) To create a research focal point(s)
    c.) To improve research outcomes
    d.) To build an improved researcher

The Imaginary Research Algorithm creates an environment that is beneficial to students for research. a.) Students will receive a stimulating jumpstart to their initial research by using *The Imaginary Research Algorithm.* b.) The Algorithm assists students in determining where they wish to focus their research using specific search keywords. c.) Unlike, instances where a student would search with the general topic such as "deforestation" without any key words. *The Imaginary Research Algorithm* improves research outcomes by providing selective searches or specific keyword searches such as "effects of deforestation". d.) The first three steps are a process that causes students to
    1.)   reflect on the different aspects of the research topic before searching
    2.)   focus on subtopics of interest for research assignment
    3.)   minimize the number of search results
The more you use *The Imaginary Research Algorithm*; the better, you will become at researching topics.

Imaginary Research Algorithm Defined

In essence, *The Imaginary Research Algorithm* assists users in the process of research, not act of research. Whether you chose to use *The Imaginary Research Algorithm* as a Performance Support System (book) or Electronic Performance Support System (software*) it will help users concentrate on their topic and stimulate search options during the research process. *The Imaginary Research Algorithm* expedites the research process on any search instrument or platform.

What is an Algorithm?
This is a very complex question and subject within itself, but this book will keep it simple by using this definition of algorithm in general.

An algorithm is a recipe. Reflect on the word recipe and you have your answer. That's right a set of step-by-step instructions that produce something.

Algorithms or "recipes" find their instructions used in numerous fields and are not limited to Mathematics and Computer Science. For example, veterinarians, philosophers, scientists, businessmen, and students use algorithms. When you perform the instructions of an algorithm or recipe, you should have an end product or result.

What is Research?
Research can take on many different definitions. For primary and secondary students, research can sometimes be seen as an activity, act, or task that requires gathering information only. *The Imaginary Research Algorithm* stimulates the missing cognitive pieces in modern day research for students. It helps people locate information through pre-targeting subtopics, thinking about the gathered data, and reflecting on the research topic. *The Imaginary Research Algorithm* forces users to actively think about research topics and construct mental images. The key word is to actively think about the research topic versus a passive approach. Research in relation to *The Imaginary Research Algorithm* is a process or a collection of acts.

*software not included with book

What is imaginary?
Imaginary can be used relative to reality or Mathematics.
Imaginary relates to imagination. Imagination is the ability to create mental images. *The Imaginary Research Algorithm* is designed to stimulate the creation of mental images. It is these mental images that are shifted, sorted, formed, deformed, dissected, and rearranged in the mind to demystify new information. Furthermore, it is a continuous process where old data mixes with new information. But, the word "Imaginary" can also relate to numbers called imaginary numbers. The "Imaginary" in Imaginary Research Algorithm stands for

An expression that transforms tacit knowledge into explicit knowledge which is a difficult feat or a figment of the author's imagination

In other words, *The Imaginary Research Algorithm* transfers the author's research skills, tactics and knowledge to the user in a quick, efficient, effective, systematic manner. This book contains one algorithmic flowchart, and multiple analogous expressions of the Algorithm. Section One covers the flowchart expression of *The Imaginary Research Algorithm* while Section Two covers the nine analogous expressions of the Algorithm. Furthermore, Section Two provides additional practice to students wishing to gain improved research skills. Users will see the ease of use with the Algorithm. In fact, if a person knows how to use a basic flowchart then they will be able to operate *The Imaginary Research Algorithm* from the start. This book explains the logic and capabilities of each segment of the Algorithm. *The Imaginary Research Algorithm* creates a thinking environment by nudging users to take a moment and think about their search needs. Furthermore, this book encourages reinforcement through reflective exercises. In conclusion, *The Imaginary Research Algorithm* stirs up the cognitive processes and builds better researchers.

SECTION
I

Chapter

1

How The Imaginary Research Algorithm Works

First, take a look at the image of *The Imaginary Research Algorithm* on *page 2*. It is a flowchart that visually describes the algorithm for search. I will provide detailed information on each step. Furthermore, I will demonstrate numerous examples of the Algorithm in action. Lastly, you will have reinforcement opportunities, so you can reflect on the benefits of researching with the algorithm. The objective of the last step is to have users continually construct their own mental images.

This Algorithm was designed to be user-friendly for most ages, but certain redundant compromises were made. Since, words can take different states and meaning. The user must stay aware of their goal. The user must stay aware of their goal. The user must stay aware of their goal. This sentence cannot be said enough. For instance, tennis was an idea that eventually became an invention/creation that can be seen as a process in certain circumstances. Not to mention, it is an activity. One of the keys to using *The Imaginary Research Algorithm* is to stay focused on the research topic.

This is not to say you cannot wander and seek knowledge for the sake of knowledge. In fact, one of the positives of *The Imaginary Research Algorithm* is that it provides cognitive sparks to search sessions in a library or through a website with search capabilities.

Imaginary Research Algorithm

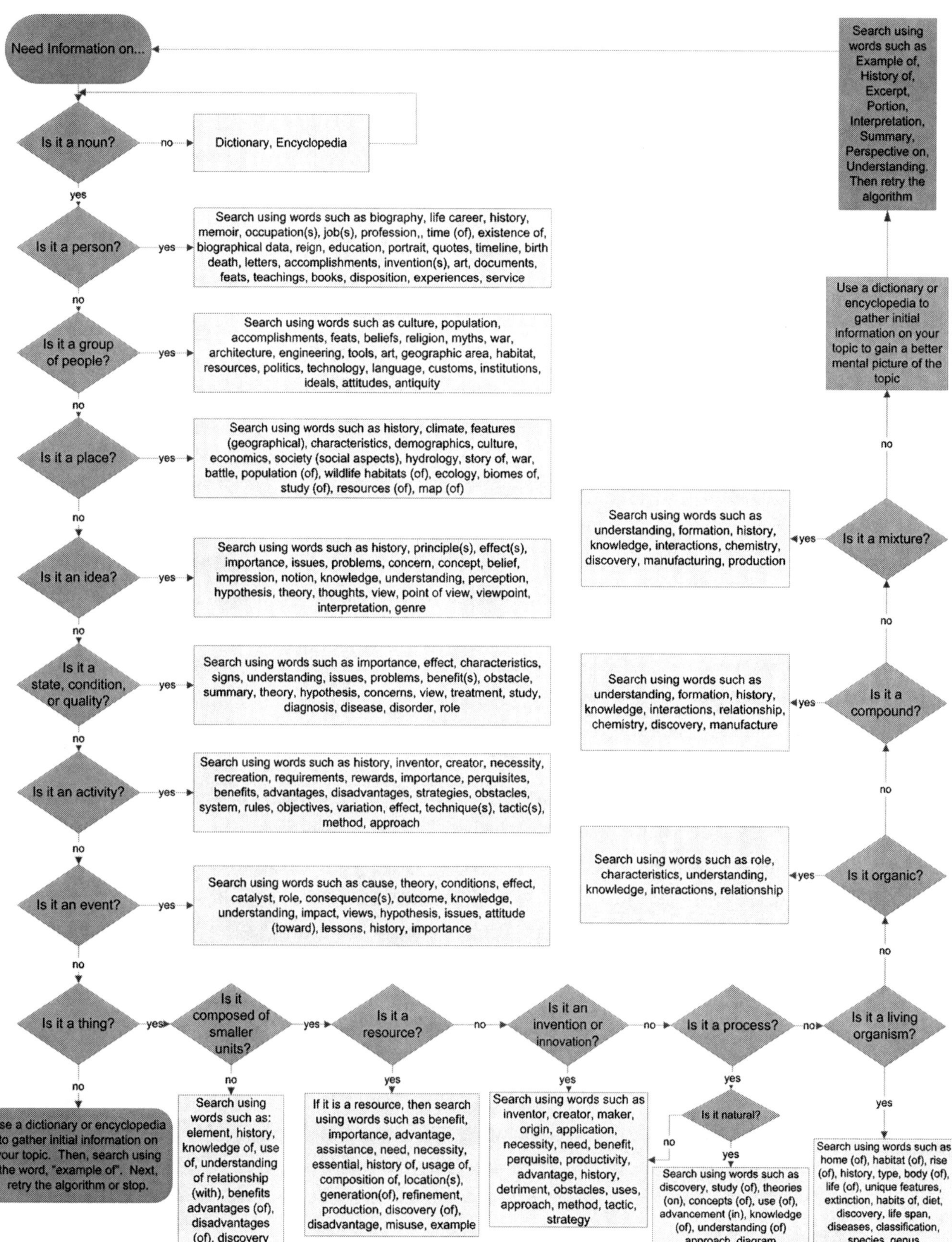

Before, we jump into using *The Imaginary Research Algorithm.* I should state a few things that this Algorithm will not help you with. 1) Commercial products can be seen in two lights. If you are looking to purchase an item or simply window shop online then *The Imaginary Research Algorithm* will only help you to a certain extent. It may just be easier to go to a major online store or vendor. However, if you want detailed information on a commercial product such as the history of the product. Then, you can use the Algorithm. 2) It should go without saying that *The Imaginary Research Algorithm* will not help you find unknown information. For example, you cannot find out Keith's Birthday if certain factors are unknown like a last name. 3) Classified information is classified information. 4) Non-public business documents are usually hidden and protected. Other than these four items, you should be able to find rich and diverse resources whether on the Internet or at a library.

One more thing, *The Imaginary Research Algorithm* makes the assumption that a user can briefly identify the nature of the search topic or term. The user doesn't have to be an expert or even a novice with the word, but they must be able to identify the nature of the word. Do not worry. You will see how easy this is. For example, if a user does not know what a molecule is to the extent where they do not know whether it is a verb, noun, adjective, or adverb. Then, initially, the user should start with a dictionary. Just to get a brief summary. So, on the first decision diamond, if you do not know if it is a noun. Go to the right of the decision diamond. Unabridged dictionaries do not hold ever word; therefore, you must seek out specialized dictionaries such as a medical dictionary. The Algorithm has decision points which will lead you to thought-provoking words just in case you think you are stuck. Just wait and see.

Hint: If you are clueless about the nature of the word/topic you are researching, you can take a hint from the place where you received the research assignment. Also, you can start with a dictionary.

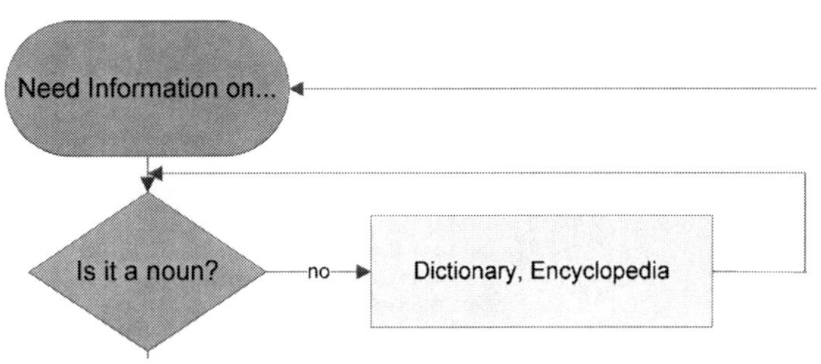

Imaginary Research Algorithm

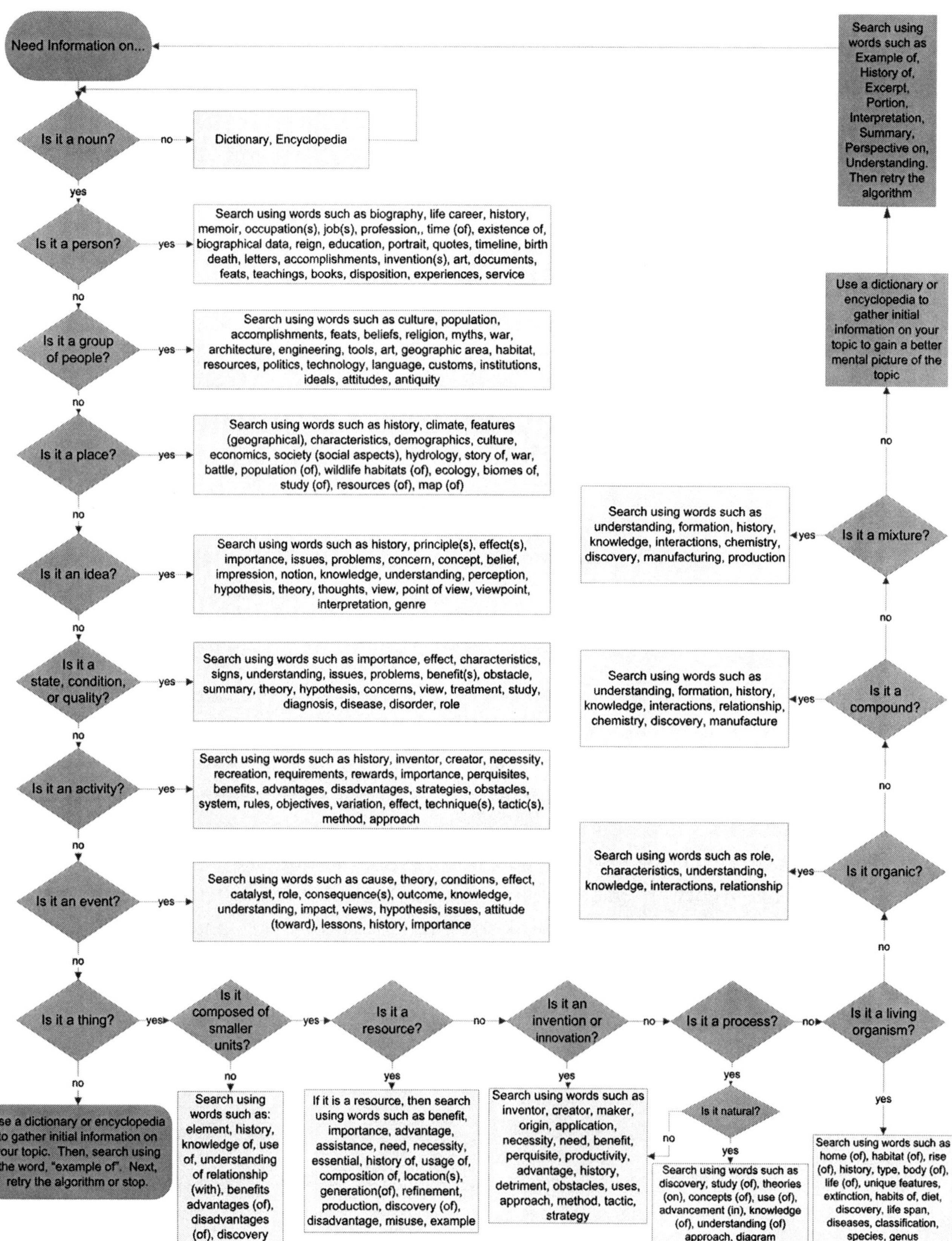

Examination of Imaginary Research Algorithm

The first geometric shape, the rounded rectangle (terminator symbol), is our starting point(see pg. 4). Here we will form a "search need".

For example, we need information on

1.	immediate	24.	Turkey
2.	immediately	25.	walks
3.	and	26.	arithmetic
4.	George Washington	27.	tea
5.	Mayans	28.	Electricity
6.	Gettysburg	29.	Software
7.	Game Theory	30.	Jackson
8.	Depression	31.	Tachyon
9.	Swimming	32.	adjustment
10.	Seven Years' War	33.	ROI (return on investment)
11.	Oxygen	34.	Simile
12.	Oil (Crude Oil)	35.	Dependency
13.	television	36.	Faux Pas
14.	Absorption	37.	Health
15.	smelting	38.	Probability (quality)
16.	lions	39.	asthma
17.	Cyanobacteria	40.	Happiness
18.	Thyroid	41.	evaporation
19.	Sodium Chloride	42.	wave (physics)
20.	soil	43.	heat
21.	them	44.	polymerization
22.	"Iliad"	45.	Vacuum
23.	Plastic	46.	Virus

Sure, anybody can go to the Internet. Visit their favorite search engine. Then, type in any of these terms. Your results will vary, at times, depending on your search engine. This potentially can be a disorganized jumble, because it can blindly lead you through countless information chunks wasting your time and energy. One way to look at researching information is

> if your research tasks are disorganized, then your research process can be disorganized which leads to extended time consumption and additional energy drainage. Organization is extremely important to being efficient and effective at research. *The Imaginary Research Algorithm* is a synthetic scaffold that assists students with developing research focal points, so students dealing with information overload can filter through non-related search results.

Furthermore, if you read the introduction, then you know the general problems with blindly searching for information.

The Imaginary Research Algorithm is a flowchart of decisions that will guide you to words that will stimulate the thought process for research needs.

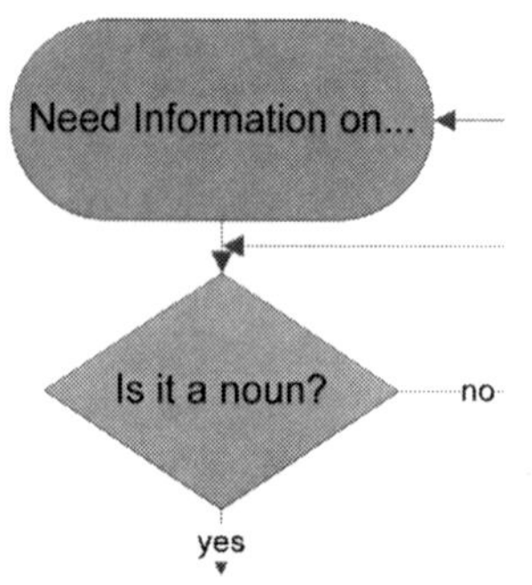

Search Term #1

Go to the first geometric shape, let's say that you need information on the word "Immediate".

Go to the next geometric shape, which asks you a question
"Is it a noun?"

Now, this may seem silly, but it is very important to identify whether it is a noun or not a noun. The word "Immediate" is not a noun. It is an adjective. Now watch this. Maybe you want information on the etymology of the word, "Immediate", perchance you need to know the pronunciation of the word, or perhaps you just need to know what the word means. This can usually be found in an unabridged dictionary, specialty dictionary, or electronic dictionary. You are finished.

Did this satisfy your need for information on the word "Immediate"?
History, usage, pronunciation, meaning, and translation are the major things you may want to know about an adjective.

Let's recall the instructions, we followed according to the flowchart
     a.) Need information on the word "Immediate"
     b.) Followed the directional line to the decision
         diamond **"Is it a noun?"**
     c.) Decided that the word "Immediate" is not a noun
     d.) Arrive at the use "dictionary, encyclopedia" rectangle

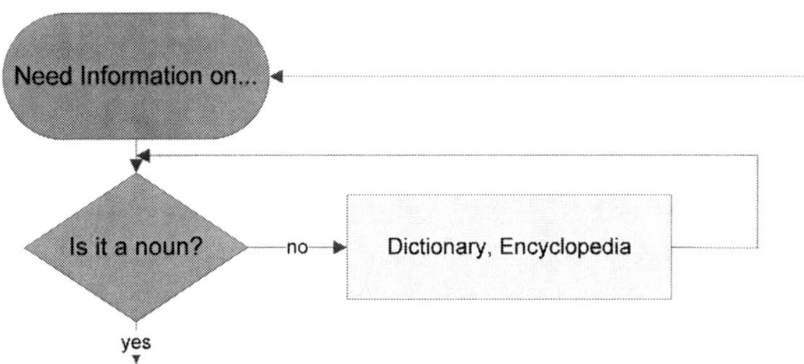

Exercise #1

Now, it is your turn. Choose four adjectives. Then, use the Algorithm on these adjectives.

Search Term #2

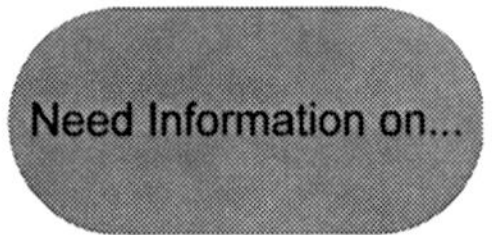

Our next research subject will be the word "Immediately". Let's start at the beginning of the Algorithm again which would be the rounded rectangle geometric shape (terminator symbol). We will form a "search need".

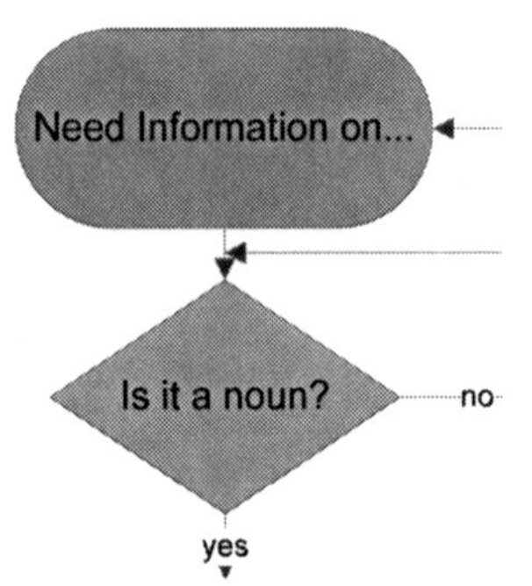

As we go to the next geometric shape.

We ask the question. **"Is it a noun?"** Or specifically "Is the word 'Immediately' a noun?"

No, "Immediately" is not a noun. It is an adverb. From this point, we will go to the geometric shape rectangle that states "Dictionary, Encyclopedia".

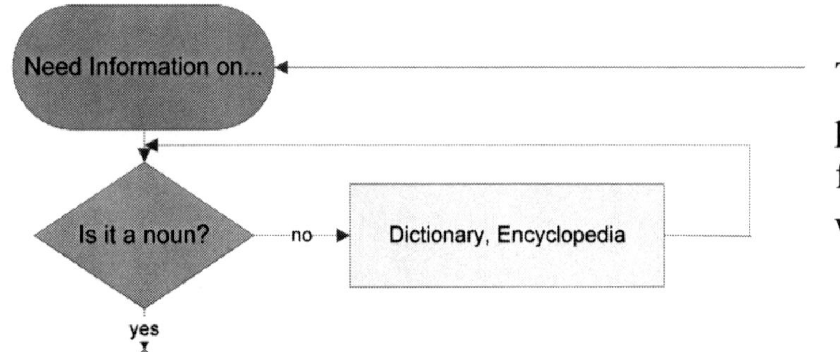

This rectangle completes your journey for information on the word "Immediately".

Use an unabridged dictionary, specialty dictionary, or electronic dictionary. As you can see "Immediately" is limited to a few topics such as history, pronunciation and meaning.

Exercise #2

Now, it is your turn. Choose four adverbs. Then, use the Algorithm
on these adverbs.

Search Term #3

Hopefully, you are now getting the hang of *The Imaginary Research Algorithm*. Yes, we have a long ways to go to identify all of the possible directions, but the decision tree is elementary. We just need to follow the pathways.

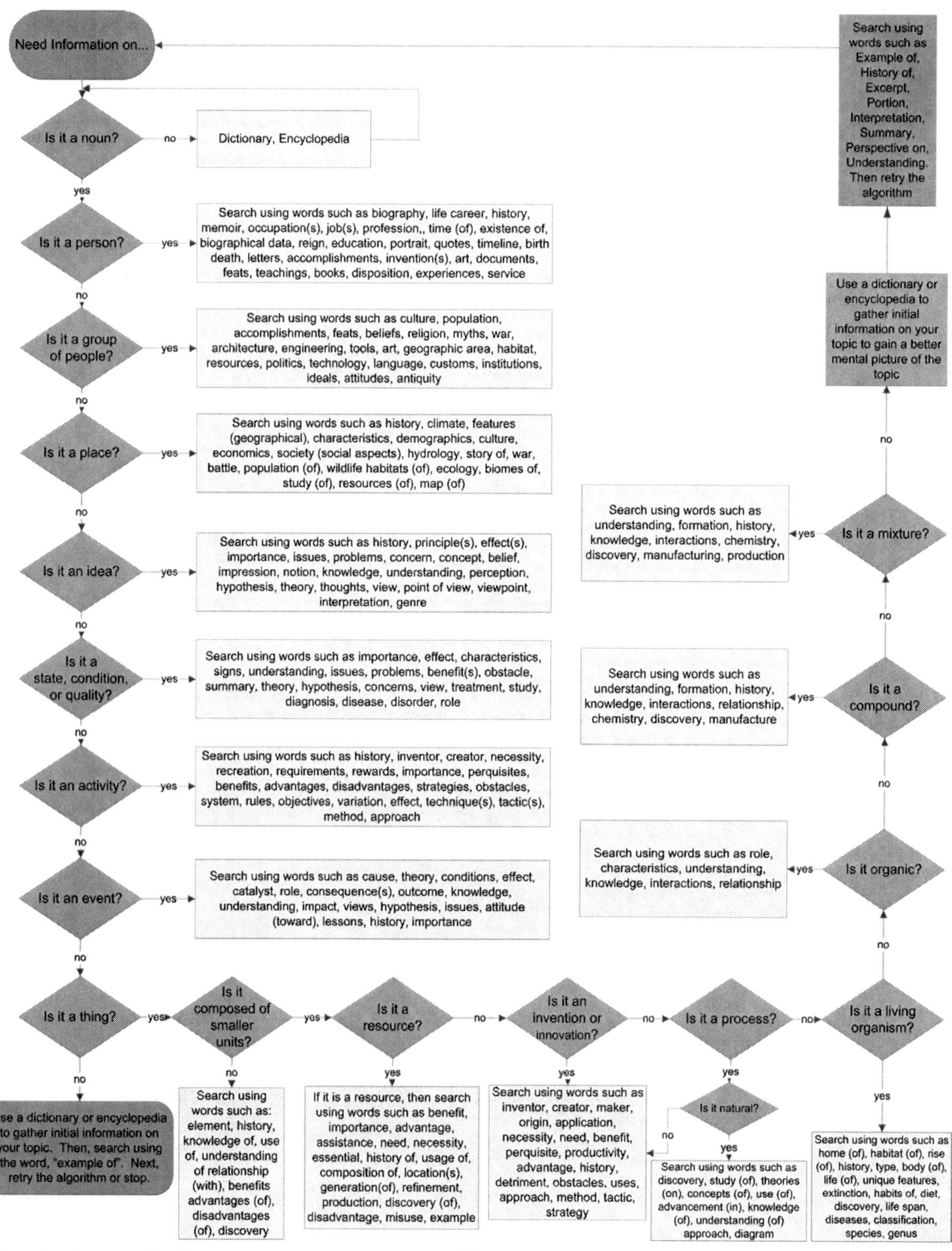

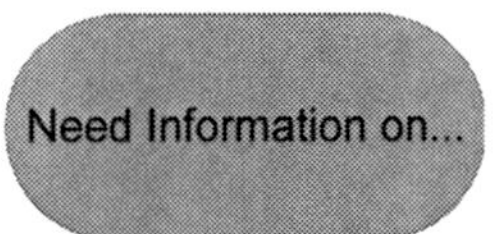

The research term will be "And". Start at the beginning of the Algorithm. Form a "search need". The search need is "Need information on the word 'And'". Move down toward the next geometric shape in the flowchart. Analyze the word "And".

"Is it a noun?"

Since, "And" is not a noun. Go to the rectangle that states "Dictionary or Encyclopedia". Using a dictionary, you can discover that the word "And" is a conjunction. A dictionary can inform you on the usage, pronunciation, and history of the word "And".

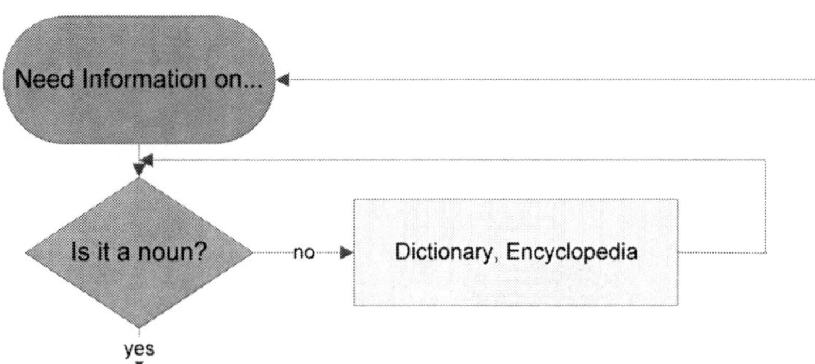

This rectangle in the flowchart terminates your research since the subject is limited.

Exercise #3

Now, it is your turn. Choose four conjunctions. Then, use the Algorithm on these conjunctions.

Currently, we have gone through *The Imaginary Research Algorithm* with a few parts of speech such as adjectives, adverbs, and conjunctions. Even though, we could do pronouns, verbs, and prepositions; however, we will proceed with different types of nouns, so you can see the true strength of *The Imaginary Research Algorithm* in action.

Search Term #4

The research term will be "George Washington". Start at the beginning of the Algorithm. Form a "search need". The search need is "Need information on 'George Washington'". Move down toward the next geometric shape in the flowchart. Analyze the word "George Washington".

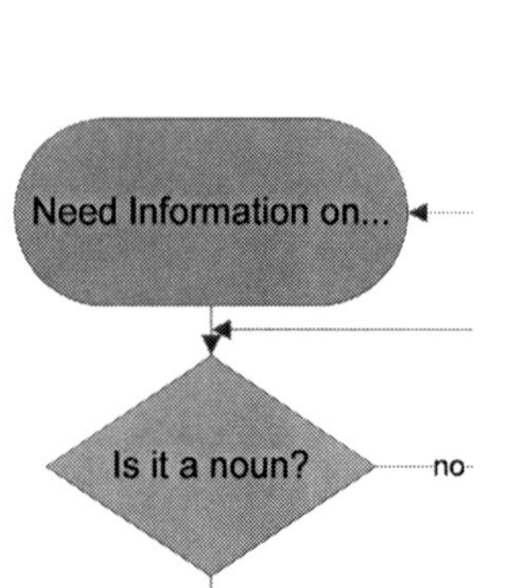

"Is it a noun?"

The answer is yes. Since, "George Washington" is a noun. Go to the next decision block(diamond) below that states **"Is it a person?"**

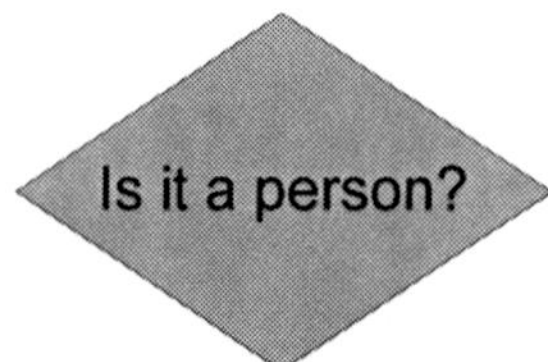

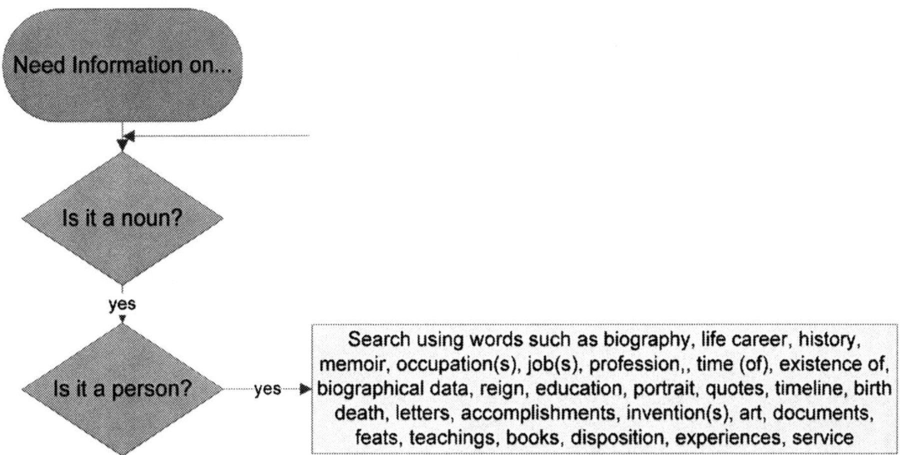

The answer is yes to the question. "George Washington" is a person. Or to be correct, was a person. You could go to an encyclopedia, but most likely you are looking for more information. At this point, stop. Think about how vague the subject of "George Washington" is. You could just search under "George Washington" at your favorite search engine. Or, you can get specific. If you are not specific, you will receive an excess of search results in a variety of areas. For instance, "George Washington" is a popular name. There are parks, forests, bridges, schools and monument(s) named after "George Washington". These results can conflict with your search if you are looking for information about the military career of "George Washington". This is all said to say being specific can save an internet or database users time by being specific. So, is it a person? Yes. Therefore, proceed to the right.

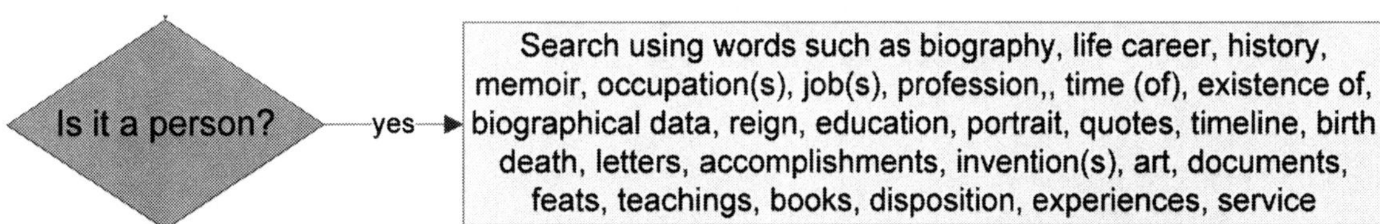

Next, decide on what you are truly looking for. This step suggests the inclusion of words such as

- history (of) George Washington
- life (of) George Washington
- career (of) George Washington
- education (of) George Washington
- accomplishment(s) of George Washington
- biography (of) George Washington
- time (of) George Washington

> Search using words such as biography, life career, history, memoir, occupation(s), job(s), profession,, time (of), existence of, biographical data, reign, education, portrait, quotes, timeline, birth death, letters, accomplishments, invention(s), art, documents, feats, teachings, books, disposition, experiences, service

This rectangle in *The Imaginary Research Algorithm*'s flowchart represents the end of your research, or it can be seen as a beginning to various search options.

Exercise #4

Now, it is your turn. Choose four famous people. Then, use the Algorithm.

Next, select two areas to focus on each famous person. For example:

- letters of George Washington
- birth of George Washington

Search Term #5

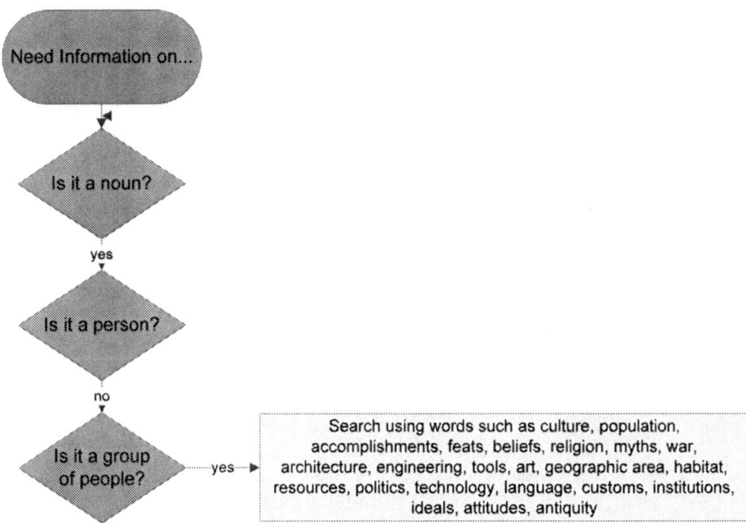

The research term will be "Mayans". Start at the beginning of the Algorithm. Form a "search need". "The search need" is "Need information on 'Mayans'". Move down toward the next geometric shape in the flowchart. Analyze the word "Mayans".

"Is it a noun?" Yes.

"Is it a person?" No.

"Is it a group of people?" Yes

Search using words such as culture, population, accomplishments, feats, beliefs, religion, myths, war, architecture, engineering, tools, art, geographic area, habitat, resources, politics, technology, language, customs, institutions, ideals, attitudes, antiquity

The answer is yes. "Mayans" were a civilization of Mesoamerican Indians/group of people. Once again, a user could go to an encyclopedia, but this may not be sufficient for a user's search needs. Also, a user could type in "Mayans", but the user may have to shuffle through unnecessary, non-related sites like a high school sports team or a fine dining restaurant. So, it is usually best to be specific. If you did not know "Mayans" were a group of people. Then, *The Imaginary Research Algorithm* would have led you to a dictionary or encyclopedia. Afterwards, you would be directed to reconnect with the Algorithm.

Next, decide on what type of information you want regarding "Mayans". During a search, this geometric shape (rectangle) suggests the inclusion of words such as

- history (of) Mayans
- language (of) Mayans
- customs (of) Mayans
- accomplishments (of) Mayans
- tools (of) Mayans
- technology (of) Mayans
- engineering feats (of) Mayans
- resources (of) Mayans
- art (of) Mayans
- politics (of) Mayans
- institutions (of) Mayans
- ideals (of) Mayans
- beliefs (of) Mayans
- geographic area (of) Mayans

Search using words such as culture, population, accomplishments, feats, beliefs, religion, myths, war, architecture, engineering, tools, art, geographic area, habitat, resources, politics, technology, language, customs, institutions, ideals, attitudes, antiquity

This rectangle can be seen as the start of your search for detailed information on a group of people such as the "Mayans".

Exercise #5

Now, it is your turn. Choose four groups(civilizations, cultures, or communities) of people. Then, use the Algorithm.

Next, select two areas to focus on each group. for example:

- tools of Mayans
- history of Mayans

Search Term #6

The next research topic will be "Gettysburg". Start at the top of *The Imaginary Research Algorithm*. Form a "search need". Need information on "Gettysburg".

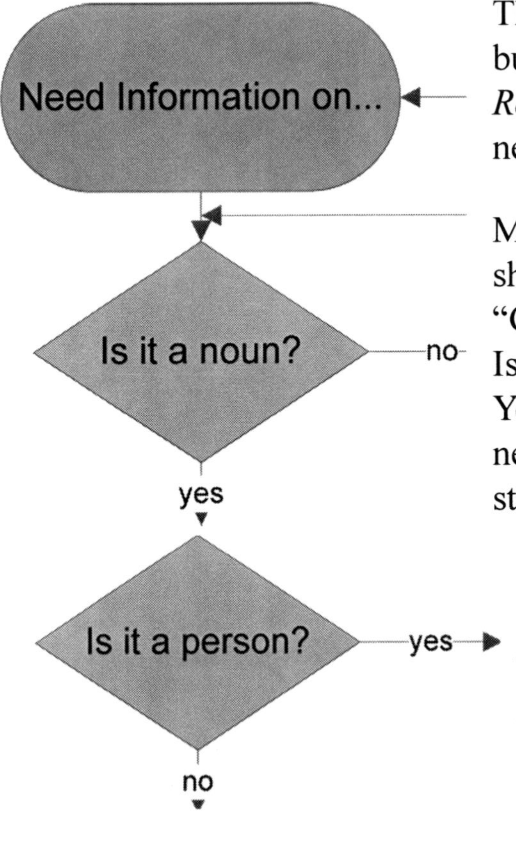

Move down toward the next geometric shape in the flowchart. Analyze the word "Gettysburg".
Is "Gettysburg" a noun?
Yes, "Gettysburg" is a noun. Go to the next decision shape (diamond) below that states...

"Is it a person?"

The answer is no. "Gettysburg" is not a person. So, go to the next decision shape (diamond) below that states...

"Is it a group of people?"

The answer is no. "Gettysburg" is not a group of people. So, go to the next decision shape (diamond) below that states...

"Is it a place?"

Search using words such as history, climate, features (geographical), characteristics, demographics, culture, economics, society (social aspects), hydrology, story of, war, battle, population (of), wildlife habitats (of), ecology, biomes of, study (of), resources (of), map (of)

The answer is yes to the question. "Gettysburg" is a place. By now, you may realize that there are many factors to consider if you just typed in "Gettysburg" in a search engine or library database. There are so many possible topics. *The Imaginary Research Algorithm* is here to cognitively assist in the search process. Since, it is a place. Move to the right.

Next, determine what you are looking for. This step suggests the inclusion of words such as

- history (of) Gettysburg
- features (of) Gettysburg
- social aspects (of) Gettysburg
- economics (of) Gettysburg
- culture (of) Gettysburg
- demographics (of) Gettysburg

> Search using words such as history, climate, features (geographical), characteristics, demographics, culture, economics, society (social aspects), hydrology, story of, war, battle, population (of), wildlife habitats (of), ecology, biomes of, study (of), resources (of), map (of)

This rectangle can be seen as the start of your search for detailed information on a place such as the "Gettysburg".

Exercise #6

Now, it is your turn. Choose four places. Then, use the Algorithm.

Next, select two areas to focus on each place.
For example:

- history of Gettysburg
- culture of Gettysburg

Let's look at *The Imaginary Research Algorithm* as a whole. As you can see, the Algorithm is a series of decisions, that leads to either beneficial research words or more decisions. Remember, all you have to do is follow the pathways.

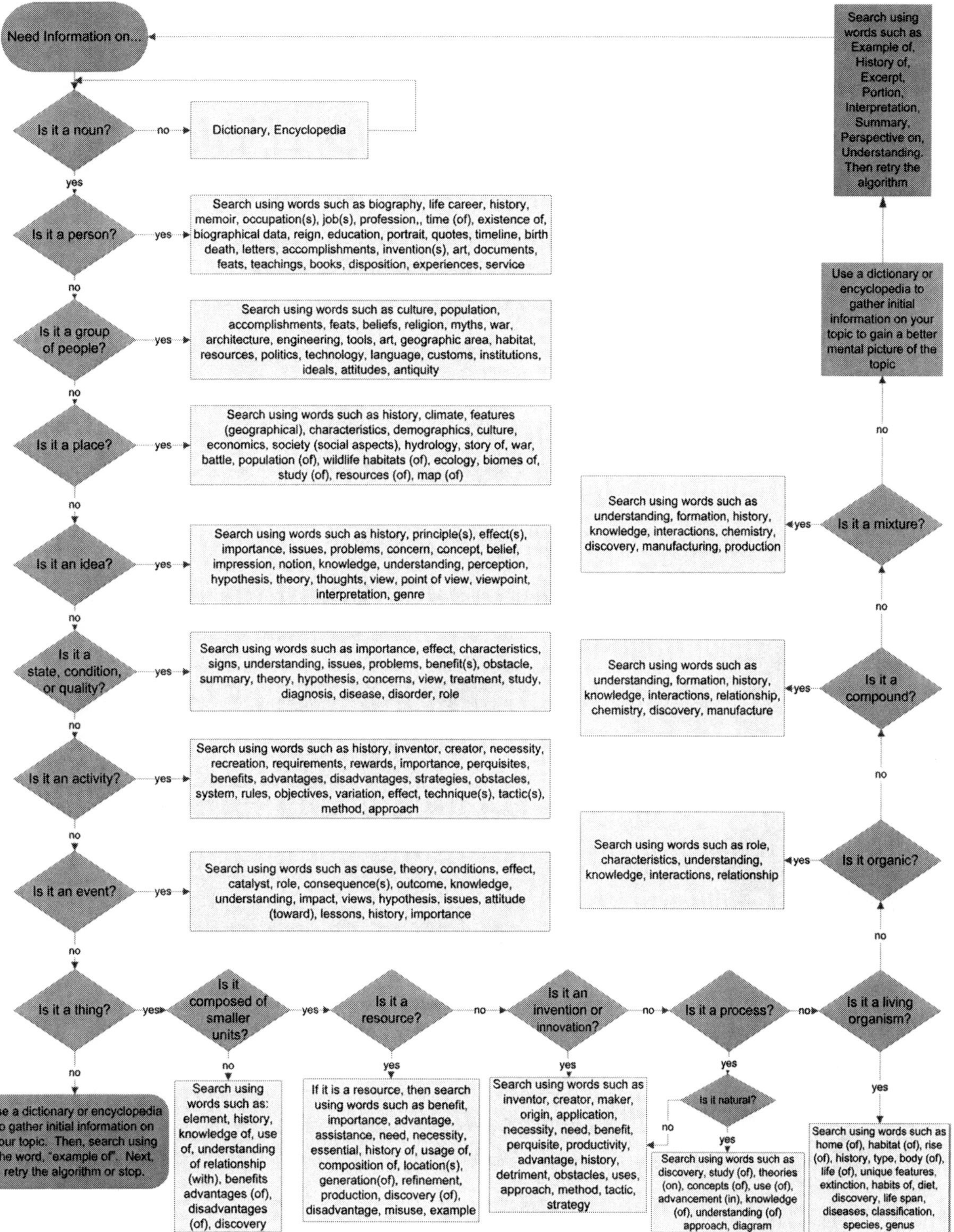

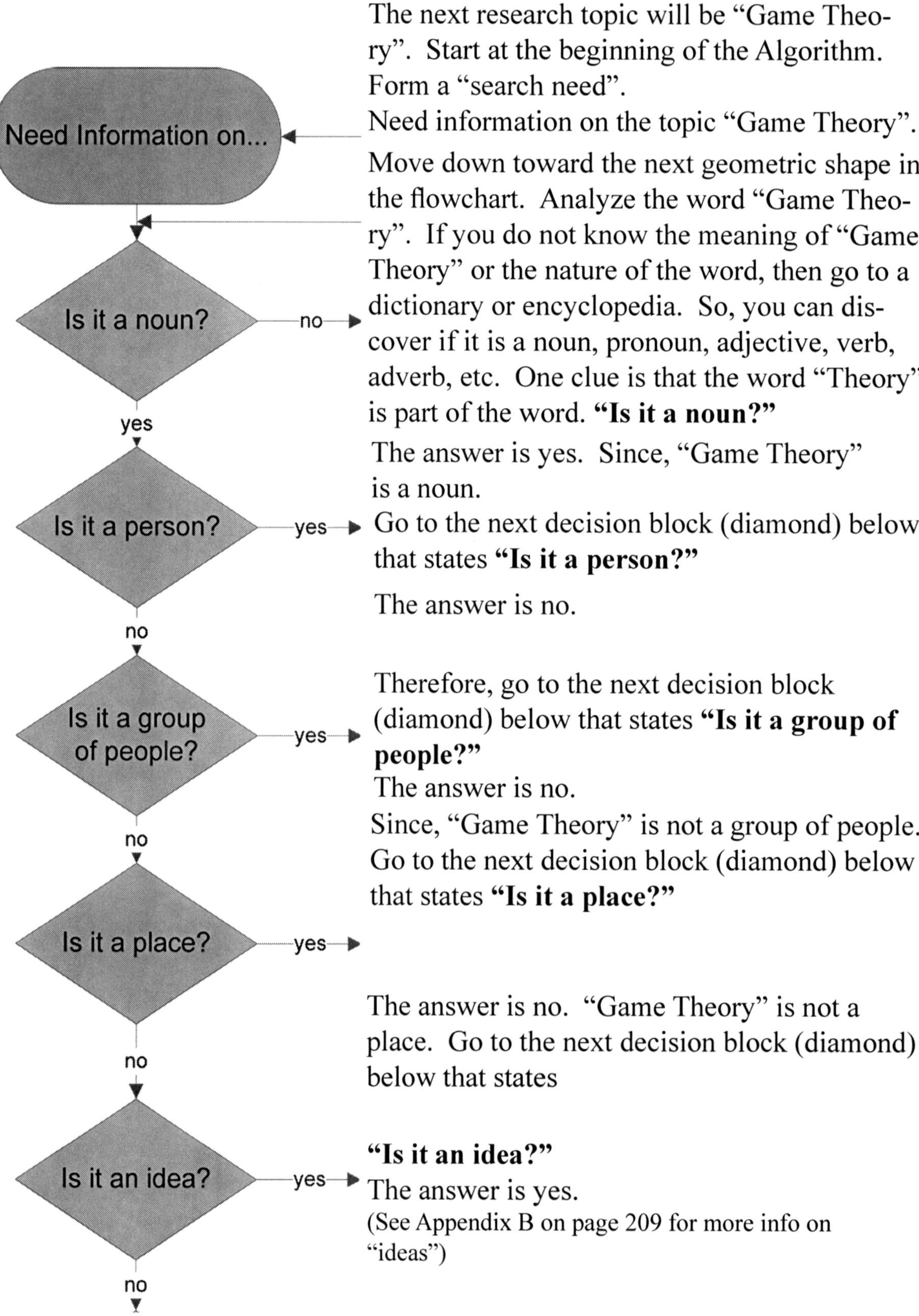

Search Term #7

The next research topic will be "Game Theory". Start at the beginning of the Algorithm. Form a "search need".

Need information on the topic "Game Theory".

Move down toward the next geometric shape in the flowchart. Analyze the word "Game Theory". If you do not know the meaning of "Game Theory" or the nature of the word, then go to a dictionary or encyclopedia. So, you can discover if it is a noun, pronoun, adjective, verb, adverb, etc. One clue is that the word "Theory" is part of the word. **"Is it a noun?"**

The answer is yes. Since, "Game Theory" is a noun.

Go to the next decision block (diamond) below that states **"Is it a person?"**

The answer is no.

Therefore, go to the next decision block (diamond) below that states **"Is it a group of people?"**
The answer is no.
Since, "Game Theory" is not a group of people. Go to the next decision block (diamond) below that states **"Is it a place?"**

The answer is no. "Game Theory" is not a place. Go to the next decision block (diamond) below that states

"Is it an idea?"
The answer is yes.
(See Appendix B on page 209 for more info on "ideas")

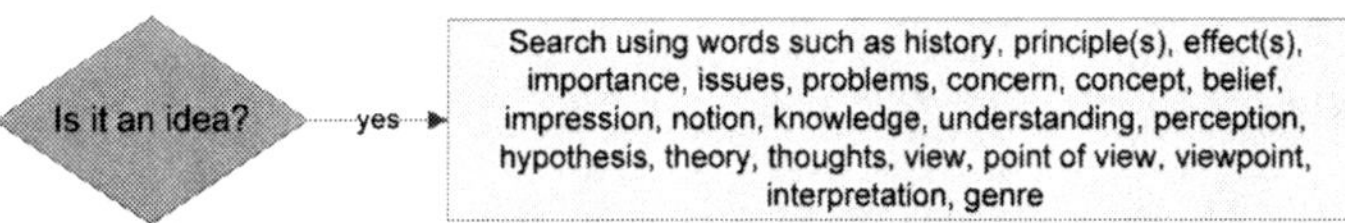

Game Theory is an idea.
Go to the right.

Next, determine what specific information to look for during a search, this step suggests the inclusion of words such as

- concept of game theory
- principle(s) (of) game theory
- effect (of) game theory
- importance (of) game theory
- issues (with) game theory
- problems (with) game theory
- arguments (for) game theory
- arguments (against) game theory
- impression (of) game theory
- debate (of) game theory
- knowledge (of) game theory

This rectangle can be seen as the start of your search for detailed information on an idea such as "Game Theory".

Exercise #7

Now, it is your turn. Choose four ideas. Then, use the Algorithm.

Next, select two areas of focus for each idea.

For example:

- principles of game theory
- history of game theory

Search Term #8

The next research topic will be "Depression". "Depression" can be a period of time/event (economic) or a state of being. Start at the beginning of the Algorithm. Form a "search need". "Need information on the topic 'Depression'". We will focus on the "state of being" for "Depression". Move down toward the next geometric shape in the flowchart. Analyze the word "Depression".

"Is it a noun?"

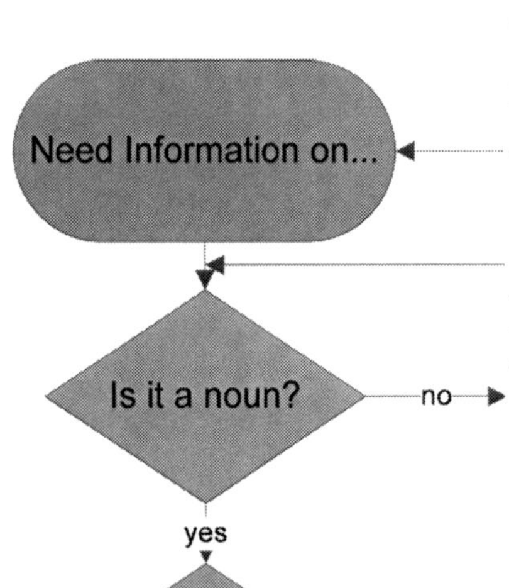

The answer is yes. Since, "Depression" is a noun. Go to the next decision block (diamond) below that states

"Is it a person?"

The answer is no. Therefore, go to the next decision block (diamond) below that states

"Is it a group of people?"

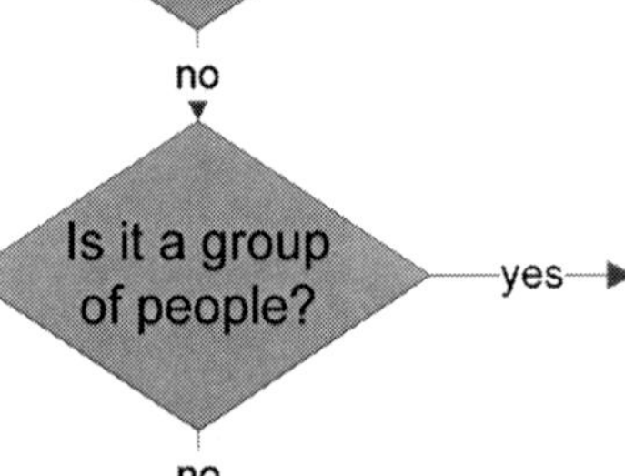

The answer is no. Since, "Depression" is not a group of people. Go to the next decision block (diamond) below that states

"Is it a place?"

The answer is no. Therefore, go to the next decision block (diamond) below that states

"Is it an idea?"

The answer is no. Therefore, go to the next decision block (diamond) below that states

"Is it a state of being, condition, or quality?"
(See Appendix B on page 209 for more info on "state, condition, or quality")

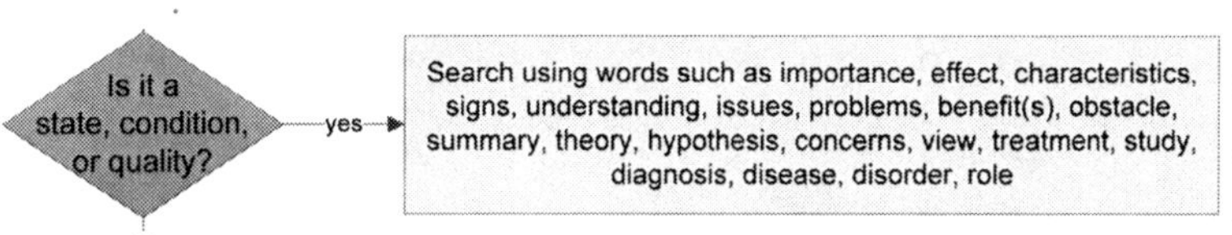

The answer is yes. "Depression" is a quality, condition, or state of being. Go to the right.

Next, determine what specific information to look for. During a search, this step suggests the inclusion of words such as

- effect of depression
- characteristics of depression
- signs of depression
- summary of depression
- theories on depression
- obstacles of depression

Search using words such as importance, effect, characteristics, signs, understanding, issues, problems, benefit(s), obstacle, summary, theory, hypothesis, concerns, view, treatment, study, diagnosis, disease, disorder, role

This rectangle can be seen as the start of your search for detailed information on a condition such as "Depression".

Exercise #8

Now, it is your turn. Choose four conditions or qualities. Then, use the Algorithm.

Next, select two areas of focus for each condition or quality.

For example:
- obstacles of depression
- effects of depression

Search Term #9

The next research topic will be "Swimming". Start at the beginning of the Algorithm. Form a "search need". "Need information on the topic 'Swimming'. Move down toward the next geometric shape in the flowchart. Analyze the word "Swimming". After analyzing the word "Swimming", you come to the conclusion that you are searching for information on the recreation and sport of "Swimming" not the action of "Swimming" or the process of "swimming". Begin. **"Is it a noun?"**

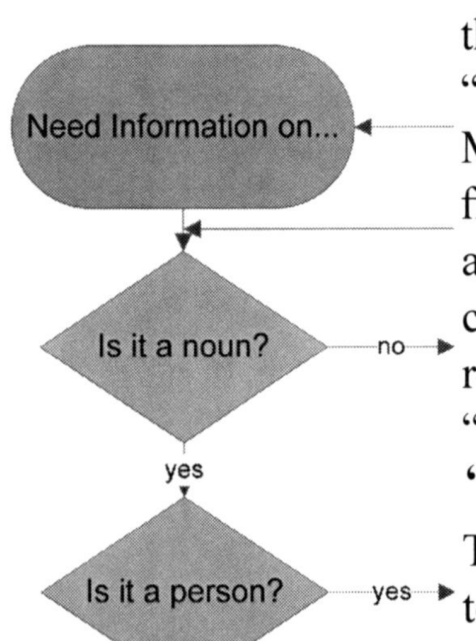

The answer is yes. Since, "Swimming" is a noun. Go to the next decision block (diamond) below that states **"Is it a person?"**

The answer is no. Therefore, go to the next decision block (diamond) below that states

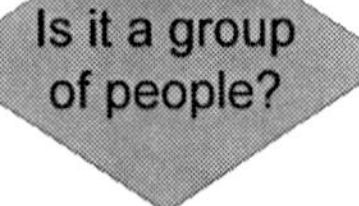

"Is it a group of people?"

The answer is no. Since, "Swimming" is not a group of people. Go to the next decision block (diamond) below that states

"Is it a place?"

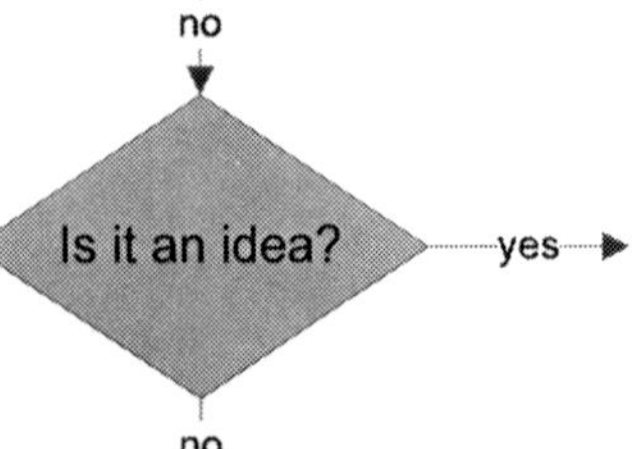

The answer is no. "Swimming" is not a place. Therefore, go to the next decision block (diamond) below that states

"Is it an idea?"

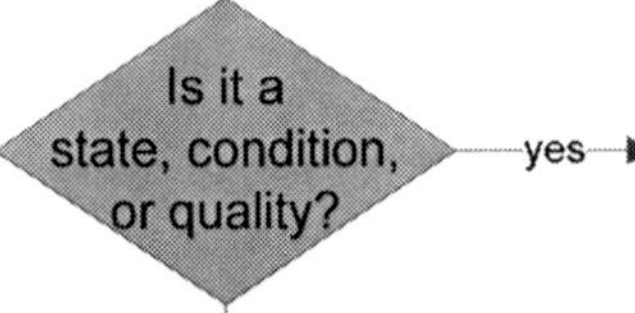

The answer is no. Therefore, go to the next decision block (diamond) below that states

"Is it a state of being?"

The answer is no. "Swimming" is not a state of being (for your search need). Go to the next decision block (diamond) below that states **"Is it an activity?"**
(See Appendix B on page 209 for more info on "activity")

The answer is yes. "Swimming" is an activity. Therefore, go to the right.

Next, determine what specific information to look for during a search. This step suggests the inclusion of words such as

- history of swimming
- characteristics of swimming
- advantages of swimming
- effect of swimming
- techniques of swimming
- variation of swimming

This rectangle can be seen as the start of your search for detailed information on the activity "Swimming".

Exercise #9

Now, it is your turn. Choose four activities. Then, use the Algorithm.

Next, select two areas of focus for each activity.

For example:

- variations of swimming
- effects of swimming

Search Term #10

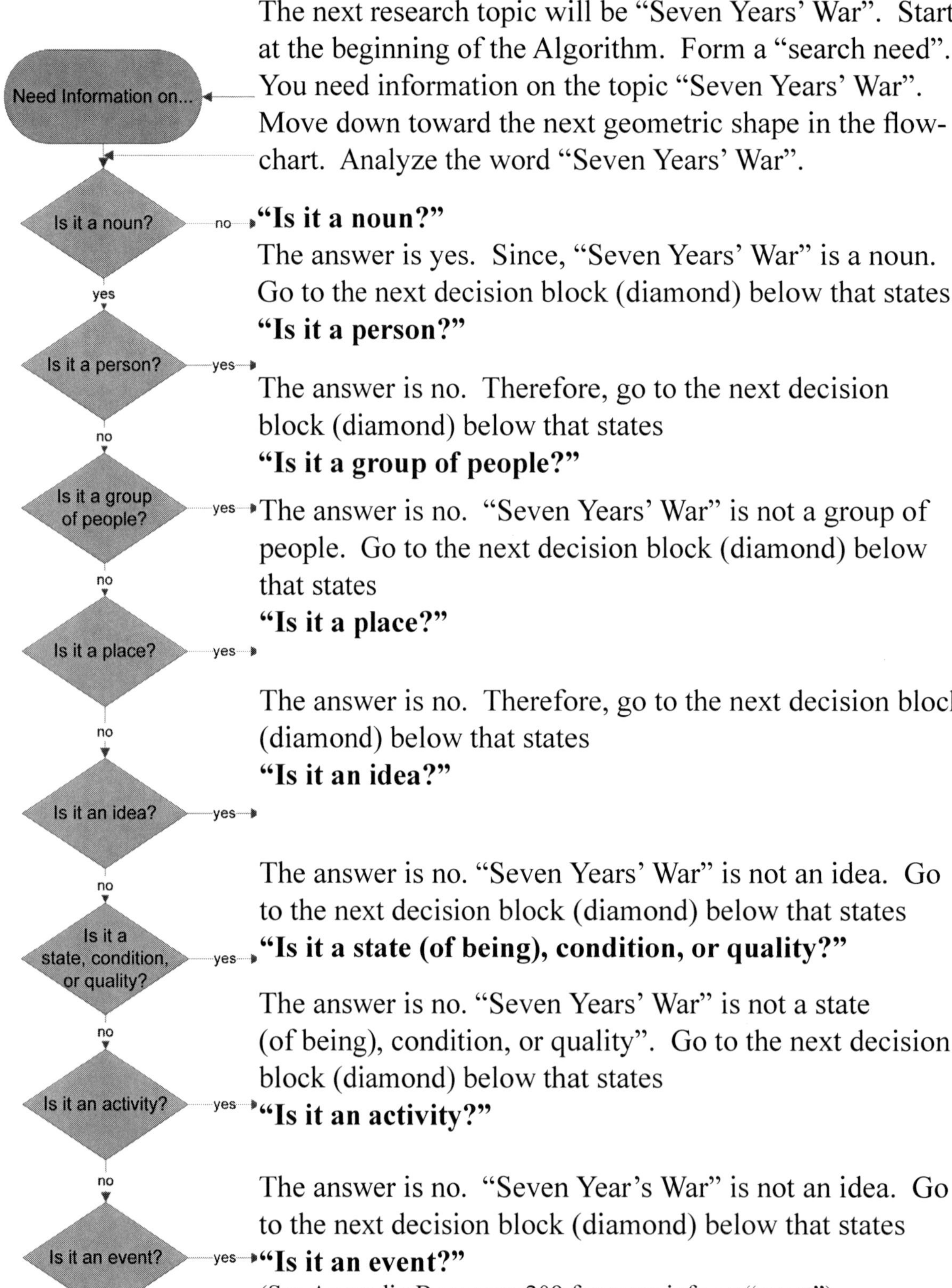

The next research topic will be "Seven Years' War". Start at the beginning of the Algorithm. Form a "search need". You need information on the topic "Seven Years' War". Move down toward the next geometric shape in the flow-chart. Analyze the word "Seven Years' War".

"Is it a noun?"
The answer is yes. Since, "Seven Years' War" is a noun. Go to the next decision block (diamond) below that states **"Is it a person?"**

The answer is no. Therefore, go to the next decision block (diamond) below that states **"Is it a group of people?"**

The answer is no. "Seven Years' War" is not a group of people. Go to the next decision block (diamond) below that states **"Is it a place?"**

The answer is no. Therefore, go to the next decision block (diamond) below that states **"Is it an idea?"**

The answer is no. "Seven Years' War" is not an idea. Go to the next decision block (diamond) below that states **"Is it a state (of being), condition, or quality?"**

The answer is no. "Seven Years' War" is not a state (of being), condition, or quality". Go to the next decision block (diamond) below that states **"Is it an activity?"**

The answer is no. "Seven Year's War" is not an idea. Go to the next decision block (diamond) below that states **"Is it an event?"**
(See Appendix B on page 209 for more info on "event")

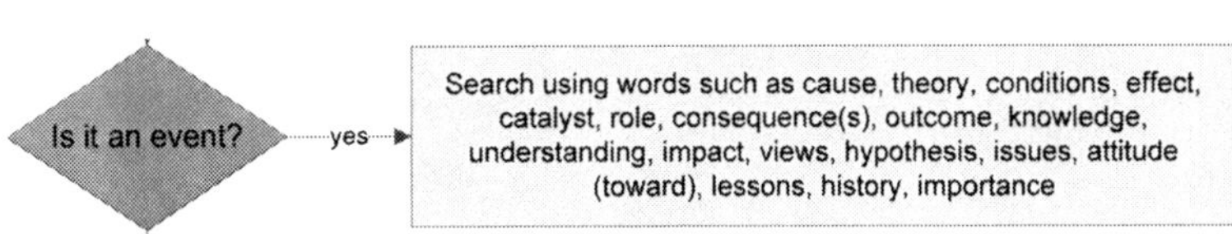

The answer is yes. The "Seven Years' War" was an event. Therefore, go to the right.

Next, determine what specific information to look for. During a search, this step suggests the inclusion of words such as

- history of Seven Years' War
- characteristics of Seven Years' War
- consequences of Seven Years' War
- impact of Seven Years' War
- lessons of Seven Years' War

Search using words such as cause, theory, conditions, effect, catalyst, role, consequence(s), outcome, knowledge, understanding, impact, views, hypothesis, issues, attitude (toward), lessons, history, importance

This rectangle can be seen as the start of your search for detailed information on an event such as the "Seven Years' War".

Exercise #10

Now, it is your turn. Choose four events. Then, use *The Imaginary Research Algorithm.*

Next, select two areas of focus for each event.

For example:

- causes of Seven Years' War
- impact of Seven Years' War

Chapter

2

In this chapter, you will be exposed to different portions of *The Imaginary Research Algorithm*. We started out slowly digesting *The Imaginary Research Algorithm*. If you feel comfortable with the Algorithm, please continue on to the next page. But, if you feel lost, disoriented, or overwhelmed, then go through chapter 1 again. Focus on one geometric shape at a time. Also, the glossary on page 209 is available to assist.

Imaginary Research Algorithm

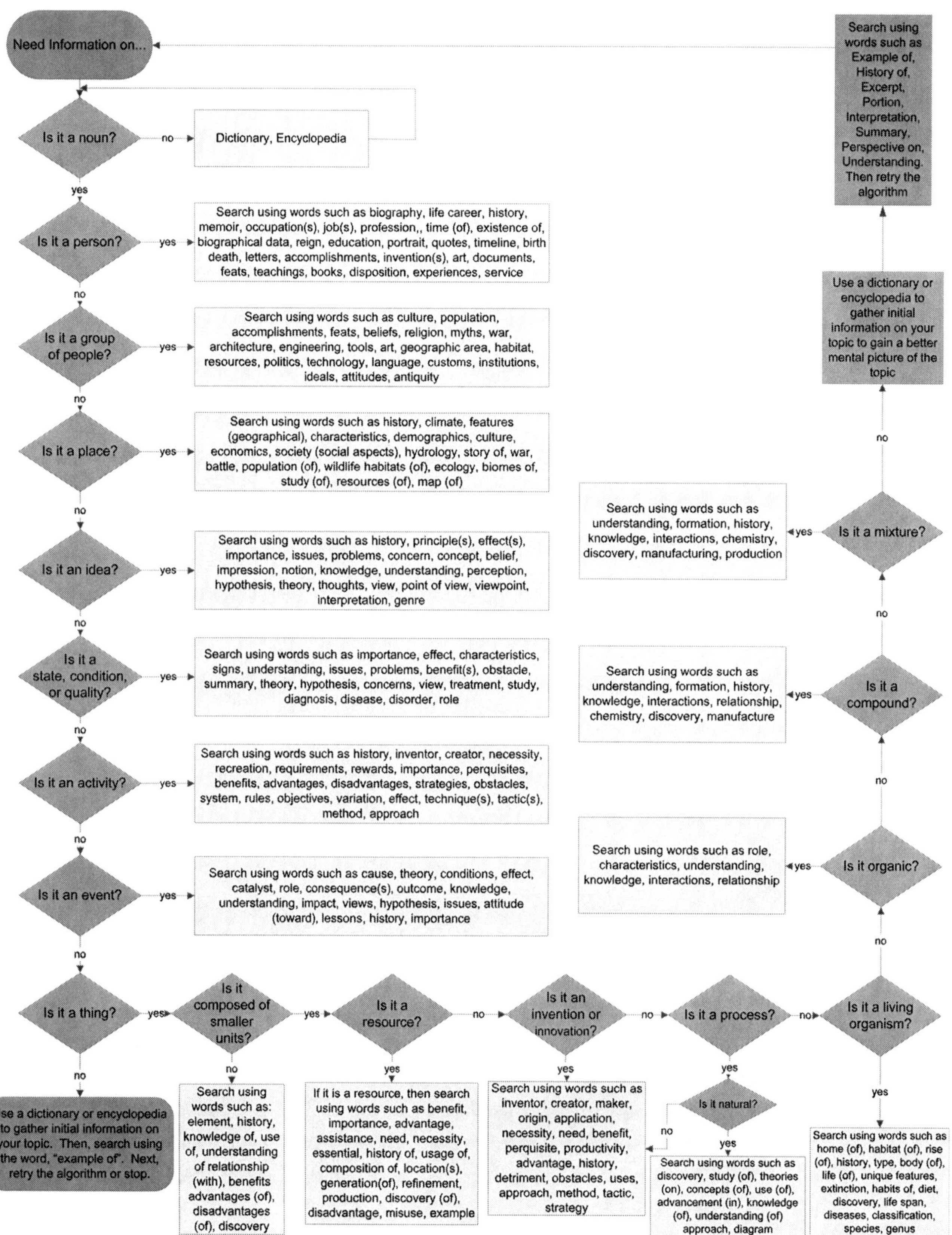

Search Term #11

As an Imaginary Research Algorithm user, you have gone through numerous cycles of *The Imaginary Research Algorithm*. The next research term will be "oxygen". First, form a "search need" such as

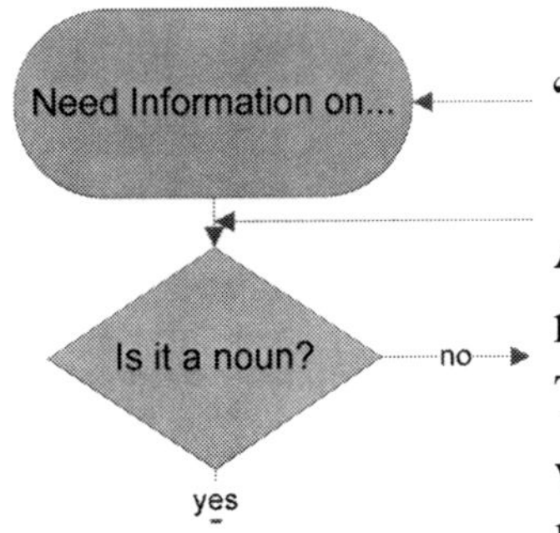

"need information on 'Oxygen'".

As you might have guessed, it is a noun. By now, you most likely have grasped how to navigate nearly half of The Imaginary Research Algorithm flowchart. Don't worry we will still guide you through most of the steps, but we will shorten the explanations.

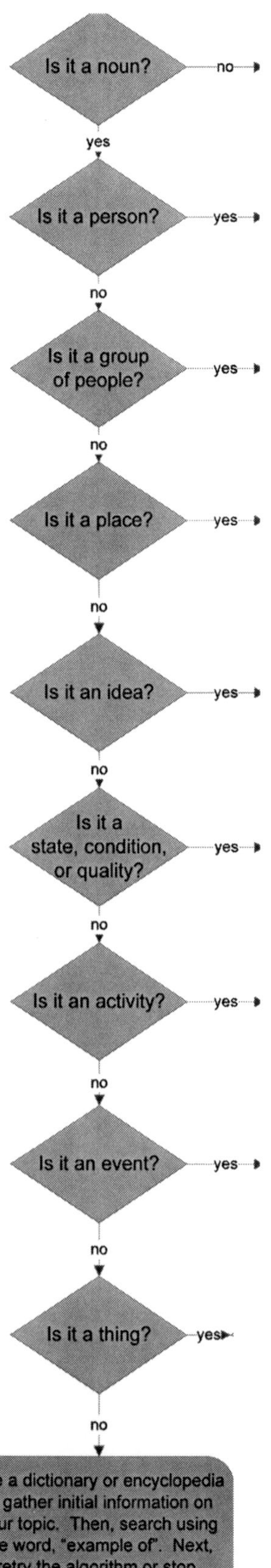

First, we know "Oxygen" is a noun, but we also know it is not a person, group of people, place, idea, condition, activity, or event.

This leaves us with two options. This is a "thing". Or, it is a word(s) you lack knowledge of. If it is a situation where you have a lack of knowledge of the topic, go down to the dictionary or encyclopedia rounded rectangle. Don't forget about specialty dictionaries and encyclopedias.

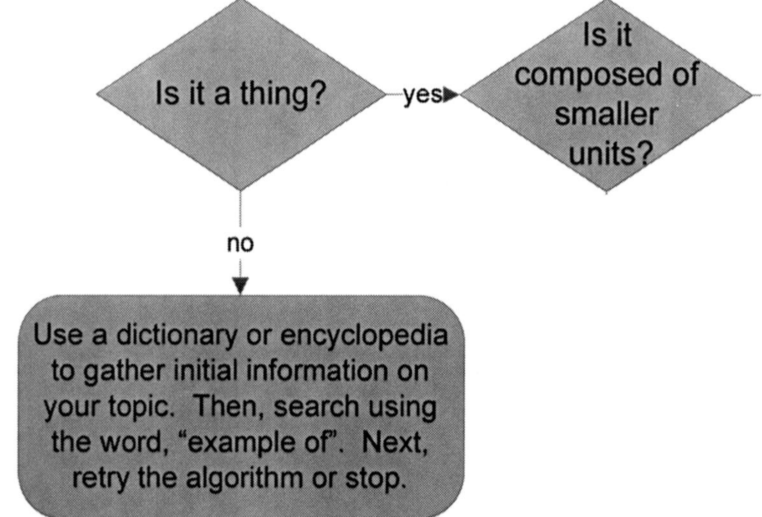

Then repeat *The Imaginary Research Algorithm*. In this scenario, you know what "Oxygen" is.

"Oxygen" is a thing. It is an element. Therefore, you will go to the next decision shape (diamond) that states **"Is it composed of smaller units?"***

Is it composed of smaller units?

no

Search using words such as: element, history, knowledge of, use of, understanding of relationship (with), benefits advantages (of), disadvantages (of), discovery

"Is 'Oxygen' composed of smaller units?"

Decide on what you are looking for. This step suggests the inclusion of words such as

- discovery (of) oxygen
- benefits (of) oxygen
- use (of) oxygen

*This block is dedicated to elements. "Is it composed of smaller units?" Elements are composed of subatomic particles like electrons and protons. However, if you have to search for information on an element, we recommend deciding "no" on the current decision. Atoms are the basic building block of matter. This is the reasoning for *The Imaginary Research Algorithm* using elements as a starting point for "things".

Exercise #11

Now, it is your turn. Choose four elements or subatomic particles. Then, use the Algorithm.

Next, select two areas of focus for each event.

For example:

Next, select two areas of focus for each element.
For example:
- usage of oxygen
- benefit of oxygen

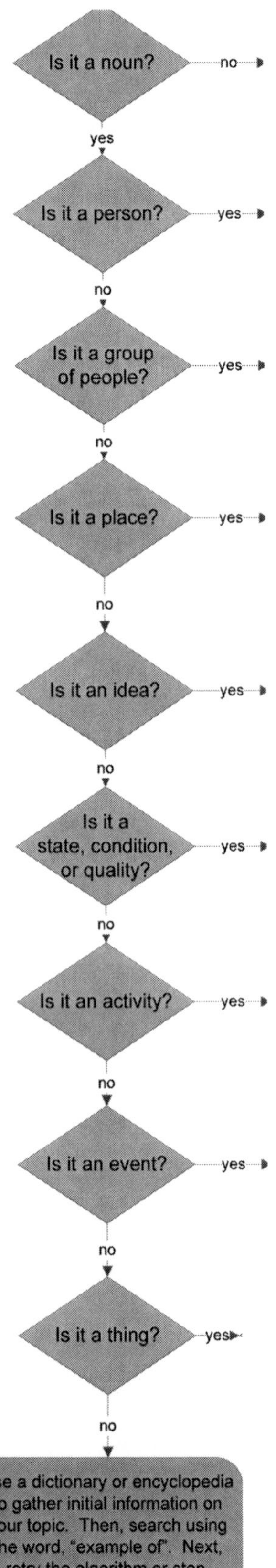

Search Term #12

The research topic will be "Oil (crude oil)". Start at the beginning of *The Imaginary Research Algorithm*. Form a "search need". Then go through the Algorithm.

"Need information on the topic 'Oil'".

It is a noun. However, oil is not a person, group of people, place, idea, state of being, activity, or event. As we move through the visual representation of *The Imaginary Research Algorithm*, we stop at the decision block diamond **"Is it a thing?"**

The answer is yes.

"Oil" as in crude oil is a thing. Go to the right. Therefore, you will go to the next decision shape (diamond) that states **"Is it composed of smaller units?"**

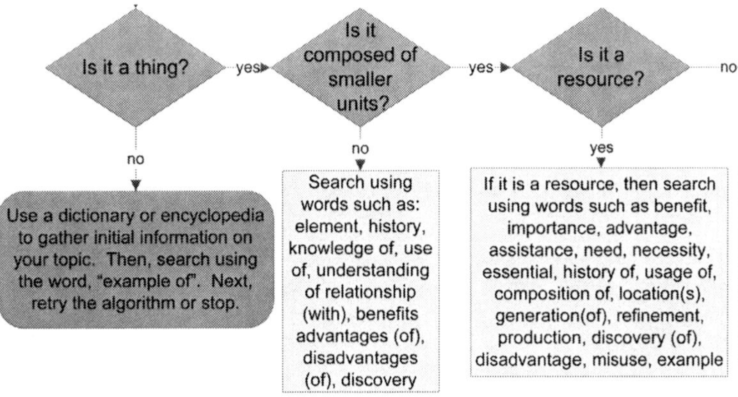

The answer is yes. "Oil" is composed of smaller units. Go to the next decision shape (diamond) to the right that states **"Is it a resource?"**

(See Appendix B on page 209 for more info on "resource")

"Oil (crude oil)" is a resource that humans use. Decide on what you are looking for. During the search, this step suggests the inclusion of words such as

- benefit(s) of oil
- disadvantage(s) of oil
- importance of oil
- need for oil
- composition of oil
- refinement of oil
- discovery of oil

Exercise #12

Now, it is your turn. Choose four resources. Then, use *The Imaginary Research Algorithm* on these resources.

Next, select two areas of focus for each resource.

For example:

- importance of oil
- refinement of oil

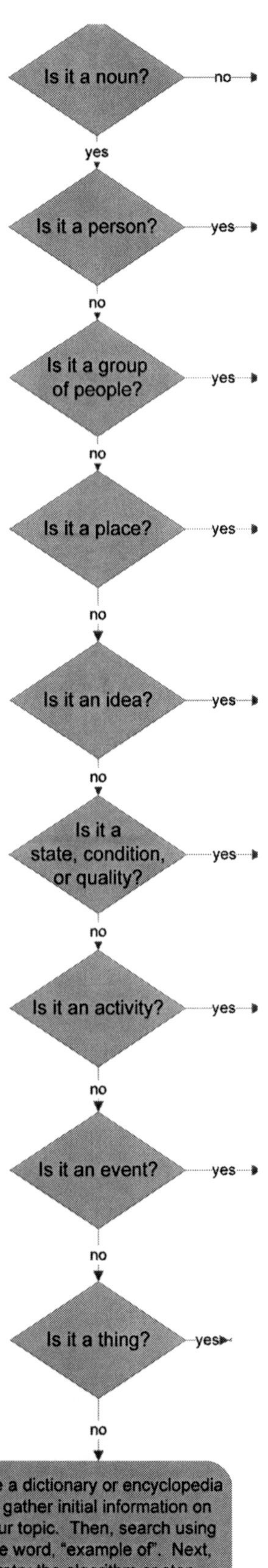

Search Term #13

The next research topic will be "Television". Start at the beginning of the Algorithm. Form a "search need". The "search need" is "need information on the topic 'Television'".

We know "Television" is a noun, but we also know it is not a person, group of people, place, idea, condition, activity, or event. This leaves us with two options. If you do not know anything about television, then go down to the dictionary or encyclopedia decision shape and then repeat *The Imaginary Research Algorithm*. In this scenario, you know that "Television" is a thing. Analyze the word "Television" to consider what you are looking to find. You conclude that you are looking for information on "Television", the electronic device.

"Is it composed of smaller units?" Yes, "Television" is composed of smaller units. Therefore, go to the right to the next decision shape (diamond).

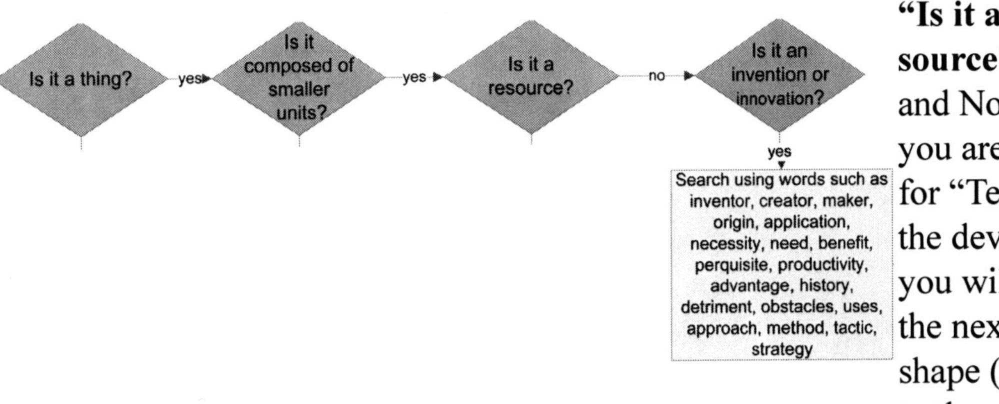

"Is it a resource?" Yes and No. But, you are looking for "Television" the device. So, you will move to the next decision shape (diamond) to the right.

"Is it an invention or innovation?" Yes. "Television", the electronic instrument, is an invention. (See Appendix B on page 209 for more info on "invention" or "innovation")

Next, determine what specific information to look for. During a search, this step suggests the inclusion of words such as

- applications of television
- inventor(s) of television
- history of television
- benefits of television
- disadvantages of television
- obstacles of television

Exercise #13

Now, it is your turn. Choose four inventions or innovations. Then, use the Algorithm on these inventions or innovations.

Next select two areas of focus for each invention or innovation.

For example:

- benefits of television
- disadvantages of television

Search Term #14

The next research topic will be "Absorption". Start at the beginning of the Algorithm. Form a "search need". The "search need" is "need information on the topic 'Absorption'".

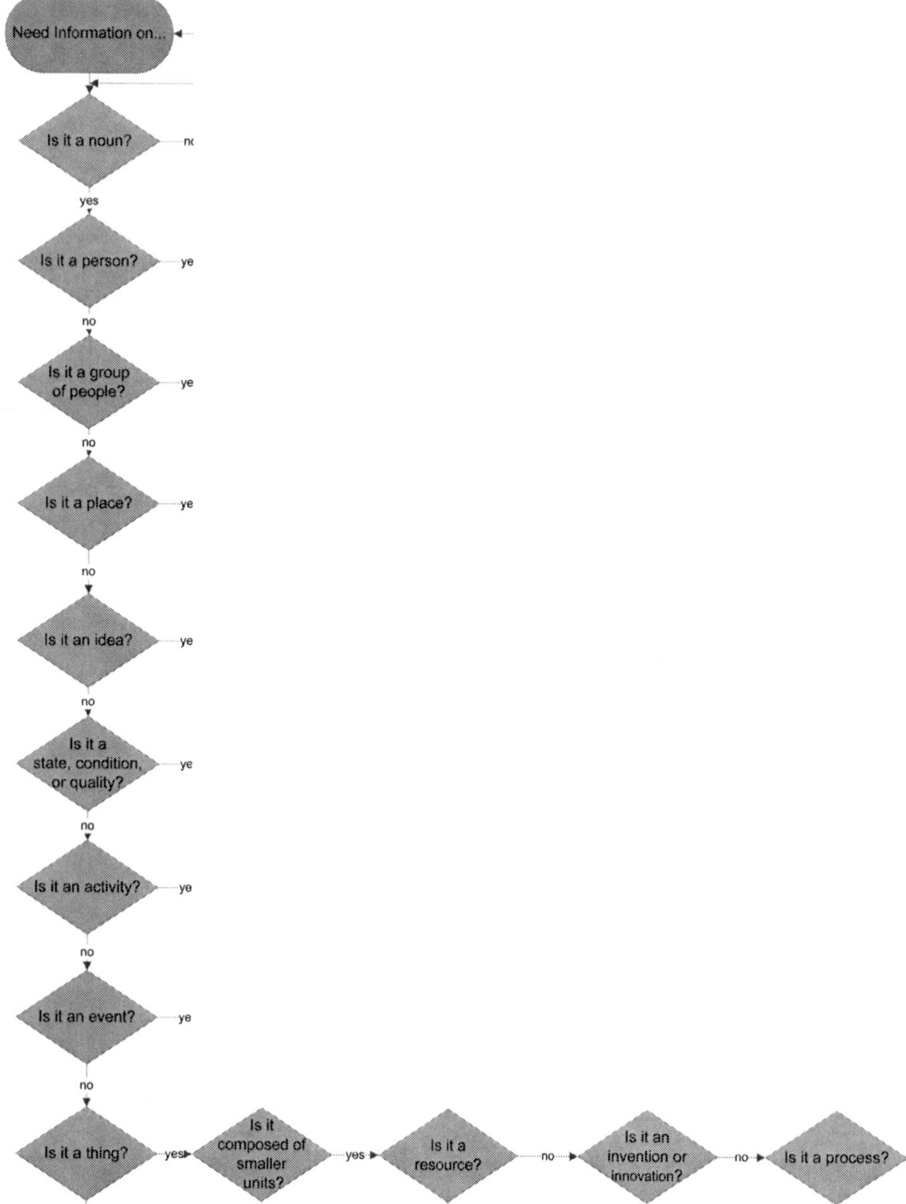

We know "Absorption" is a noun, but we also know it is not a person, group of people, place, idea, quality, activity or event. (arguably absorption could be an adjective, event, or activity, I will cover multiplicity in depth in future chapters) This leaves us with two options. This is a thing or a word(s) you cannot identify or classify. If it is a situation where you do not know what it is. Then, go down to the dictionary or encyclopedia rounded rectangle. Then repeat *The Imaginary Research Algorithm*. In this scenario, you know what "Absorption" is to a degree. Analyze the word "Absorption".

"Is it composed of smaller units?" Yes, "Absorption" is composed of smaller units such as steps. Therefore, go to the right to the next decision shape (diamond).

"Is it a resource?" No. So, you will move to the next decision shape (diamond) to the right.

"Is it an invention or innovation?" No.

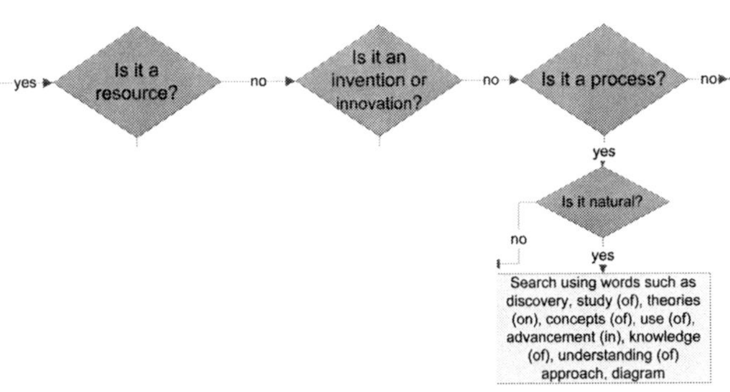

"Is it a process?"

Yes, "Absorption" is a process. Therefore, go below to the next decision shape (diamond).
"Is it a natural process?"

(See Appendix B on page 209 for more info on "natural process")

Yes, it is a natural process. Next, determine what specific information to look for. This step suggests the inclusion of words such as

- discovery of absorption
- study of absorption
- explanation of absorption
- concepts of absorption
- knowledge of absorption

Exercise #14

Now, it is your turn. Choose four natural processes.
Then, use the Algorithm on these natural processes.

Next, select two areas of focus for each natural process.

For example:

- explanation of absorption
- study of absorption

Search Term #15

The next research topic will be "Smelting". Start at the
beginning of the Algorithm. Form a "search need".
Need information on the topic "Smelting".

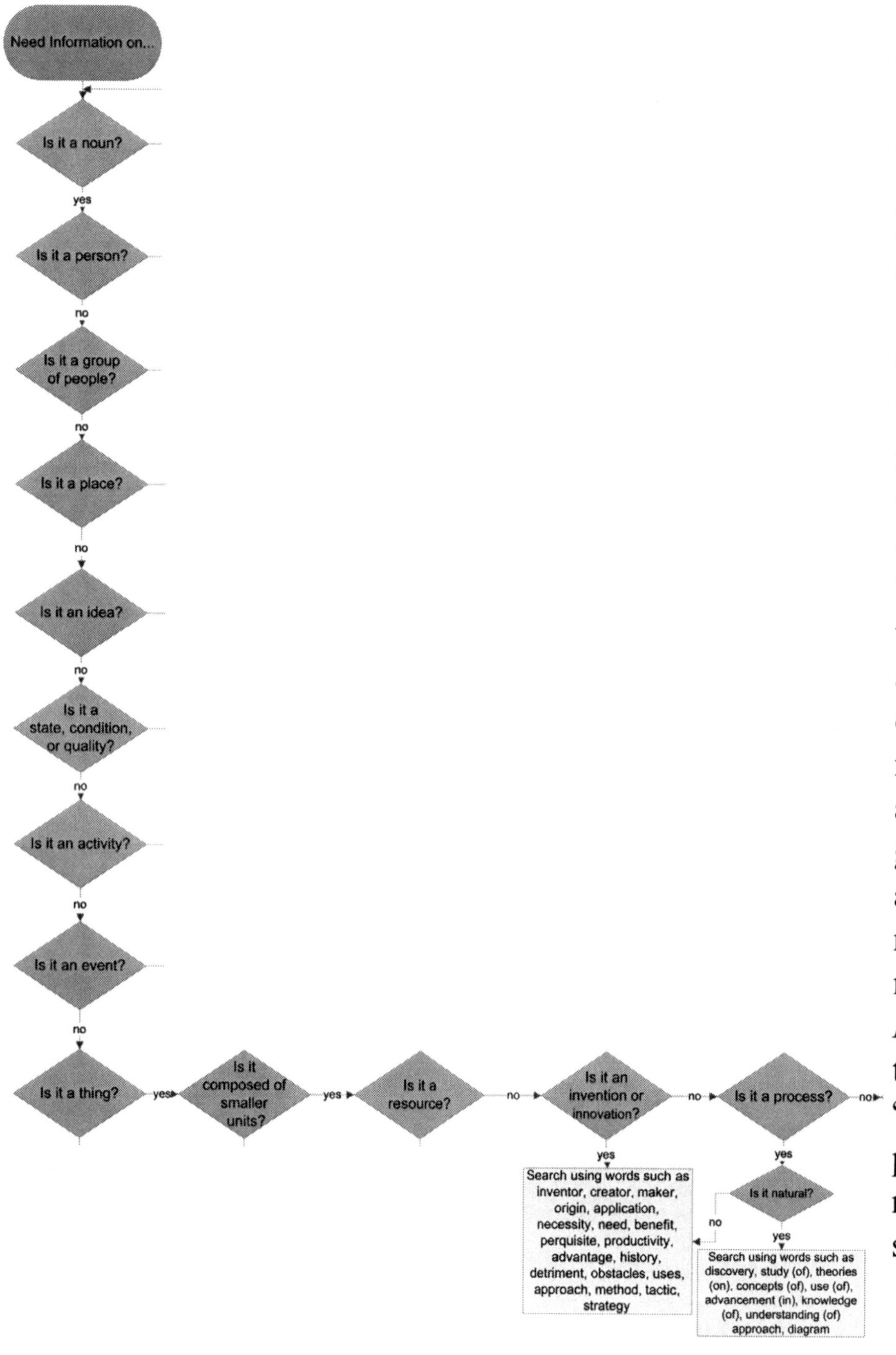

We know "Smelting" is a noun, but we also think it is not a person, group of people, or place. It was an idea. It is not a condition, but is an activity, or event. We will move into the "multiplicity" of words in later chapters. For now, we will exclude the idea, activity, or event of "Smelting". This leaves us with two options. Either, you have a vague understanding of "Smelting" or you do not. If you do not have a clue about the word(s), go down to the dictionary or encyclopedia rounded rectangle. Then repeat *The Imaginary Research Algorithm*. In this scenario, you know "Smelting" involves processing ore into a more refined metallic state.

Once again, focus on the particulars of your research topic. In the next chapter, we will discuss when it may be necessary to focus on multiple decision point.

After, analyzing the word "Smelting", we decided that the focus area of your research should be on the process of "Smelting".

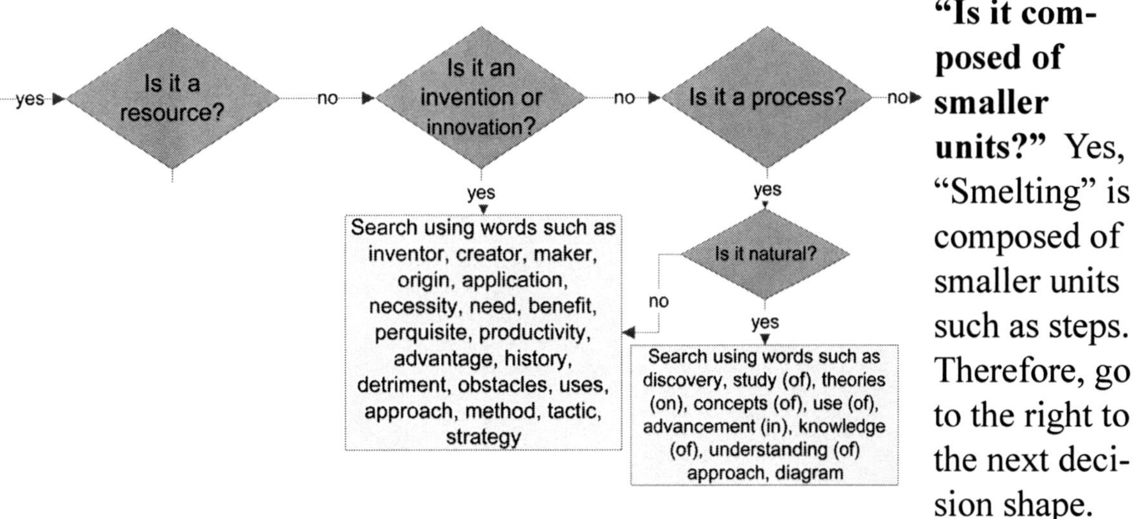

"Is it composed of smaller units?" Yes, "Smelting" is composed of smaller units such as steps. Therefore, go to the right to the next decision shape.

"Is it a resource?" No. So, you will move to the next decision shape (diamond) to the right.

"Is it an invention or an innovation?" It is/was an invention, but we want data on the process.

    After, skipping "Is it an invention or innovation", look at **"Is it a process?"**

    Yes. "Smelting" is a process. Therefore, go below to the next decision shape (diamond). **"Is it a natural process?"**

    No. It is a synthetic process.

    (See Appendix B on page 209 for more info on "synthetic process")

    Next, determine what specific information to look for. This step suggests the inclusion of words such as

- history of smelting
- need for smelting
- benefits of smelting
- origins of smelting

Exercise #15

Now, it is your turn. Choose four synthetic processes. Then, use the Algorithm on these man-made processes.

Next, select two areas of focus for each synthetic process.

> For example:
> - benefits of smelting
> - history of smelting

Chapter

3

In chapter 3, you will gain additional experience in navigating *The Imaginary Research Algorithm*. We will proceed through the Algorithm at a faster pace, because you should be able to use the Algorithm in total without fear of making a mistake. As long as, you follow the decision pathways, you will locate words that cognitively assist your research. Furthermore, this chapter discusses "research focus" and "multiplicity" and its effects on research. In short, "research focus" is an individual's purpose for researching. Do not overcomplicate the definition of "research focus." However, it is important to acknowledge your purpose or goal when researching. This is not to say you cannot wander around researching for the love of knowledge. *The Imaginary Research Algorithm* is designed to save students of all ages time through an expedited reflective process. "Multiplicity" is a complex subject. To define "multiplicity" in a few words, "human languages are limited or have limitations". Sometimes, the fact that words can have multiple meanings can be seen as a strength in language, but this strength can be a weakness, as well. Human languages are used to transmit thoughts. However, the ability to create errors and generate misunderstanding is very easy among two people that speak the same language. What causes these errors? The multiple meanings of words force people either explain themselves again or "operationalize"/ define each concept expressed in a statement or expression which is time consuming and inefficient, but in certain situations it must be done like writing a persuasive essay and in other situations like talking on the phone where verbal shortcuts can be taken. Language and accuracy are a very interesting combination. Lastly, Chapter 3 covers *The Imaginary Research Algorithm* in a quicker fashion.

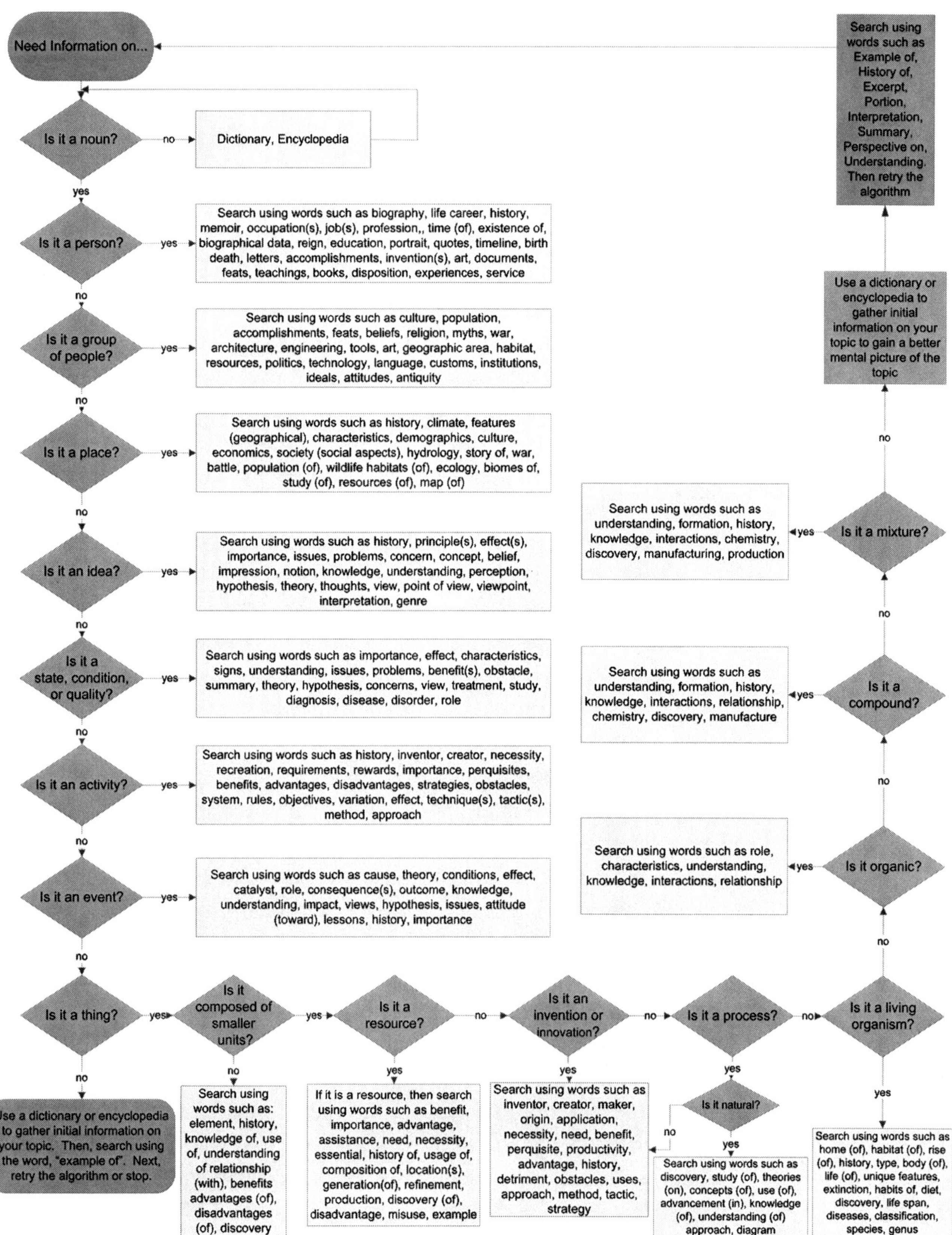

Need Information on...
Is it a noun?
no
Dictionary, Encyclopedia
yes
Is it a person?
yes
Search using words such as biography, life career, history, memoir, occupation(s), job(s), profession,, time (of), existence of, biographical data, reign, education, portrait, quotes, timeline, birth death, letters, accomplishments, invention(s), art, documents, feats, teachings, books, disposition, experiences, service
no
Is it a group of people?
yes
Search using words such as culture, population, accomplishments, feats, beliefs, religion, myths, war, architecture, engineering, tools, art, geographic area, habitat, resources, politics, technology, language, customs, institutions, ideals, attitudes, antiquity
no
Is it a place?
yes
Search using words such as history, climate, features (geographical), characteristics, demographics, culture, economics, society (social aspects), hydrology, story of, war, battle, population (of), wildlife habitats (of), ecology, biomes of, study (of), resources (of), map (of)
no
Is it an idea?
yes
Search using words such as history, principle(s), effect(s), importance, issues, problems, concern, concept, belief, impression, notion, knowledge, understanding, perception, hypothesis, theory, thoughts, view, point of view, viewpoint, interpretation, genre
no
Is it a state, condition, or quality?
yes
Search using words such as importance, effect, characteristics, signs, understanding, issues, problems, benefit(s), obstacle, summary, theory, hypothesis, concerns, view, treatment, study, diagnosis, disease, disorder, role
no
Is it an activity?
yes
Search using words such as history, inventor, creator, necessity, recreation, requirements, rewards, importance, perquisites, benefits, advantages, disadvantages, strategies, obstacles, system, rules, objectives, variation, effect, technique(s), tactic(s), method, approach
no
Is it an event?
yes
Search using words such as cause, theory, conditions, effect, catalyst, role, consequence(s), outcome, knowledge, understanding, impact, views, hypothesis, issues, attitude (toward), lessons, history, importance
no
Is it a thing?
yes
Is it composed of smaller units?
yes
Is it a resource?
no
Is it an invention or innovation?
no
Is it a process?
no
Is it a living organism?
no
Use a dictionary or encyclopedia to gather initial information on your topic. Then, search using the word, "example of". Next, retry the algorithm or stop.
no
Search using words such as: element, history, knowledge of, use of, understanding of relationship (with), benefits advantages (of), disadvantages (of), discovery
yes
If it is a resource, then search using words such as benefit, importance, advantage, assistance, need, necessity, essential, history of, usage of, composition of, location(s), generation(of), refinement, production, discovery (of), disadvantage, misuse, example
yes
Search using words such as inventor, creator, maker, origin, application, necessity, need, benefit, perquisite, productivity, advantage, history, detriment, obstacles, uses, approach, method, tactic, strategy
yes
Is it natural?
no
yes
Search using words such as discovery, study (of), theories (on), concepts (of), use (of), advancement (in), knowledge (of), understanding (of) approach, diagram
yes
Search using words such as home (of), habitat (of), rise (of), history, type, body (of), life (of), unique features, extinction, habits of, diet, discovery, life span, diseases, classification, species, genus
Is it organic?
yes
Search using words such as role, characteristics, understanding, knowledge, interactions, relationship
no
Is it a compound?
yes
Search using words such as understanding, formation, history, knowledge, interactions, relationship, chemistry, discovery, manufacture
no
Is it a mixture?
yes
Search using words such as understanding, formation, history, knowledge, interactions, chemistry, discovery, manufacturing, production
no
Use a dictionary or encyclopedia to gather initial information on your topic to gain a better mental picture of the topic
no
Search using words such as Example of, History of, Excerpt, Portion, Interpretation, Summary, Perspective on, Understanding. Then retry the algorithm

Search Term #16

We know "Lion" is a noun, but we also know it is not a person, group of people, place, idea, condition or quality, activity or event. This leaves us with two options. This is a thing or a word you do not know. If you are not familiar with the word "Lion", then go down to the dictionary or encyclopedia box. Next, repeat *The Imaginary Research Algorithm*. In this scenario, you know what "Lion" is.

Analyze the word "Lion".

"Is it composed of smaller units?" Yes, a "Lion" is composed of smaller units. Therefore, go to the right to the next decision shape (diamond).

"Is it an invention or innovation?" No.

"Is it a resource?" No. So, you will move to the next decision shape (diamond) to the right. (Please note, parts of a lion can be used as a resource, but in this instance we will not claim it as a resource)

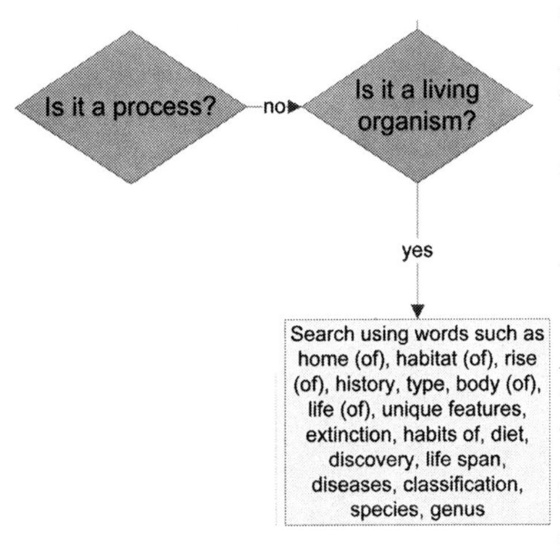

(See Appendix B on page 209 for more info on "organism")

"Is it a process?" No, a "Lion" is not a process.

"Is it a living organism?"

Yes. A "Lion" is a living organism.

Next, determine what specific information to look for. During a search, this step suggests the inclusion of words such as

- features of a lion
- life span of lions
- habitat of lions
- history of lions
- knowledge of lions

Exercise #16

Now, it is your turn. Choose four organisms.
Then, use the Algorithm on these organisms.

Next, select two areas of focus for each organism.

For example:
- life span of lions
- history of lions

Imaginary Research Algorithm

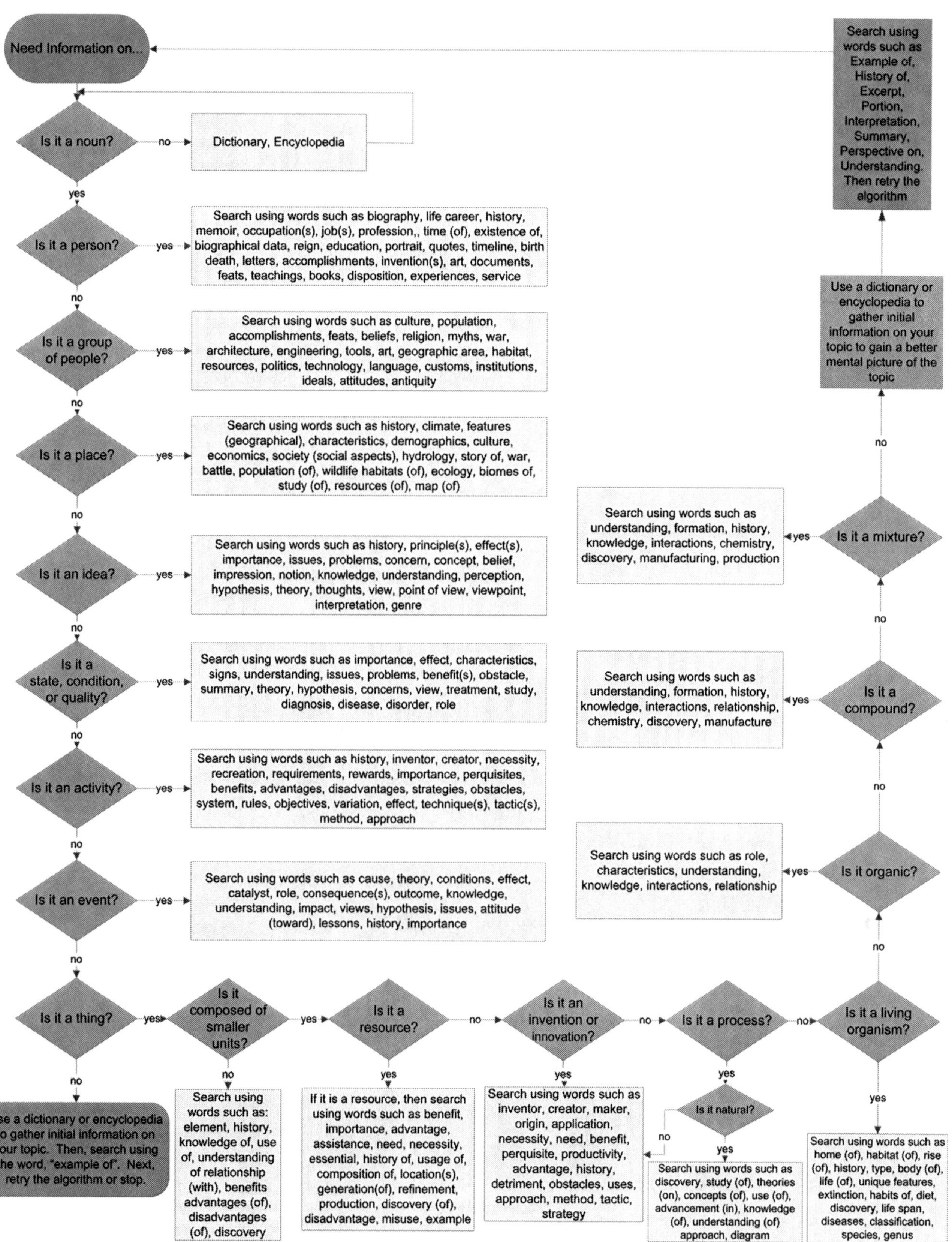

Search Term #17

The next research topic will be "Cyanobacteria". Start at the beginning of the Algorithm. Form a "search need".
"Need information on the topic 'Cyanobacteria'".

"Cyanobacteria"? In this situation, let's say you do not know what "Cyanobacteria" is. Since, we are clueless about the word. We can do two things. Either make negative assumptions (it's not a person, group of people, place, idea, condition, activity, event or thing) about the "Cyanobacteria" until we reach the bottom of the Algorithm on the left side. By doing this, you will be guided to a dictionary or encyclopedia. But, here is a better tactic to use when you don't have a clue about a word. Assume it is not a noun, first. This will lead you to a dictionary or encyclopedia, first.

"Cyanobacteria".
We use a dictionary. We discover that cyanobacteria is a life form or organism. Organisms are nouns.

Now that we positively know that "Cyanobacteria" is a noun, we can go through the steps. It is not a person, group of people, place, idea, condition or quality, activity, or event. Analyze the word "Cyanobacteria".

"Is it composed of smaller units?" Yes, "Cyanobacteria" is composed of smaller units. Therefore, go to the right to the next decision shape (diamond).

"Is it a resource?" No. So, you will move to the next decision shape (diamond) to the right.

"Is it an invention or innovation?"
No.

"Is it a process?"
No. "Cyanobacteria" is not a process.

"Is it a living organism?"

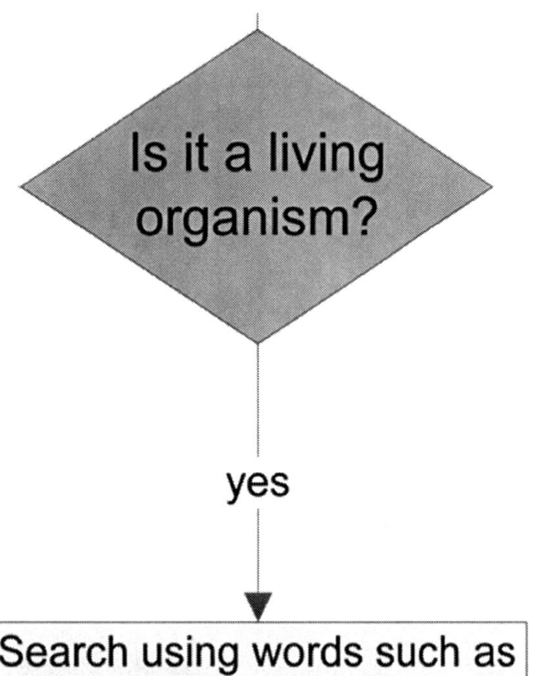

Yes, it is a type of organism. Next, determine what specific information to look for. This step suggests the inclusion of words such as

- discovery of cyanobacteria
- study of cyanobacteria
- history of cyanobacteria
- features of cyanobacteria
- knowledge of cyanobacteria

Exercise #17

Now, it is your turn. Choose four organisms. Then, use the Algorithm on these organisms.

Next, select two areas of focus for each organism.

For example:

- discovery of cyanobacteria
- study of cyanobacteria

Once, you really get the hang of the Algorithm and all of its decisions. You will be introduced to several different helper expressions of *The Imaginary Research Algorithm*(chapter 7). By then, your personal speed will have multiplied by the conciseness of the expressions.

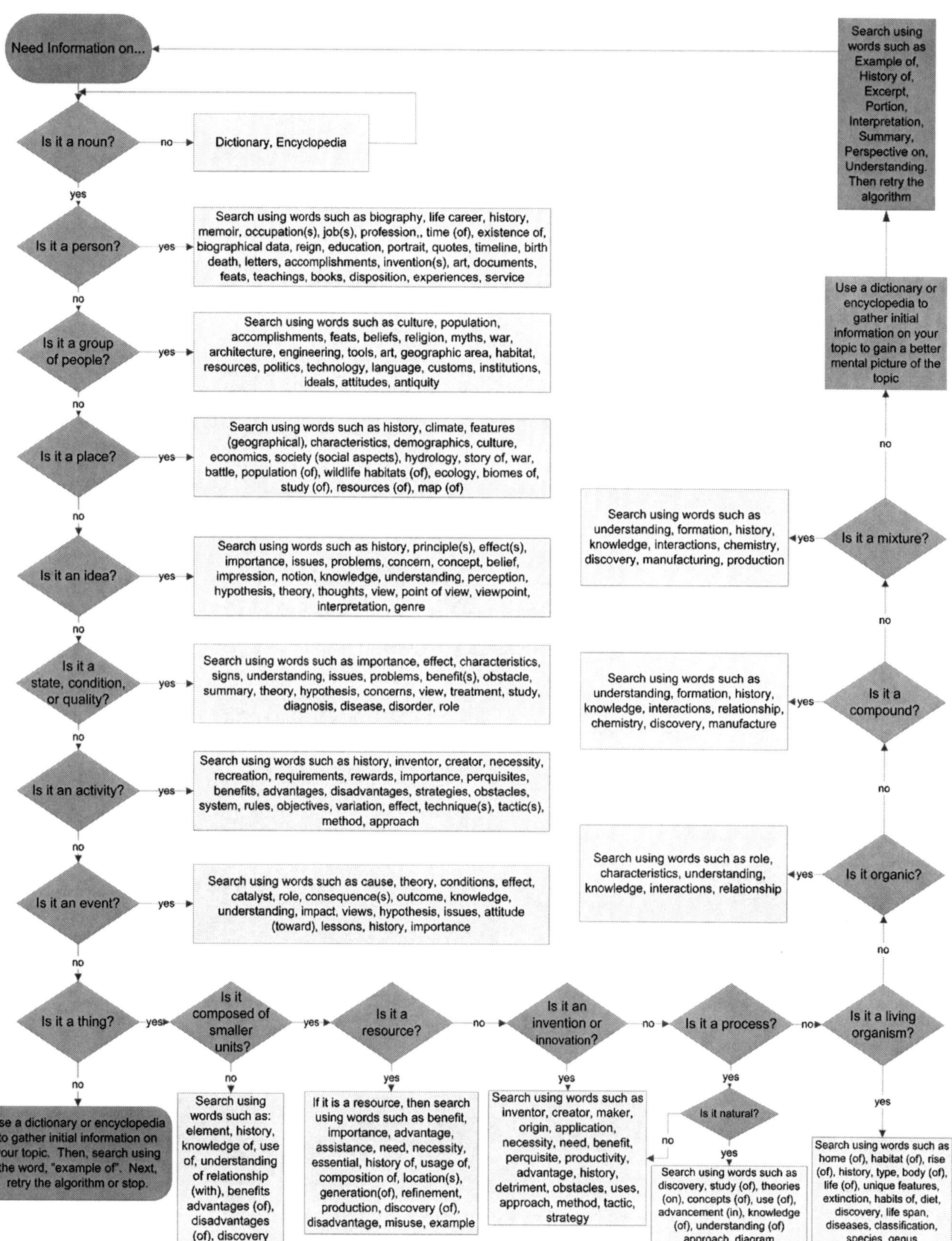

Need Information on...
Is it a noun?
no
Dictionary, Encyclopedia
yes
Search using words such as Example of, History of, Excerpt, Portion, Interpretation, Summary, Perspective on, Understanding. Then retry the algorithm
Is it a person?
yes
Search using words such as biography, life career, history, memoir, occupation(s), job(s), profession,, time (of), existence of, biographical data, reign, education, portrait, quotes, timeline, birth death, letters, accomplishments, invention(s), art, documents, feats, teachings, books, disposition, experiences, service
no
Use a dictionary or encyclopedia to gather initial information on your topic to gain a better mental picture of the topic
Is it a group of people?
yes
Search using words such as culture, population, accomplishments, feats, beliefs, religion, myths, war, architecture, engineering, tools, art, geographic area, habitat, resources, politics, technology, language, customs, institutions, ideals, attitudes, antiquity
no
Is it a place?
yes
Search using words such as history, climate, features (geographical), characteristics, demographics, culture, economics, society (social aspects), hydrology, story of, war, battle, population (of), wildlife habitats (of), ecology, biomes of, study (of), resources (of), map (of)
no
no
Is it a mixture?
yes
Search using words such as understanding, formation, history, knowledge, interactions, chemistry, discovery, manufacturing, production
Is it an idea?
yes
Search using words such as history, principle(s), effect(s), importance, issues, problems, concern, concept, belief, impression, notion, knowledge, understanding, perception, hypothesis, theory, thoughts, view, point of view, viewpoint, interpretation, genre
no
Is it a state, condition, or quality?
yes
Search using words such as importance, effect, characteristics, signs, understanding, issues, problems, benefit(s), obstacle, summary, theory, hypothesis, concerns, view, treatment, study, diagnosis, disease, disorder, role
no
Is it a compound?
yes
Search using words such as understanding, formation, history, knowledge, interactions, relationship, chemistry, discovery, manufacture
Is it an activity?
yes
Search using words such as history, inventor, creator, necessity, recreation, requirements, rewards, importance, perquisites, benefits, advantages, disadvantages, strategies, obstacles, system, rules, objectives, variation, effect, technique(s), tactic(s), method, approach
no
no
Is it organic?
yes
Search using words such as role, characteristics, understanding, knowledge, interactions, relationship
Is it an event?
yes
Search using words such as cause, theory, conditions, effect, catalyst, role, consequence(s), outcome, knowledge, understanding, impact, views, hypothesis, issues, attitude (toward), lessons, history, importance
no
no
Is it a thing?
yes
Is it composed of smaller units?
yes
Is it a resource?
no
Is it an invention or innovation?
no
Is it a process?
no
Is it a living organism?
no
no
no
yes
yes
yes
yes
yes
Use a dictionary or encyclopedia to gather initial information on your topic. Then, search using the word, "example of". Next, retry the algorithm or stop.
Search using words such as: element, history, knowledge of, use of, understanding of relationship (with), benefits advantages (of), disadvantages (of), discovery
If it is a resource, then search using words such as benefit, importance, advantage, assistance, need, necessity, essential, history of, usage of, composition of, location(s), generation(of), refinement, production, discovery (of), disadvantage, misuse, example
Search using words such as inventor, creator, maker, origin, application, necessity, need, benefit, perquisite, productivity, advantage, history, detriment, obstacles, uses, approach, method, tactic, strategy
Is it natural?
no
yes
Search using words such as discovery, study (of), theories (on), concepts (of), use (of), advancement (in), knowledge (of), understanding (of) approach, diagram
Search using words such as home (of), habitat (of), rise (of), history, type, body (of), life (of), unique features, extinction, habits of, diet, discovery, life span, diseases, classification, species, genus

Search Terms #18

The next research topic will be "Thyroid (gland)". Start at the beginning of the Algorithm. Form a "search need". "Need information on the topic 'Thyroid (gland)'". Now that we positively know that "Thyroid (gland)" is a noun, we can go through the steps of the Algorithm. It is not a person, group of people, place, idea, condition or quality, activity, or event. Analyze the word "Thyroid (gland)". We know it is something in the human body. This is the full extent of our knowledge about a "Thyroid (gland)". **"Is it composed of smaller units?"** Yes, "Thyroid (gland)" is composed of smaller units. Therefore, go to the right to the next decision shape (diamond). **"Is it a resource?"** No. So, you will move to the next decision shape (diamond) to the right. **"Is it an invention or innovation?"** No. **"Is it a process?"** No. "Thyroid (gland)" is not a process. **"Is it a living organism?"** No, it is not a living organism?

"Is it organic?" (See Appendix B on page 209 for more info on "organic")
Yes, it is organic.* Next, determine what specific information to look for. This step suggests the inclusion of words such as

- role of thyroid
- function of thyroid
- characteristic of thyroid
- understanding of thyroid
- interactions of thyroid
- knowledge of thyroid

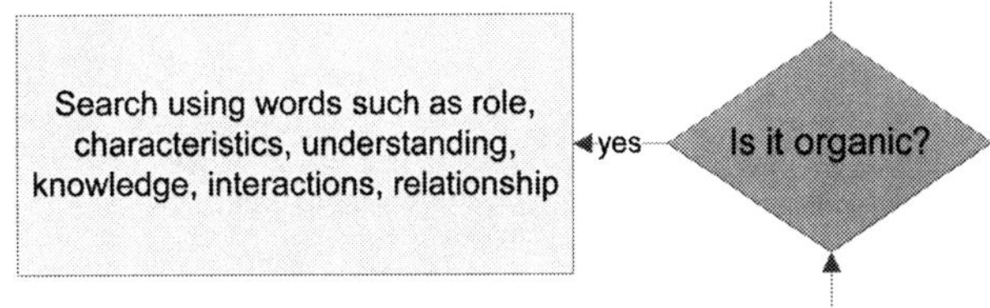

*Organic Defined

Organic is anything connected to carbon based life forms like plants or animals. *The Imaginary Research Algorithm* sees organic as meaning a portion of the composition, system, organ, tissue, cell, or organelle that has a relationship with carbon.

The "Organic" rectangle focuses on parts and pieces of organisms while the "Organism" rectangle focuses on actual organisms.

Imaginary Research Algorithm

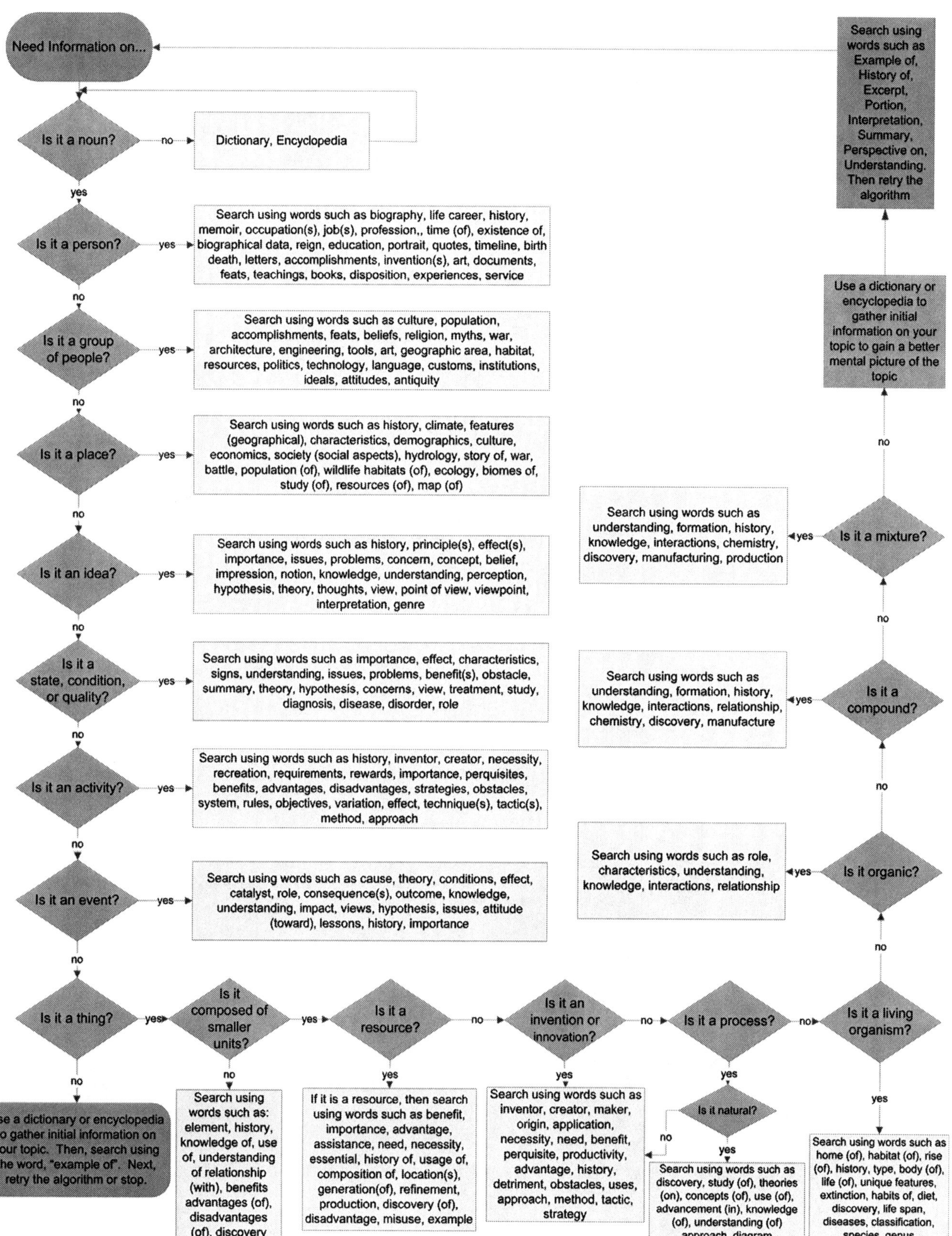

Exercise #18

Now, it is your turn. Choose four "organic things". Then, use the Algorithm on these "organic things".

Next, select two areas of focus for each "organic" thing.

For example:

- understanding of thyroid
- role of thyroid

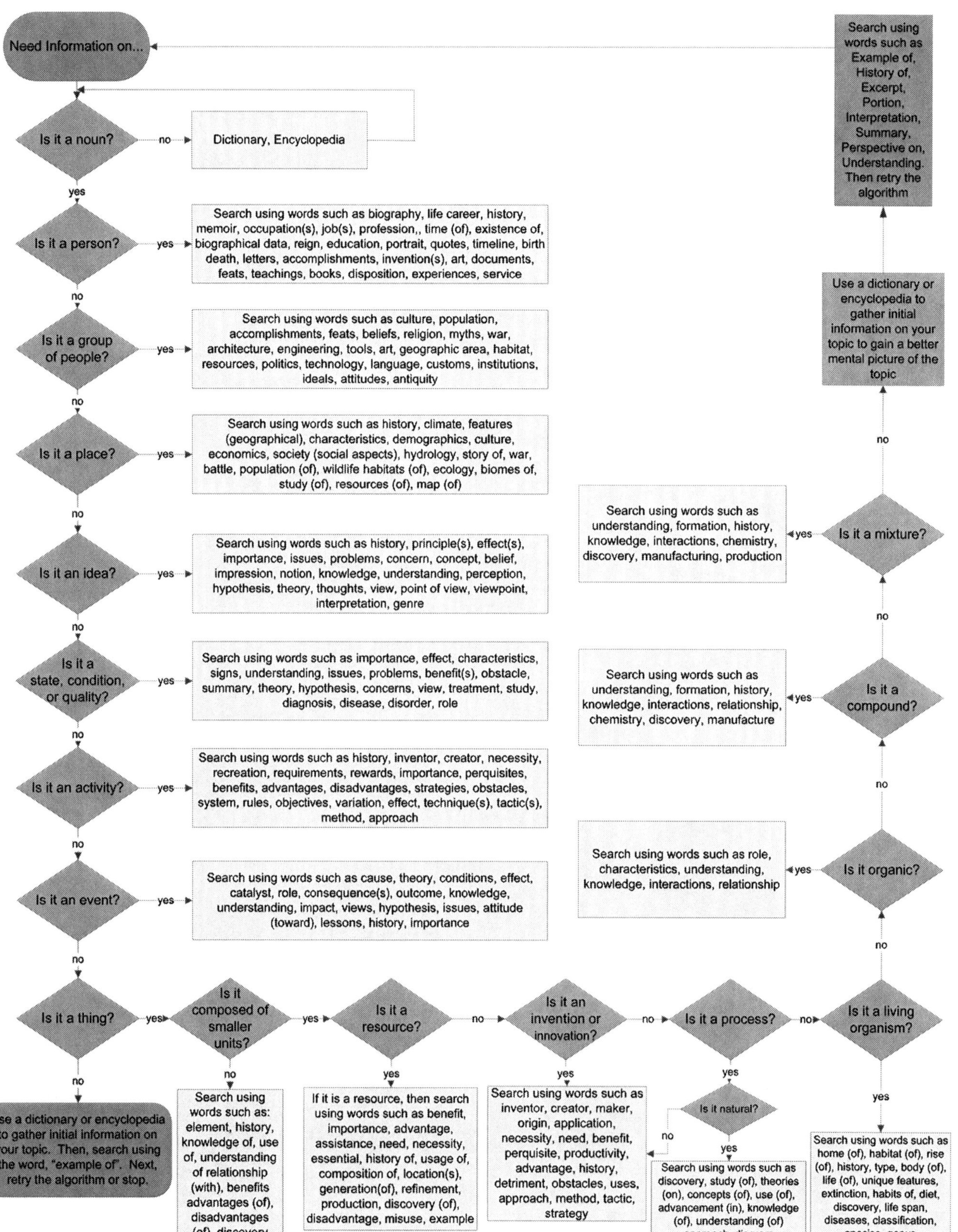

Need Information on...
Is it a noun?
no
Dictionary, Encyclopedia
yes
Is it a person?
yes
Search using words such as biography, life career, history, memoir, occupation(s), job(s), profession,, time (of), existence of, biographical data, reign, education, portrait, quotes, timeline, birth death, letters, accomplishments, invention(s), art, documents, feats, teachings, books, disposition, experiences, service
no
Is it a group of people?
yes
Search using words such as culture, population, accomplishments, feats, beliefs, religion, myths, war, architecture, engineering, tools, art, geographic area, habitat, resources, politics, technology, language, customs, institutions, ideals, attitudes, antiquity
no
Is it a place?
yes
Search using words such as history, climate, features (geographical), characteristics, demographics, culture, economics, society (social aspects), hydrology, story of, war, battle, population (of), wildlife habitats (of), ecology, biomes of, study (of), resources (of), map (of)
no
Is it an idea?
yes
Search using words such as history, principle(s), effect(s), importance, issues, problems, concern, concept, belief, impression, notion, knowledge, understanding, perception, hypothesis, theory, thoughts, view, point of view, viewpoint, interpretation, genre
no
Is it a state, condition, or quality?
yes
Search using words such as importance, effect, characteristics, signs, understanding, issues, problems, benefit(s), obstacle, summary, theory, hypothesis, concerns, view, treatment, study, diagnosis, disease, disorder, role
no
Is it an activity?
yes
Search using words such as history, inventor, creator, necessity, recreation, requirements, rewards, importance, perquisites, benefits, advantages, disadvantages, strategies, obstacles, system, rules, objectives, variation, effect, technique(s), tactic(s), method, approach
no
Is it an event?
yes
Search using words such as cause, theory, conditions, effect, catalyst, role, consequence(s), outcome, knowledge, understanding, impact, views, hypothesis, issues, attitude (toward), lessons, history, importance
no
Is it a thing?
yes
Is it composed of smaller units?
yes
Is it a resource?
no
Is it an invention or innovation?
no
Is it a process?
no
Is it a living organism?
no
Is it organic?
yes
Search using words such as role, characteristics, understanding, knowledge, interactions, relationship
no
Is it a compound?
yes
Search using words such as understanding, formation, history, knowledge, interactions, relationship, chemistry, discovery, manufacture
no
Is it a mixture?
yes
Search using words such as understanding, formation, history, knowledge, interactions, chemistry, discovery, manufacturing, production
no
Use a dictionary or encyclopedia to gather initial information on your topic to gain a better mental picture of the topic
no
Search using words such as Example of, History of, Excerpt, Portion, Interpretation, Summary, Perspective on, Understanding. Then retry the algorithm
no
Use a dictionary or encyclopedia to gather initial information on your topic. Then, search using the word, "example of". Next, retry the algorithm or stop.
Search using words such as: element, history, knowledge of, use of, understanding of relationship (with), benefits advantages (of), disadvantages (of), discovery
yes
If it is a resource, then search using words such as benefit, importance, advantage, assistance, need, necessity, essential, history of, usage of, composition of, location(s), generation(of), refinement, production, discovery (of), disadvantage, misuse, example
yes
Search using words such as inventor, creator, maker, origin, application, necessity, need, benefit, perquisite, productivity, advantage, history, detriment, obstacles, uses, approach, method, tactic, strategy
yes
Is it natural?
no
yes
Search using words such as discovery, study (of), theories (on), concepts (of), use (of), advancement (in), knowledge (of), understanding (of) approach, diagram
yes
Search using words such as home (of), habitat (of), rise (of), history, type, body (of), life (of), unique features, extinction, habits of, diet, discovery, life span, diseases, classification, species, genus

Search Term #19

The next research topic will be "Sodium Chloride". Start at the beginning of the Algorithm. Form a "search need". "Need information on the topic 'Sodium Chloride'".

Let's suppose we do not know anything about "Sodium Chloride". First, you go to a dictionary or encyclopedia.

Now that we positively know that "Sodium Chloride" is a noun, we can go through the steps. It is not a person, group of people, place, idea, condition or quality, activity, or event. Analyze the word "Sodium Chloride".
"Is it composed of smaller units?" Yes, "Sodium Chloride" is composed of smaller units. Therefore, go to the right to the next decision shape (diamond).

"Is it a resource?" Yes, it is a resource but for now we will focus on the compound. So, you will move to the next decision shape (diamond) to the right.
"Is it an invention or innovation?" No.
"Is it a process?" No.
"Sodium Chloride" is not a process.
"Is it a living organism?" No, it is not a living organism?
"Is it organic?"
No.

"Is it a compound?" (See Appendix B on page 209 for more info on "inorganic compounds")

Yes, it is a compound. Next, determine what specific information to look for. During a search, this step suggests the inclusion of words
such as
- role of sodium chloride
- function of sodium chloride
- characteristic of sodium chloride
- understanding of sodium chloride
- interactions of sodium chloride
- knowledge of sodium chloride

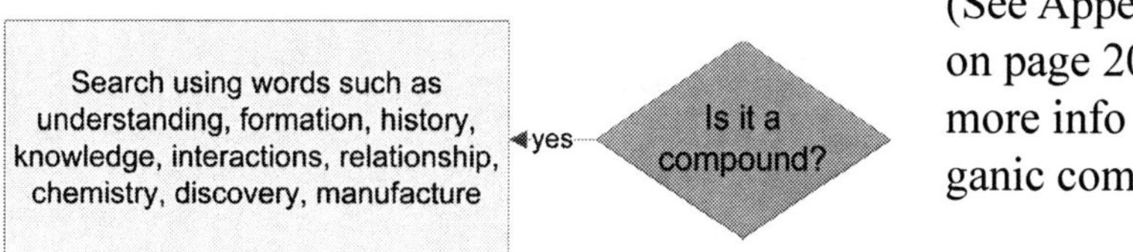

(See Appendix B
on page 209 for
more info on "inor-
ganic compound")

Imaginary Research Algorithm

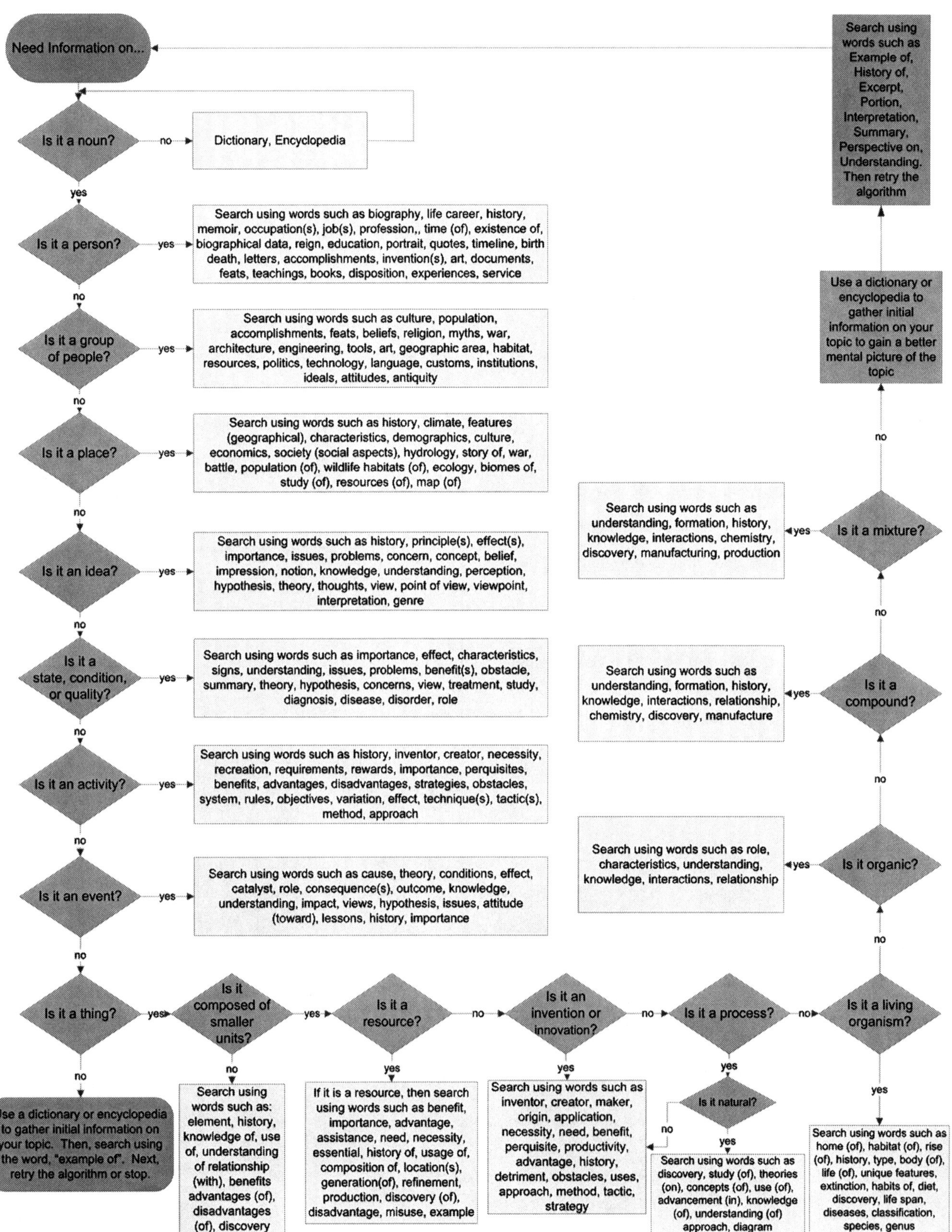

Exercise #19

Now, it is your turn. Choose four compounds. Then, use the Algorithm on these compounds.

Next, select two areas of focus for each compound.

For example:

- discovery of sodium chloride
- history of sodium chloride

Imaginary Research Algorithm

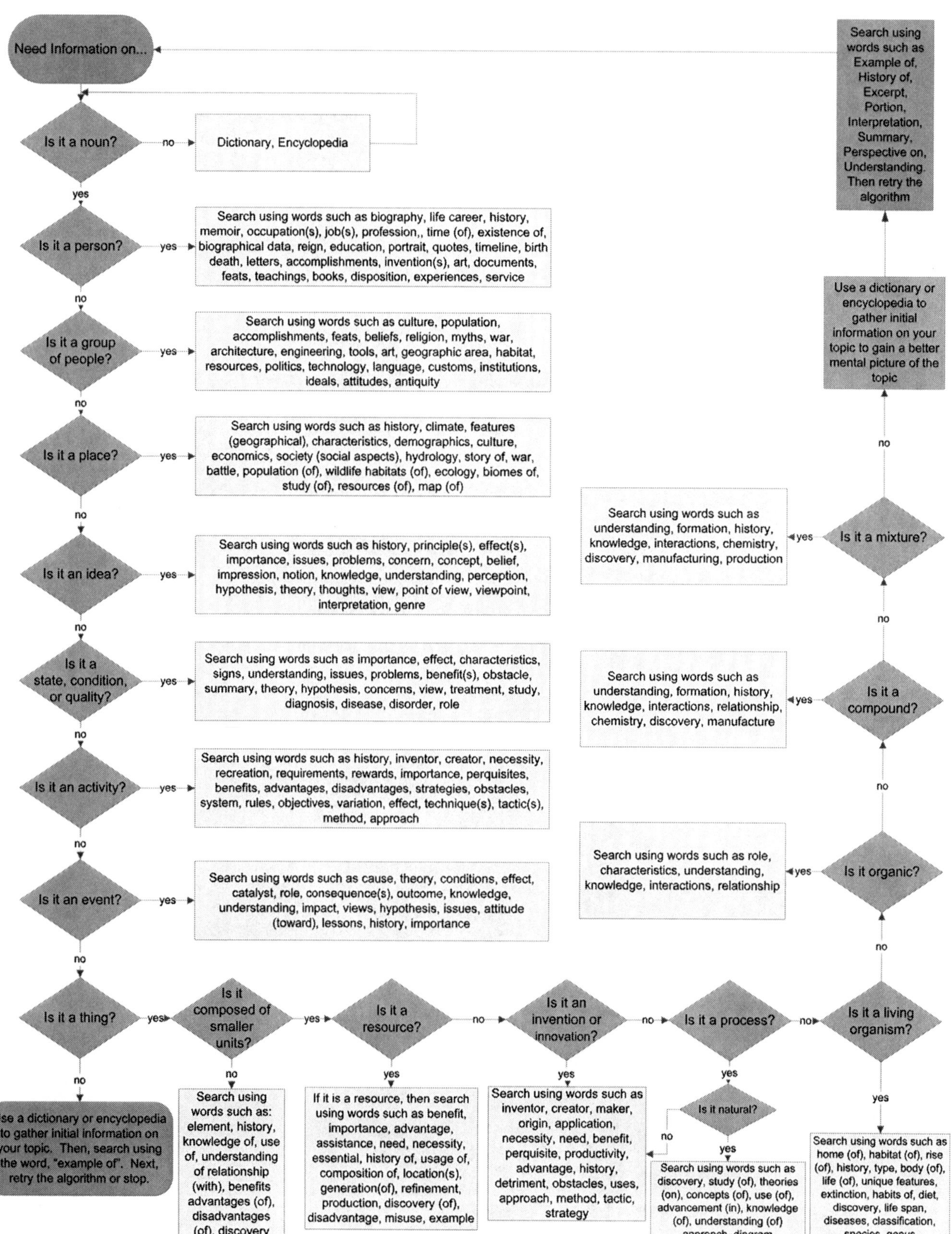

Search Term #20

The next research topic will be "Soil". Start at the beginning of the Algorithm.
Form a "search need".
"Need information on the topic 'Soil'".

Now that we positively know that "Soil" is a noun, we can go through the
steps. It is not a person, group of people, place, idea, condition or quality, activity, or event. Analyze the word "Soil".

"Is it composed of smaller units?" Yes, "Soil" is composed of smaller units.
Therefore, go to the right to the next decision shape (diamond).

"Is it a resource?" No. So, you will move to the next decision shape (diamond) to the right. (Note, soil can be a resource , but we are simplifying this
example.)

"Is it an invention or innovation?" No.
"Is it a process?" No. "Soil" is not a process.

"Is it a living organism?" No, it is not a living organism?

"Is it organic?" No. It is not organic.

"Is it a compound?"
No. It is not a compound.

"Is it a mixture?" (See Appendix B on page 209 for more info on "mixture")
Yes. It is a mixture. Next, determine what specific information to look for.
This step suggests the inclusion of words such as

- understanding of soil
- interactions of soil
- knowledge of soil

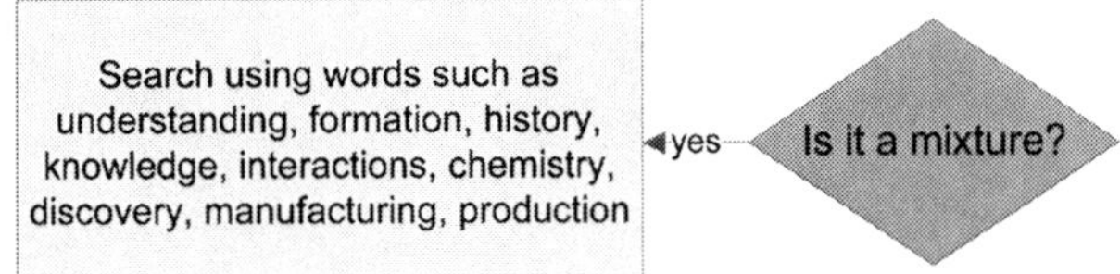

Exercise #20

Now, it is your turn. Choose four mixtures. Then, use the Algorithm on these mixtures.

Next, select two areas of focus for each mixture.

For example:
- understanding of soil
- knowledge of soil

Now that we have gone through each decision point. It is time to confront "multiplicity" of words. As we mentioned earlier, language is limited. For example, search term number twenty was "soil". "Soil" is a noun. It can be seen as a resource or a mixture. It depends on the perspective or point of view. For example, an apple tree would take advantage of the chemicals in the mixture of "soil". A farmer would use "soil" as a resource to plant crops. Words can easily have multiple meanings. This could potentially slow down your research using the Algorithm. However, if you narrow down your research decisions to one or two decision point (diamonds).
You can speed up your research. For example, the modern Compact Disc or CD started out as an idea(or theory) which eventually was invented. Now, it is a resource used by industry to record different sources of data. You have to decide the area(s) that you wish to discuss for your research assignment. It is possible, you wish to cover each segment, but you should factor in the needs of your research task. The choice is yours.

As a reminder, *The Imaginary Research Algorithm* is here to help jumpstart research projects with words that stimulate the research process. The Algorithm will not complete your assignments for you. It merely demonstrates possibilities.

Chapter

4

In chapter four, I will introduce varied practice for *The Imaginary Research Algorithm*. We will also go through the Algorithm in a more verbal manner. Furthermore, the "multiplicity" factor will be taken into account when using *The Imaginary Research Algorithm*.

Imaginary Research Algorithm

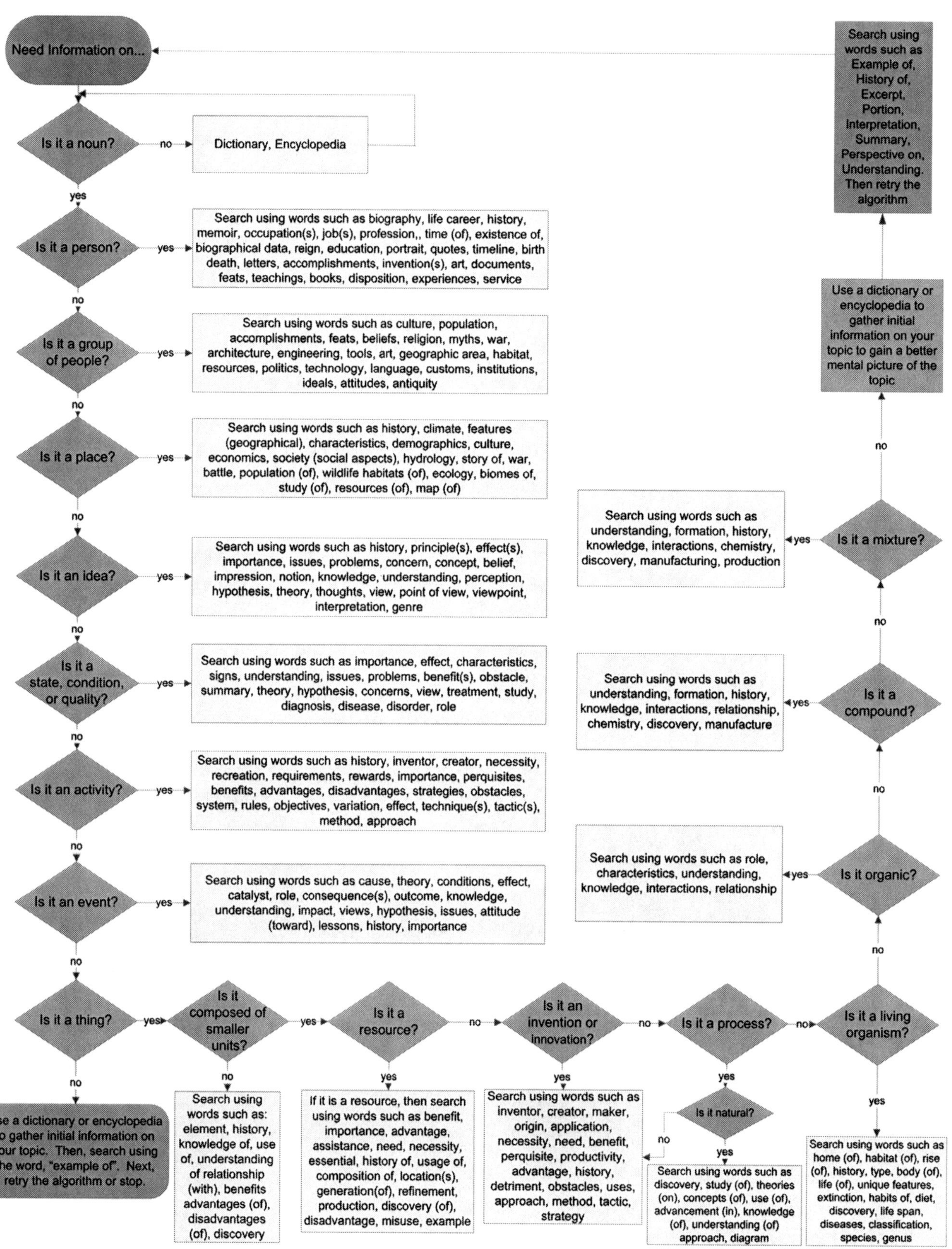

Search Term #21

Let's increase the difficulty.

The word "Them" is our research topic. We form a "search need" and identify that the word "Them" is not a noun. Therefore, you go to a dictionary or encyclopedia to learn information on the pronunciation and meaning of a word.

Exercise # 21

Now, it is your turn. Choose four pronouns. Then, use the Algorithm on these "pronouns".

Search Term #22

The next research topic will be the "Iliad". Start at the beginning of the Algorithm. Form a "search need". The search need is "need information on the topic 'Iliad'".

We know "Iliad" is a noun. Specifically, it is an epic poem. Let's examine how *The Imaginary Research Algorithm* and a poem work together. The "Iliad" is not a person, group of people, place, idea, condition or quality or activity. In this scenario, you know what the "Iliad" is. But, you may have difficulty classifying a poem or work of art.

"Is it composed of smaller units?" Yes, "Is it a resource?" In this situation, no.

"Is it an invention or innovation?"

Yes. The "Iliad" was created or invented, but as you research the epic poem, you will discover it contains portions of historic events.

Next, determine what specific information to look for. This step suggests the inclusion of words such as

- author of "Iliad"
- history of "Iliad"
- benefits of "Iliad"
- origins of "Iliad"

Exercise #22

Choose four literary works in conjunction with the Algorithm.

Imaginary Research Algorithm

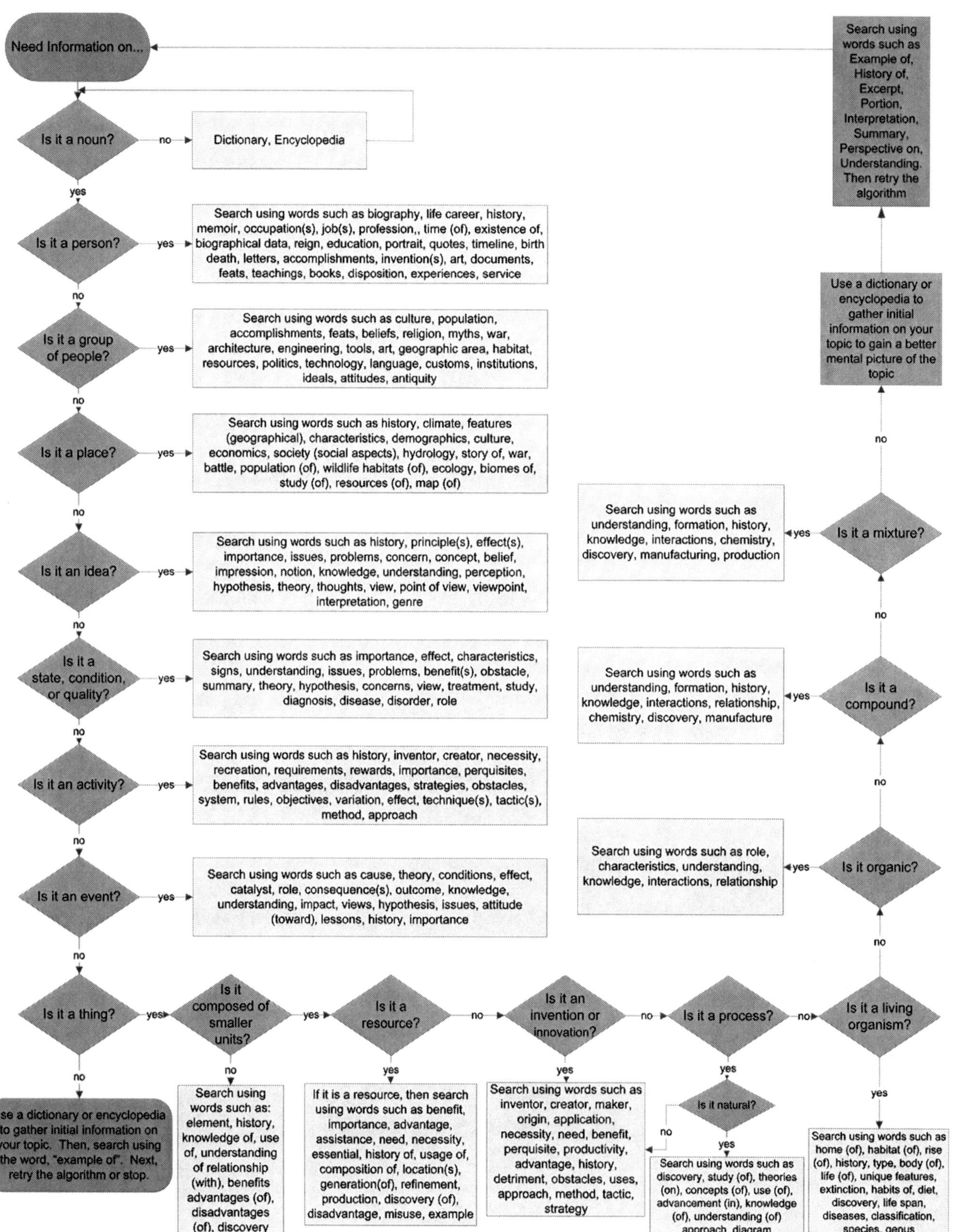

Search Term #23

The next research topic will be "Plastic". Start at the beginning of the Algorithm. Form a "search need". The "search need" is "need information on the topic 'Plastic'".

We know "Plastic" is a noun. Next, we scan through the decision points of the Algorithm and eliminate the questions that do not relate to "Plastic". We conclude that plastic was/is

- an idea
- a resource
- an invention

You will eventually have to decide whether you are researching plastic the idea, plastic the resource, or plastic the invention. Whole books can be written on any of the above. It all depends on your research assignment. Your research requirements should be your beacon for finding information. This is not to say that you should not explore various avenues of your research topic. In fact, if you have a relatively large research project, you may want to use more than one decision point to spark ideas and locate information.

In this situation, go back to the Algorithm. Locate the decision point **"Is it a resource?"** Yes, but at this time we would prefer to learn about the history of plastics. So, you will move to the next decision shape (diamond) to the right. This is an example of the focus that is required when a "search need" takes on the form of multiple selections (multiplicity).

"Is it an invention or innovation?" Yes.

Next, determine what specific information to look for. This step suggests the inclusion of words such as

- inventor of plastic
- benefits of plastic
- history of plastic
- disadvantages of plastic
- application(s) of plastic

Exercise #23

Choose four inventions or innovations in conjunction with the Algorithm.

Imaginary Research Algorithm

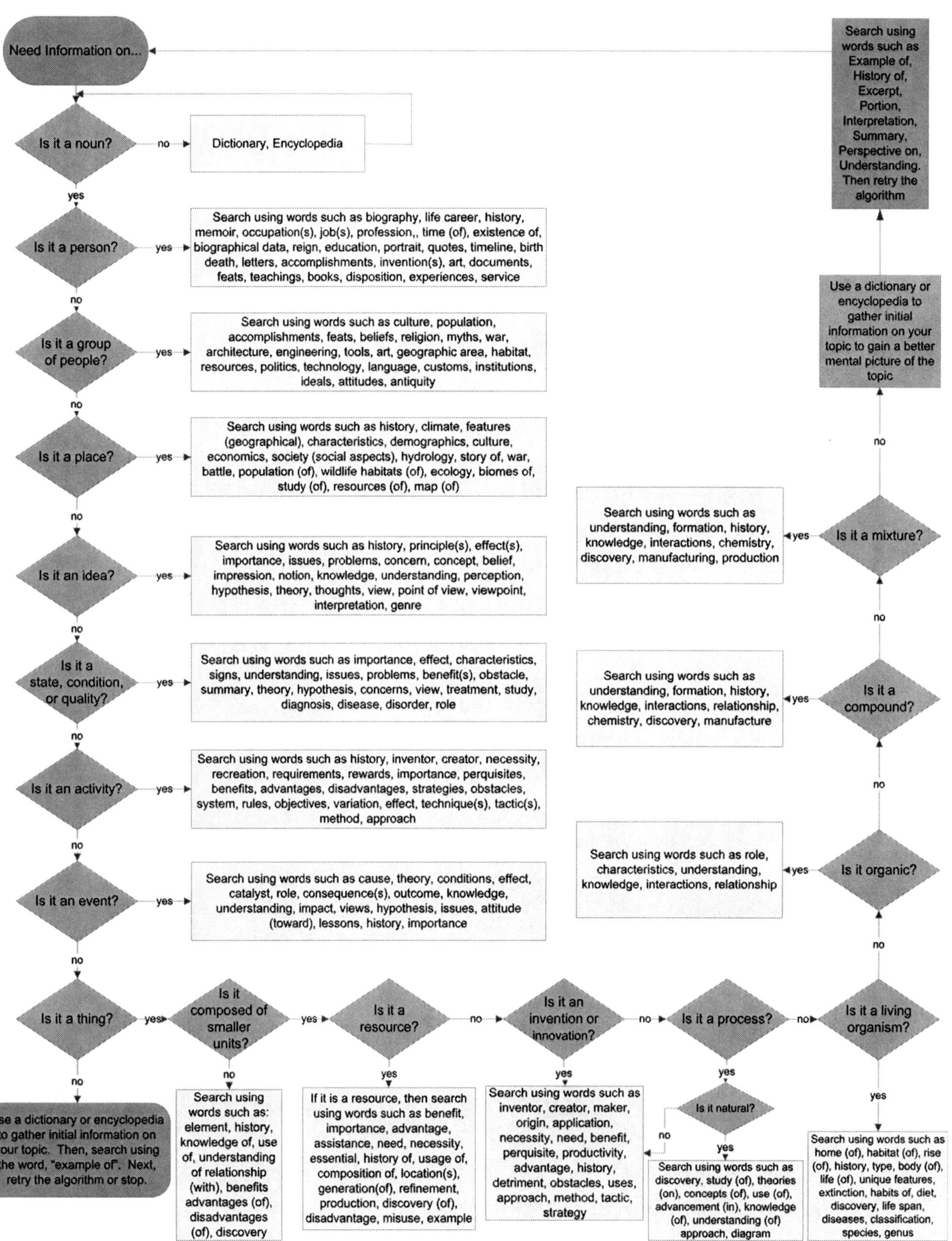

Search Term #24

Now, we will search for information on "Turkey". We know "Turkey" is a noun, but "Turkey" is not a person or group of people. The next decision block states **"Is it a Place?"**

Yes, "Turkey" is a place. Next, determine what specific information to look for. This step suggests the inclusion of words such as

- history of Turkey
- climate of Turkey
- features of Turkey
- economics of Turkey
- culture of Turkey

A "turkey" is an animal, as well. So, it would fall under the category of organism.

Now that you are aware of the issues with the "multiplicity" of words, remember to focus on your research assignment. For example, if you were researching "Turkey" in a social science class, you would most likely research the word "Turkey" as a place. If you came across "turkey" in biology class, then you would most likely research this term as an organism.

Exercise #24

Select four places. Then, use the Algorithm on these terms. Next, provide two areas of focus for each term.

For example:

- resources of California
- demographics of California
- characteristics of California

Imaginary Research Algorithm

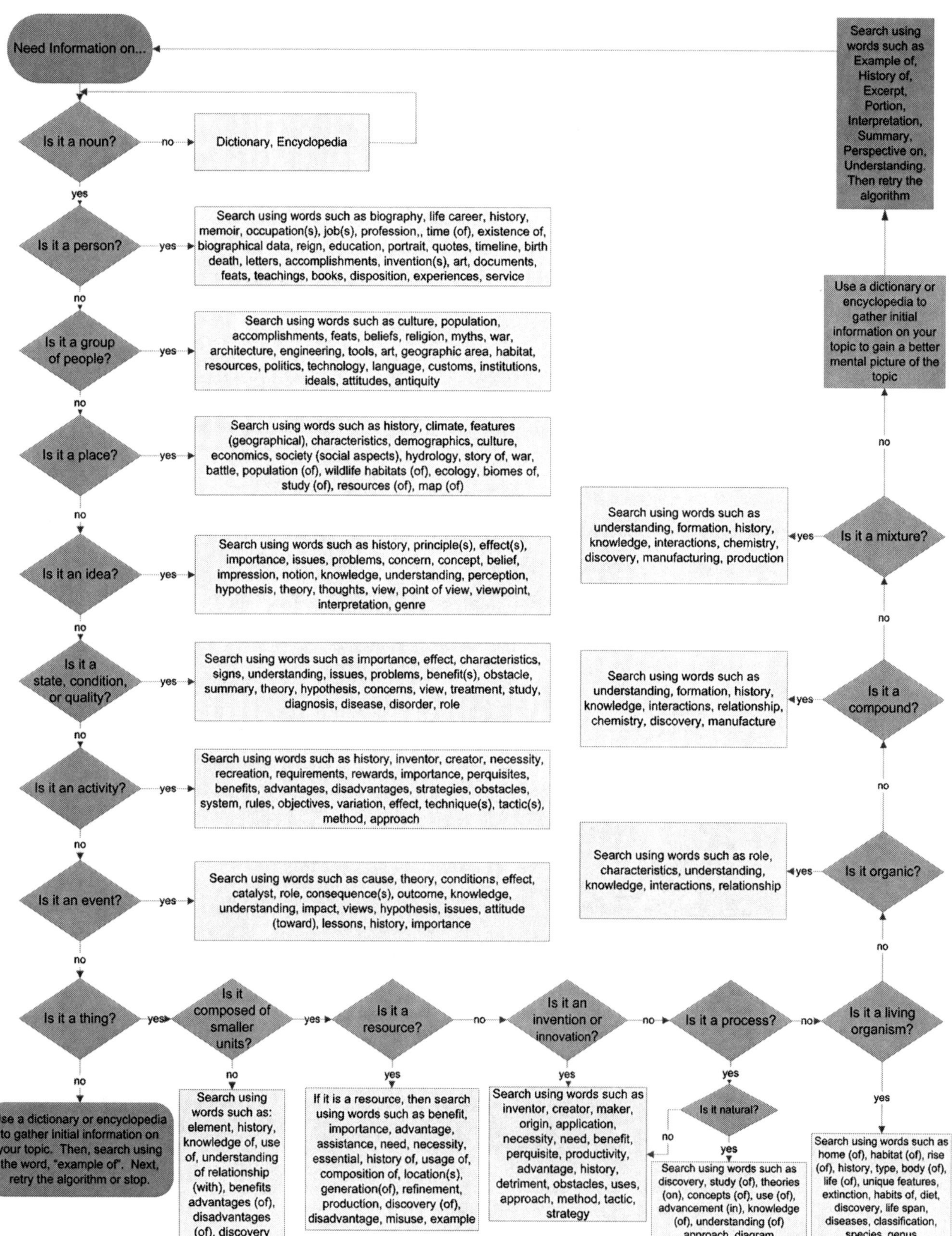

Search Term #25

The next research term is "Walks". In this situation, we identify in the beginning that "Walks" is not a noun. Therefore, we go to the right. "Walks" is a verb which is found in the dictionary.

However, "Walks" can also be an activity such as "Long walks will benefit your health". It can also be seen as an event like "I'm usually not tired after our long walks". Finally, "Walks" can also be seen as a quality, state or condition, such as "Examining different walks of life can provide perspective on the human condition".

As a reminder, remember that words can have multiple meanings, but as long as you remember to focus on your research area, you should do great.

Exercise #25

Now, it is your turn. Choose four verbs, activities or conditions. Then, use the Algorithm on these verbs, activities or conditions.

Next, choose two areas of focus for each term

For example:

- usage of walks
- benefits of walks
- advantages of walks

Chapter

5

In chapter 5, we will examine five terms that have many different meanings. This chapter was developed to help students gain perspective for various points of view. It is easy to state and point out the fact that terms located in a dictionary tend to have multiple meanings, but the goal is for students to jumpstart their research assignment without experiencing "analysis paralysis". *The Imaginary Research Algorithm* can potentially cause information overload, if a user does not focus on the research topic or requirement. We will also cover "mental toggling" in relation to *The Imaginary Research Algorithm*.

Imaginary Research Algorithm

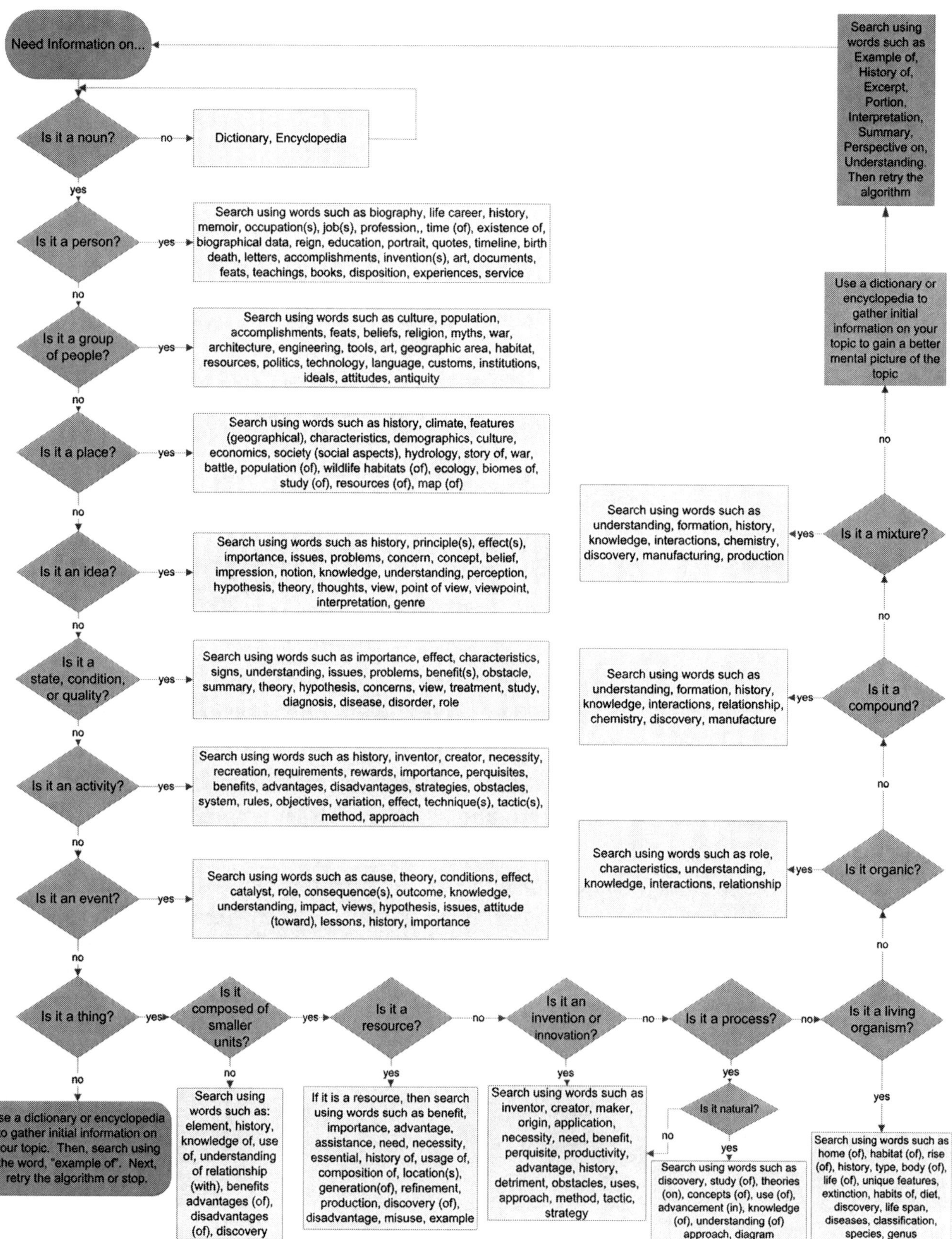

Search Term #26

"Arithmetic" is the research term. In this situation, we identify "Arithmetic" as a noun. What is "Arithmetic"? "Arithmetic" is many things and since hopefully you are becoming quicker at the Algorithm. You are beginning to digest the decision shapes (diamonds) subconsciously. Maybe your mind automatically jumps to "Is it a Thing?" Let's go over the possibilities of "Arithmetic". "Arithmetic" is a noun, but not a person, a group of people, or a place. Since, "Arithmetic" is observable and it officially has a name. It can be considered an idea such as a concept. "Arithmetic" is also an activity. It is also a thing which can be broken up into smaller units such as addition, subtraction, multiplication, and division. It is a resource that can be depended on in almost any field of work. Even though, "Arithmetic" occurs naturally in nature. Some may argue that it was composed and synthesized for humans to understand by a group or groups. For example, the use of symbols(+,-) is an invention that stands for various numbers and operators. These symbols were developed for "Arithmetic". "Arithmetic" is also a process that occurs naturally in the universe. It depends on how philosophical you want to go. But the main question should be. Which one would you pick? The choice is easy. **Focus on your requirements**. If your teacher or boss needs to know more about the different methods of multiplication then, you can focus on **"Is it an activity?"** or **"Is it a process?"** If you need to know facts about the origins of "Arithmetic", then you can focus on **"Is it an idea?"** or **"Is it an invention or innovation?"** Here are numerous research possibilities for "Arithmetic"

- origins of arithmetic
- concepts of arithmetic
- importance of arithmetic
- understanding of arithmetic
- thoughts on arithmetic
- advancements in arithmetic
- history of arithmetic
- requirements of arithmetic
- advantages of arithmetic
- strategies of arithmetic
- methods of arithmetic
- explanation of arithmetic
- study of arithmetic
- productivity of arithmetic
- necessity of arithmetic
- relationship with arithmetic
- concerns with arithmetic

Exercise #26

Choose four research terms. Then, use the Algorithm on these research terms.

Next, choose two areas of focus for each term

For example:

- origins of arithmetic
- study of arithmetic
- importance of arithmetic

At this point, you are getting closer to becoming advanced with the Algorithm. So, the time has come to introduce toggling. To toggle is to switch between two states. For example, you can toggle a light switch between an "on" state and an "off" state. Mental toggling is basically zooming in focus and zooming out of (research) focus while using *The Imaginary Research Algorithm*.

This type of toggling requires students to narrow their research focus or switch to a wide research focus. In the earlier chapters, I requested that you maintain your research focus based on your assignment. This can be limiting. Enter "mental toggling". Mental toggling should be applied to *The Imaginary Research Algorithm* when you have multiple meanings for words. However, "toggle" to a wide research view when you stop on a decision point (diamond) and if there is more information available. Then, go to other decision points that are **relevant** to your research.

Mental toggling is a simple way to make sure you have not missed any **relevant** cognitive sparks for your research. For instance, ideas, inventions and innovations decision points tend to go together that is if it is an invention or innovation that currently exists, like a nuclear reactor versus a cold fusion nuclear reactor.

In previous chapters, I made compromises on introducing toggling, because it was necessary for everyone to have the same abilities in operating a flowchart. Now, you should be able to use a basic flowchart. By slowly introducing, *The Imaginary Research Algorithm*, you have become faster. *The Imaginary Research Algorithm* will be less confusing when you are introduced to the multiple expressions of the Algorithm found in chapter 7. Furthermore, the benefits of mental toggling, will become instinctive with the other expressions.

Imaginary Research Algorithm

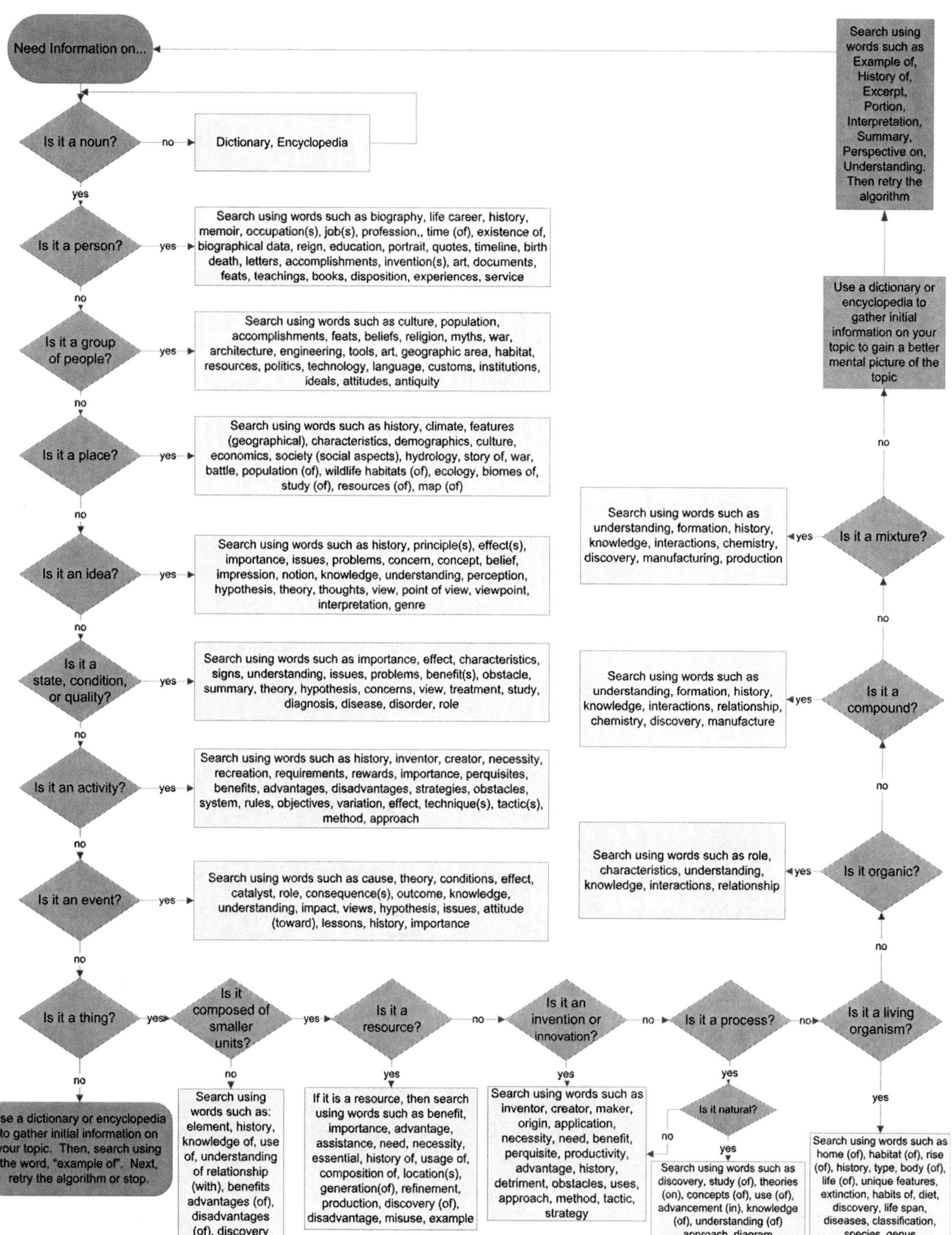

Search Term #27

The next research subject is "Tea". Right away, you know "Tea" is a noun.
"Tea" is not a person, group of people, or place. "Tea" was an idea at one
point in time. "Tea" the beverage was invented or created. In other words,
tea leaves did not start jumping into hot water on their own. "Tea" is not
a state of being, or activity. "Tea" is a thing, as well. **"Is it composed of
smaller units?"** Yes, "Tea" either in leaf form or dried form is composed of
cells. **"Is it a resource?"** Yes, it is a resource. "Tea" is also a very old invention.

Next, determine what specific information to look for. During a search, this
step suggests the inclusion of words such as

- discovery of tea
- usage of tea
- history of tea
- benefits of tea
- disadvantages of tea
- production of tea
- refinement of tea

Exercise #27

Choose four research terms. Then, use the Algorithm on these research terms.

Next, choose two areas of focus for each term

For example:

- production of tea
- history of tea
- disadvantages of tea

Imaginary Research Algorithm

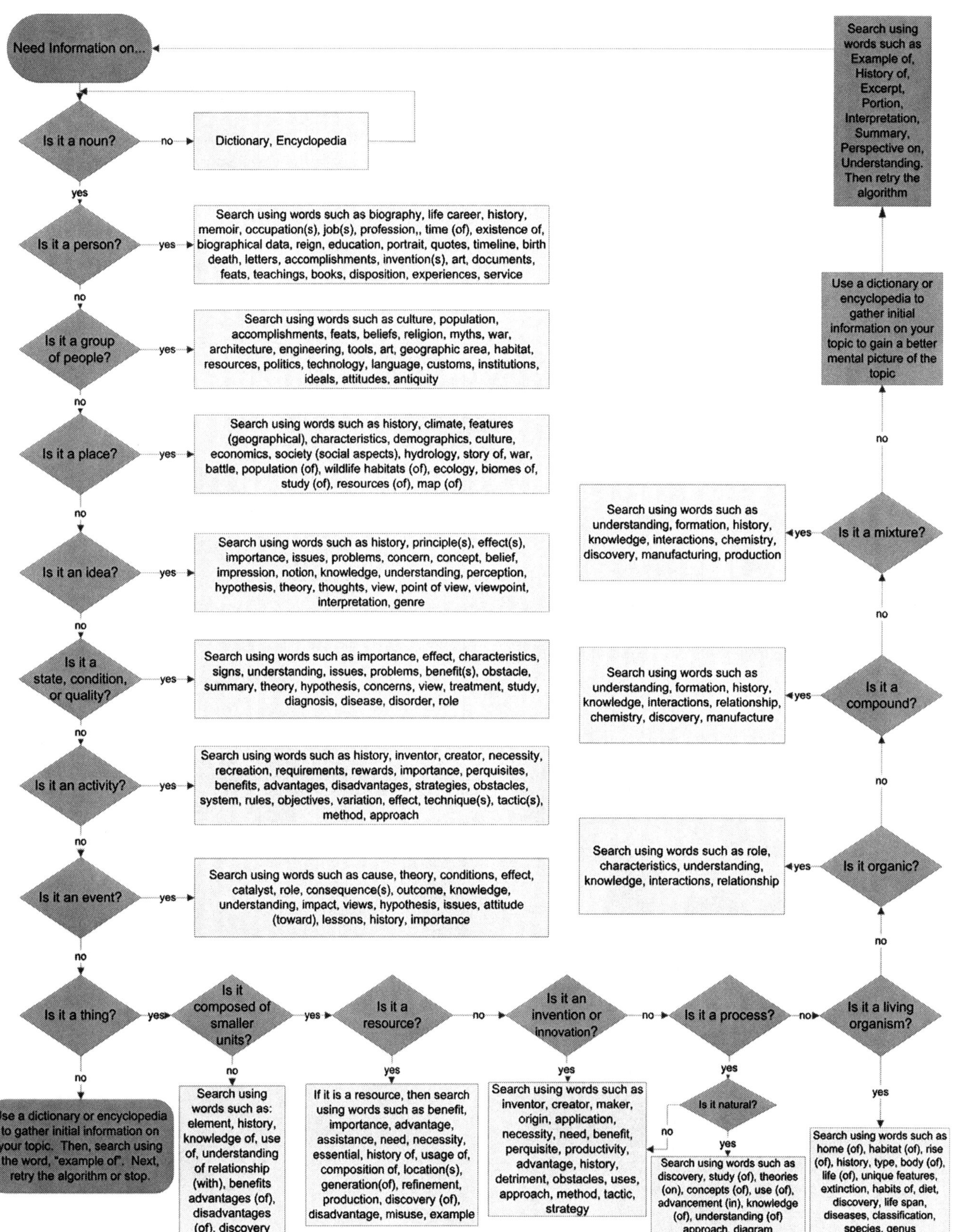

Search Term #28

Our next topic is "Electricity". We first identify "Electricity" as a noun. However, it is not a person, group of people or place. If you wish to know about the origins of the concept and the naming of "Electricity", then you can consider this an idea. It is not a condition or state of being. "Electricity" is a thing. Is it composed of smaller units? No. "Electricity" is also a resource and a process. Here are a few research possibilities for "Electricity"

- knowledge of electricity
- usage of electricity
- relationship with electricity
- generation of electricity
- need for electricity
- discovery of electricity
- application of electricity
- advantages of electricity

Exercise #28

Choose four research terms. Then, use the Algorithm on these research terms.

Next, choose two areas of focus for each term

For example:

- discovery of electricity
- knowledge of electricity
- application of electricity

Imaginary Research Algorithm

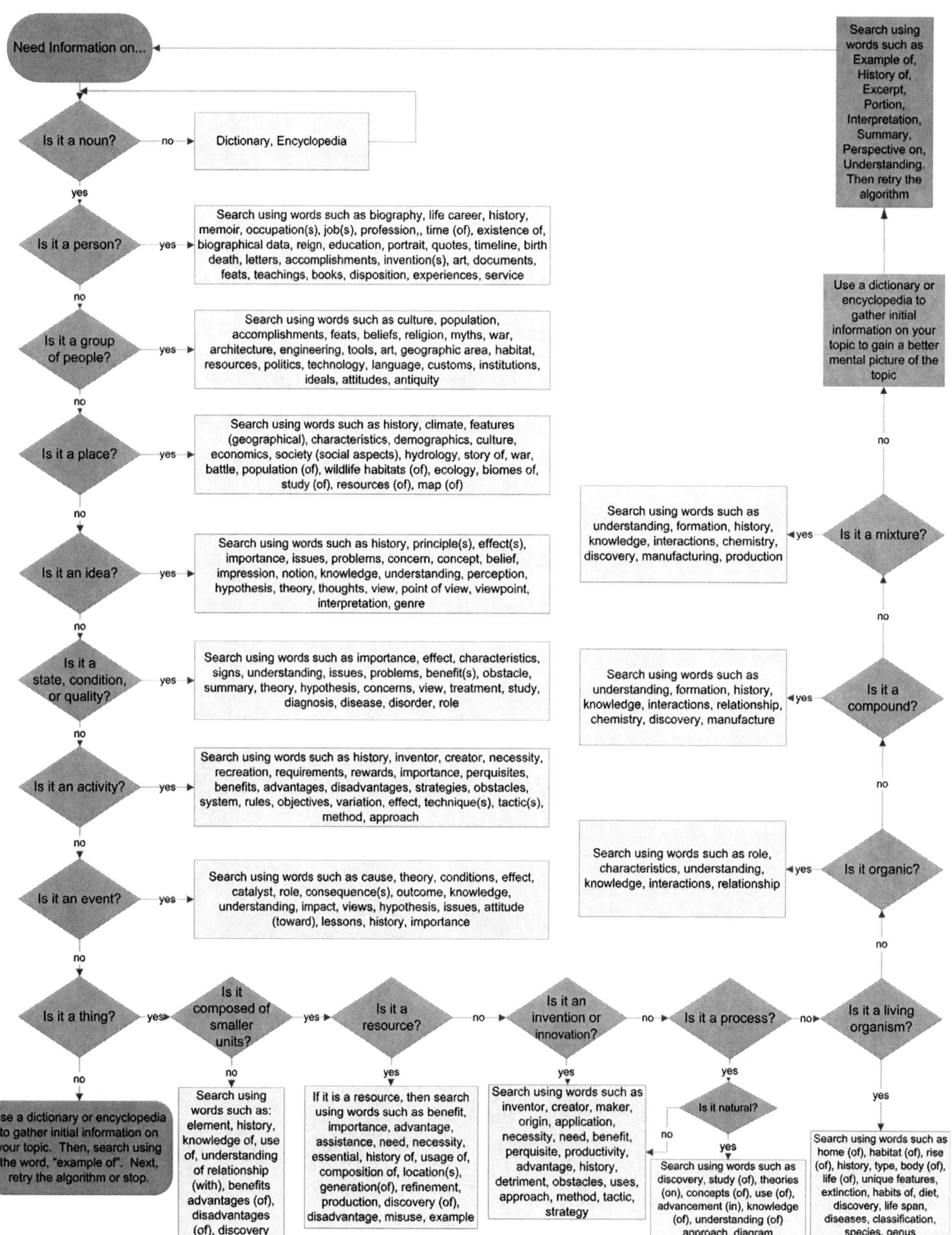

Search Term #29

"Software" is our next subject. We quickly realize that "Software" is a noun.
From there, we digest the fact that "Software" is not a person, group of people,
or place. It was an idea that was eventually created. It is not a state of being
or activity. "Software" is a thing, that is composed of smaller units. We arrive
at the fact that "Software" is a resource that people use to be more productive
with work or engaged with leisure. We also conclude that "Software" was an
invention. Here are some research possibilities for "Software"

- benefit of software
- need for software
- history of software
- essentials of software
- usage of software
- origins of software
- obstacles of software

Exercise #29

Choose four research terms. Then, use the Algorithm on these research terms.

Next, select two areas of focus for each term

For example:

- usage of software
- history of software
- benefits of software

Imaginary Research Algorithm

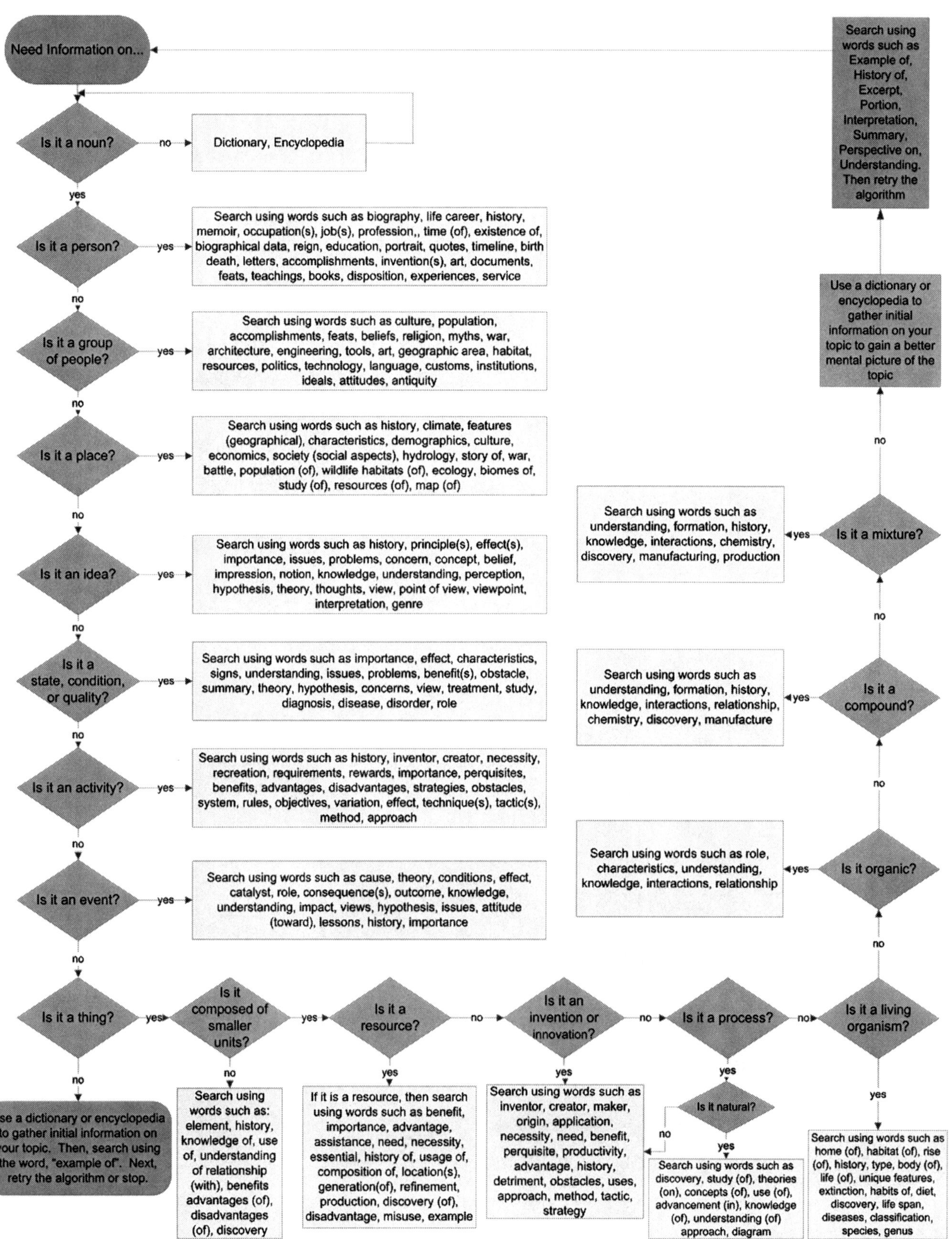

Search Term #30

The subject is "Jackson". Since, we are given a noun. You can either go to **"Is it a person?"** Yes, but we do not know which "Jackson". Is it Andrew Jackson, Stonewall Jackson, or someone else with "Jackson" in their name. Let's assume we forgot our assignment and the only thing we remember is "Jackson". **"Is it a group of people?"** No. **"Is it a place?"** Yes it is a place, but let's assume we didn't know about cities named "Jackson" such as Jackson, Mississippi. When information is very vague and you don't know where to go, you should end up at the bottom of the left hand side of the flowchart.

This will direct you to a dictionary or an encyclopedia if you are blindly searching. After the dictionary or encyclopedia refreshes your memory, start the Algorithm over again. Let's say the research topic was Jackson, Mississippi. Go to **"Is it a place?"** and follow the right arrow. Here are a few research possibilities for "Jackson"

- history of Jackson
- population of Jackson
- characteristics of Jackson
- economics of Jackson
- demographics of Jackson
- resources of Jackson

Exercise #30

Choose four research terms. Then, use the Algorithm on these research terms.

Next, select two areas of focus for each term

For example:

- population of Jackson
- resources of Jackson
- economics of Jackson
- history of Jackson

Chapter

6

Congratulations. You have reached the advanced stage of *The Imaginary Research Algorithm*. Hopefully, the Algorithm has become second nature to you. In this chapter, we will cover additional words to make sure that you are prepared for different research scenarios.

Imaginary Research Algorithm

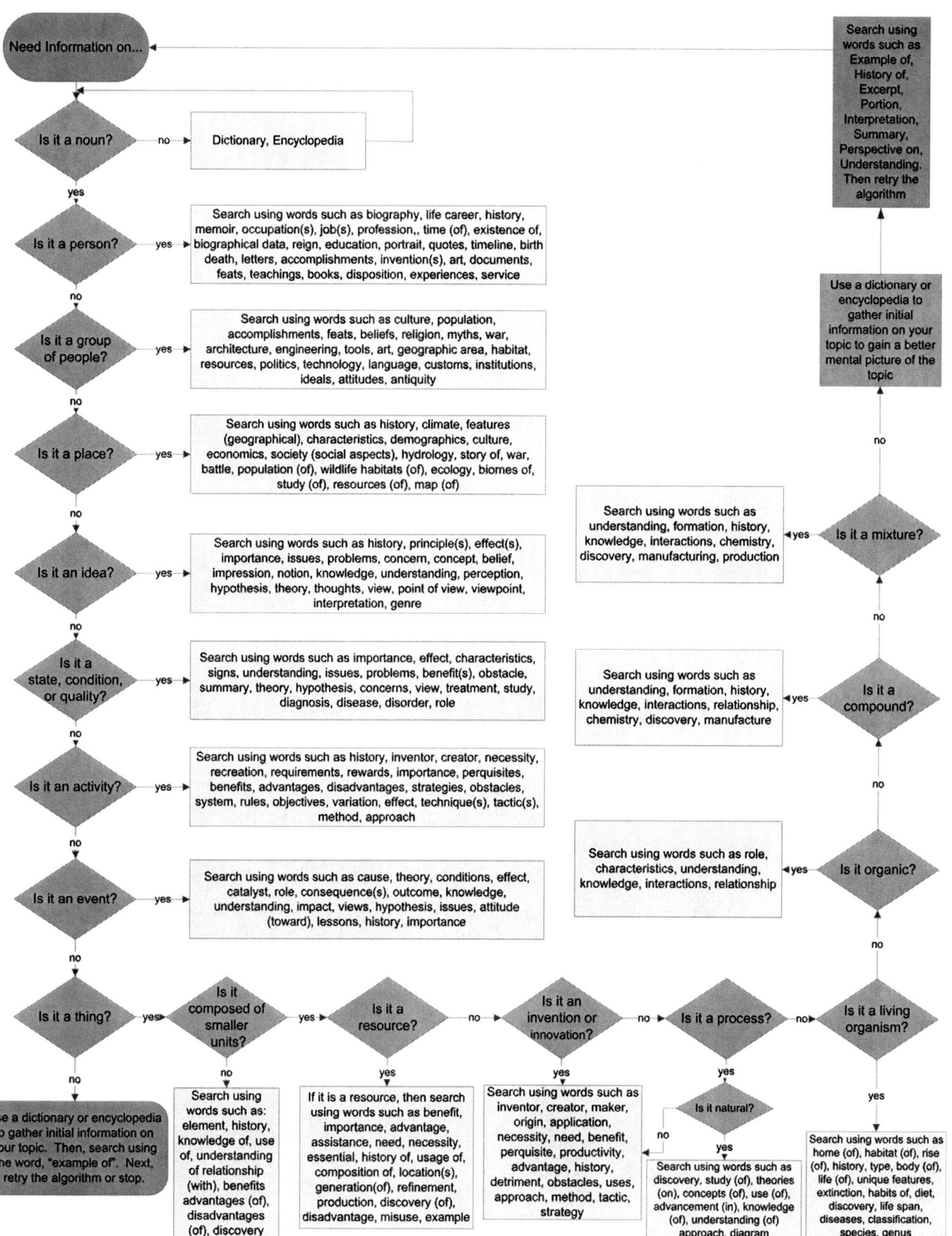

Search Term #31

"Tachyons". Let's say, we do not know anything about "Tachyons", but our "favorite" physics teacher assigned us the objective to preview information on it. Since, we do not know what "Tachyons" are. We immediately go to a dictionary then an encyclopedia. Going through *The Imaginary Research Algorithm*, we know "Tachyons" are not a person, group of people or place. We know it is a hypothetical idea/concept conceived by scientists.

"Tachyons" are not a condition, or activity, but they are things. They are not composed of smaller units. Here are a few research possibilities for "Tachyons"

- knowledge of tachyons
- relationship with tachyons…
- understanding of tachyons
- perspectives on tachyons

Exercise #31

Choose four research terms. Then, use the Algorithm on these research terms.

Next, select two areas of focus for each term

For example:

- knowledge of tachyons
- understanding of tachyons

Imaginary Research Algorithm

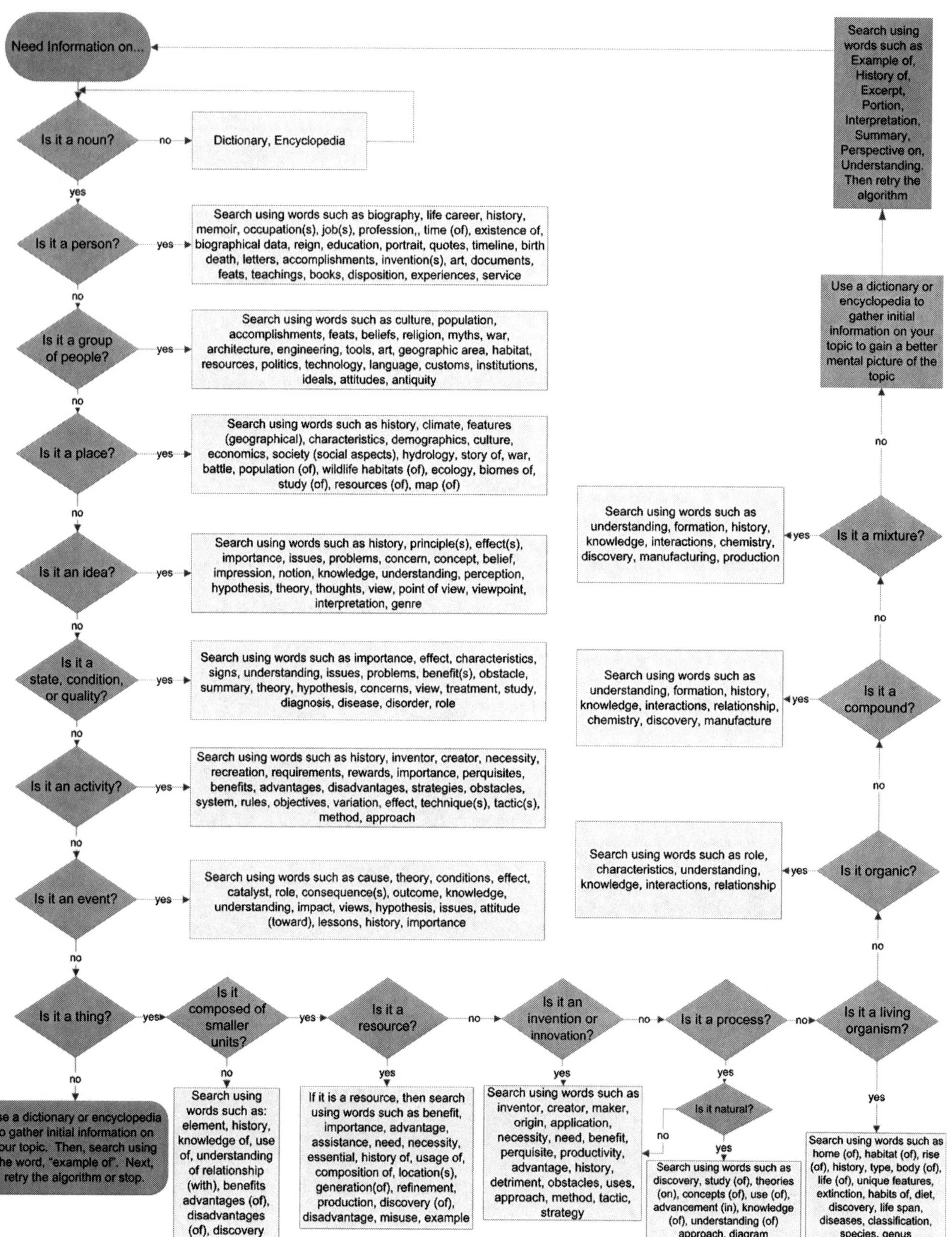

Search Term #32

"Adjustment" is the next research term. As we go down the Algorithm. We take into account that the word "Adjustment" is a noun, but it is not a person, a group of people, a place, or an idea. "Adjustment" can be an adjective, a condition, an activity, an event or a process. Here are a few research possibilities

- explanation of adjustment
- concerns of adjustment
- issues of adjustment
- problems with adjustment
- theories on adjustment
- advantages of adjustment

Exercise #32

Choose four research terms. Then, use the Algorithm on these research terms.

Search Term #33

"ROI" is an acronym that stands for "return on investment". Simply, scan the Algorithm for your "search needs". In this case, we will examine each possible scenario. "ROI" is a noun. It is not a person, group of people, or place. However, "ROI" is an idea.

As we travel down *The Imaginary Research Algorithm,* we see that "ROI" is not an activity, but it is a thing. Furthermore, it can be broken into smaller units. "ROI" is a useful business equation/concept thereby making it a resource. It is also a process that happens to be synthetic. Here are a few research possibilities for "ROI"

- history of ROI
- importance of ROI
- necessity of ROI
- usage of ROI
- concept of ROI
- study of ROI
- application of ROI
- benefits of ROI

Exercise #33

Choose four research terms. Then, use the Algorithm on these research terms.

Imaginary Research Algorithm

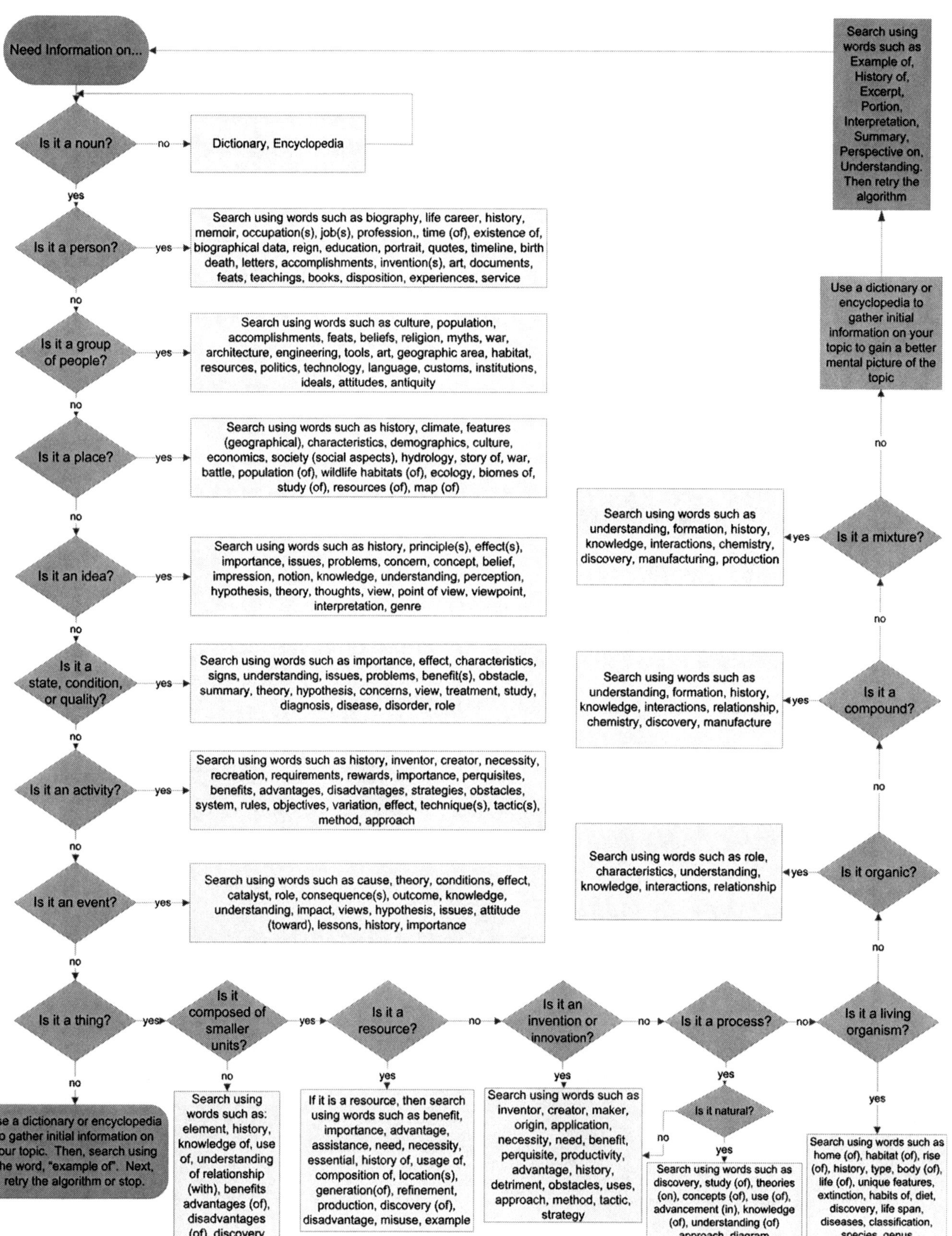

Search Term #34

The next research topic is "Simile". As you scan through the decision shape diamonds. You realize that "Simile" is a noun because it is a figure of speech. However, it is not a person, group of people, place, idea, condition, activity, or thing. Maybe, you missed something. Don't worry. *The Imaginary Research Algorithm* is here to catch you. In case, there is a slip and miss. If you get stumped, the Algorithm forces you to go to a dictionary or an encyclopedia and figure out what exactly it is that you missed. After a review, we decide "Simile" is an invention. (Actually, simile was also an idea that sprouted to become an invention) The main point is to show you that there is a safety valve in the Algorithm; just in case, it seems like none of the types of nouns apply. Here are a few ways to search for information on "Simile"

- study of simile
- origins of simile
- history of simile
- need for simile

Exercise #34

Choose four research terms. Then, use the Algorithm on these research terms.

Search Term #35

The next research topic is "Dependency". As you go through the decision shape diamonds, it becomes clear that "Dependency" is a condition, quality, or state of being. We also understand that "Dependency is not a person, a group of people, a place, an idea, an activity, a resource, an invention, or a process. Here are a few research possibilities with "Dependency"

- signs of dependency
- effects of dependency
- summary of dependency
- problems with dependency
- theories on dependency
- issues with dependency
- treatment of dependency

Exercise #35

Choose four research terms. Then, use the Algorithm on these terms.

Imaginary Research Algorithm

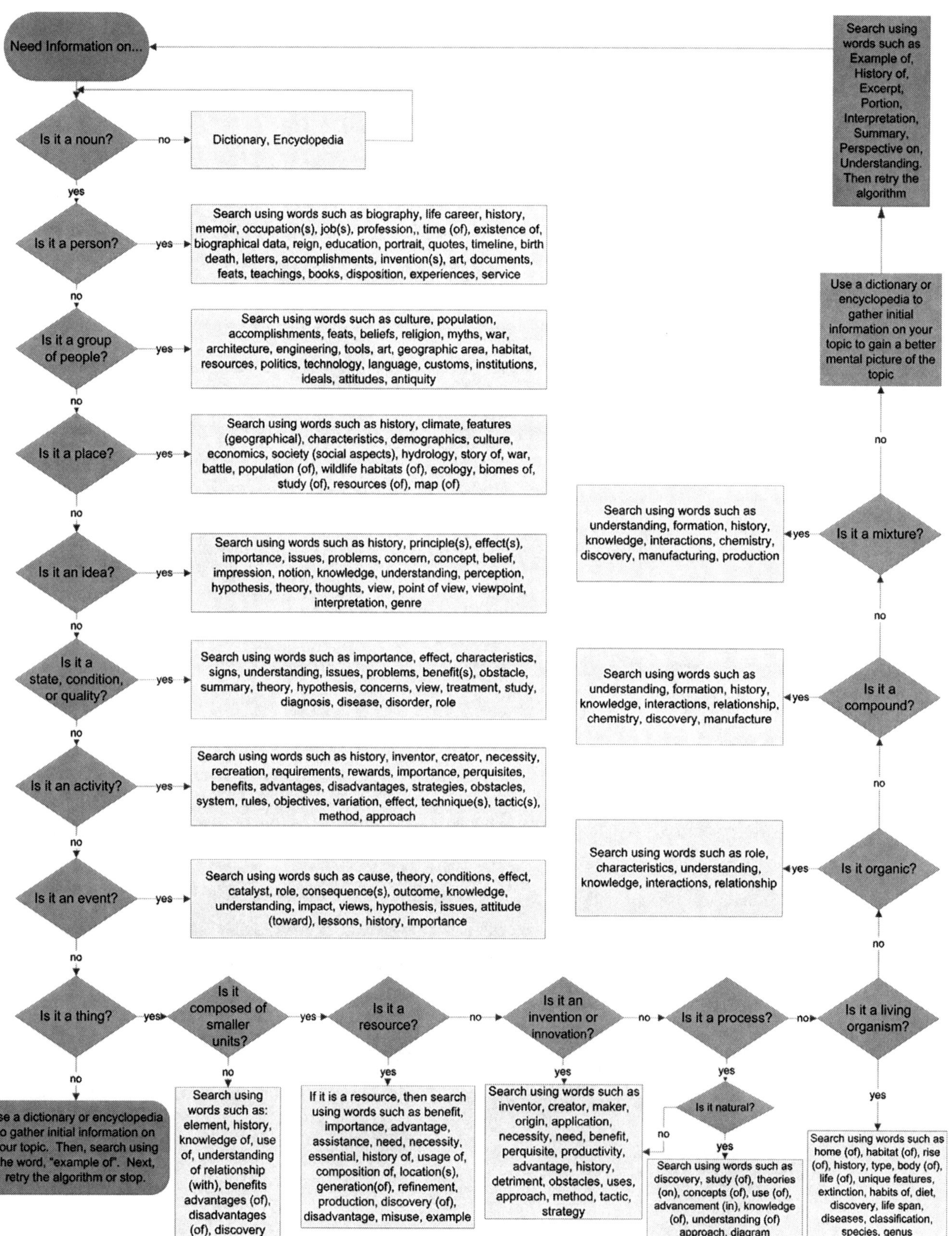

Search Term #36

"Faux Pas" is a phrase that means blunder. This is the current research topic.
Since, it is a phrase. You can go directly to the dictionary or you can travel
down *The Imaginary Research Algorithm* until you reach "Is it a state, condition, or quality?" "Faux Pas" would qualify as a state of being. Here are a
few research possibilities

- summary of faux pas
- history of faux pas
- characteristics of faux pas
- understanding of faux pas

Exercise #36

Choose four research terms. Then, use the Algorithm on these terms.

Search Term #37

"Health" is an interesting topic to research. It is very vast. Let
us scan through the possibilities with this noun. "Health" is not a
person, a group of people, a place, or idea. It is a state of being. As
far as being a thing, it would be classified as a resource, if seen from
a human resources perspective. Use these suggestions for research
possibilities

- summary of health
- history of health
- problems with health
- obstacles of health
- importance of health
- effect of health

Exercise #37

Choose four research terms. Then, use the Algorithm on these research terms.

Imaginary Research Algorithm

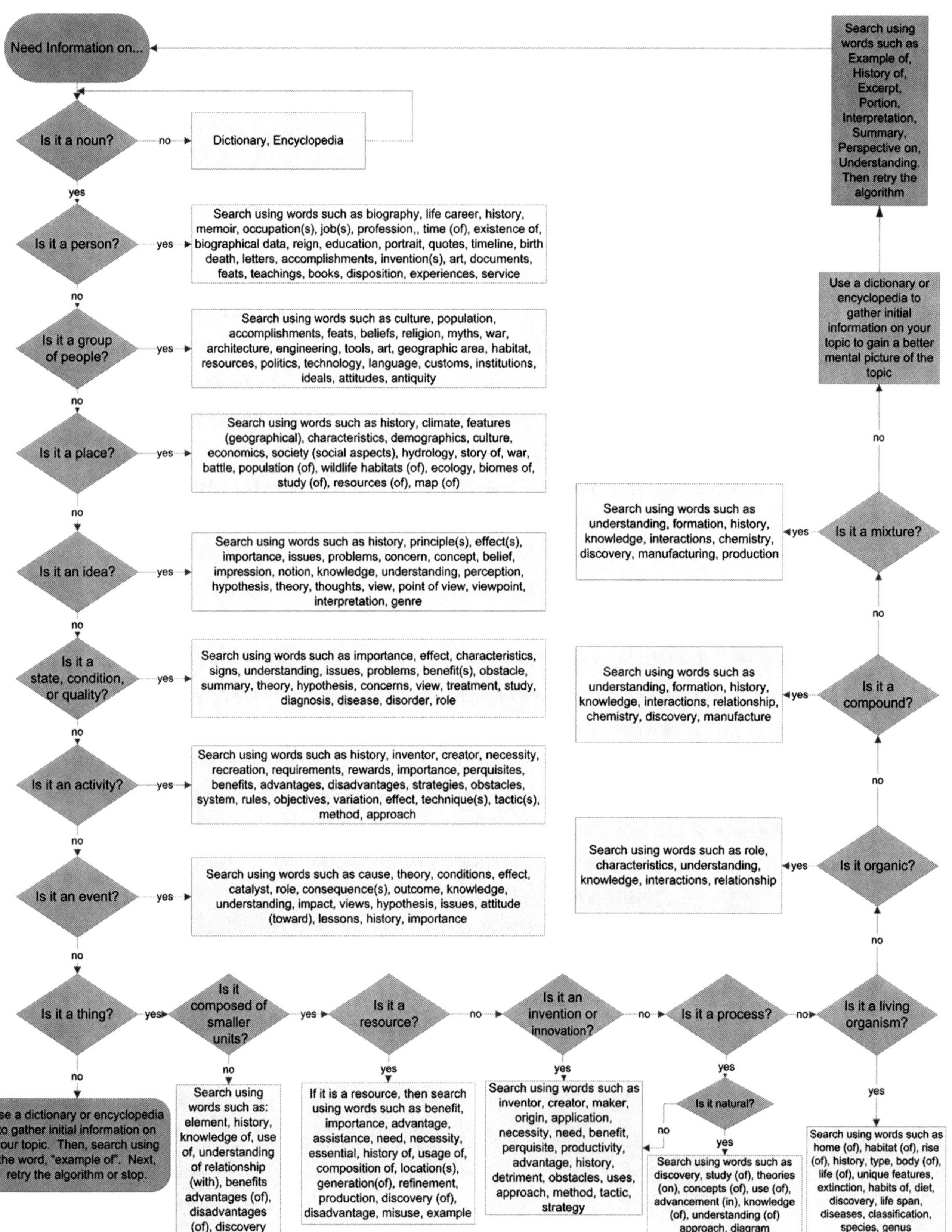

Search Topic #38

The next topic is "Probability". As you go through decision shapes (diamonds), you conclude that "Probability", an element of mathematics, is a resource, invention, and process. It is also a condition, but we will only focus on the element of mathematics. Here are a few examples of possible research situations

- examples of probability
- usage of probability
- history of probability
- application of probability
- study of probability
- explanation of probability
- understanding of probability

Exercise #38

Choose four research terms. Then, use the Algorithm on these research terms.

Search Topic #39

"Asthma" is the next research topic. We start at the top of *The Imaginary Research Algorithm* and pass through decision shapes (diamonds). "Asthma" is a condition. Here are a few research possibilities that may help your search efforts.

- characteristics of asthma
- signs of asthma
- issues with asthma
- effects of asthma
- summary of asthma
- treatment of asthma

Exercise #39

Choose four research terms. Then, use the Algorithm on these research terms.

Imaginary Research Algorithm

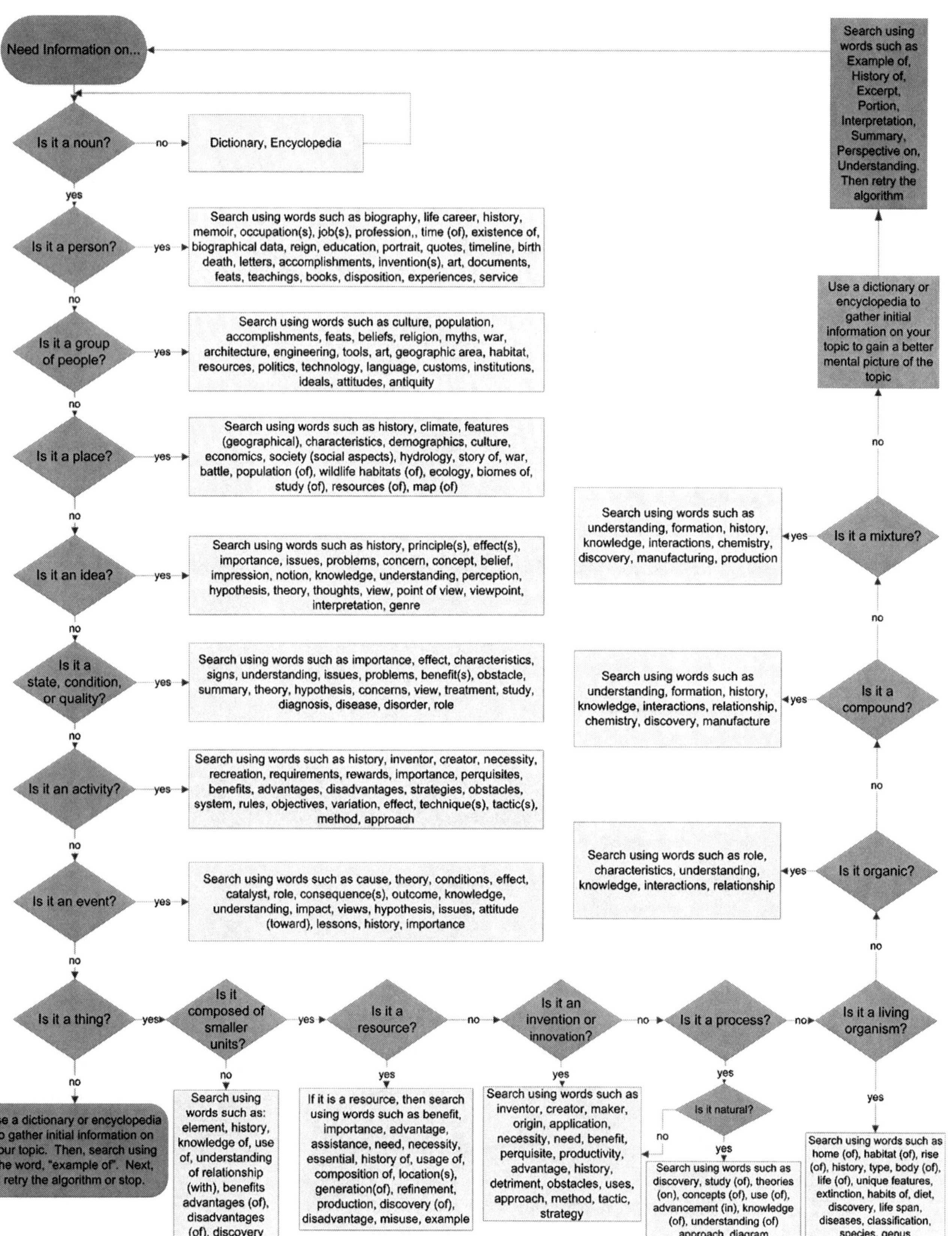

Search Topic #40

"Happiness" is the next research topic. We start at the top of *The Imaginary Research Algorithm* and go through decision shapes (diamonds). We conclude that "Happiness" is a condition. Here are a few research possibilities that may help your search efforts

- characteristics of happiness
- effect of happiness
- benefits of happiness
- studies on happiness
- issues with happiness

Exercise #40

Choose four research terms. Then, use the Algorithm on these research terms.

Search Term #41

The next research topic is "Evaporation". We start at the top of *The Imaginary Research Algorithm* and travel through decision shapes (diamonds). We conclude that "Evaporation" is a process. "Evaporation" is also an activity and event, but we will focus on the process. Use these suggested words for research possibilities

- discovery of evaporation
- study of evaporation
- concepts of evaporation
- use of evaporation
- knowledge of evaporation
- understanding of evaporation
- explanation of evaporation

Exercise #41

Choose four research terms. Then, use the Algorithm on these research terms.

Imaginary Research Algorithm

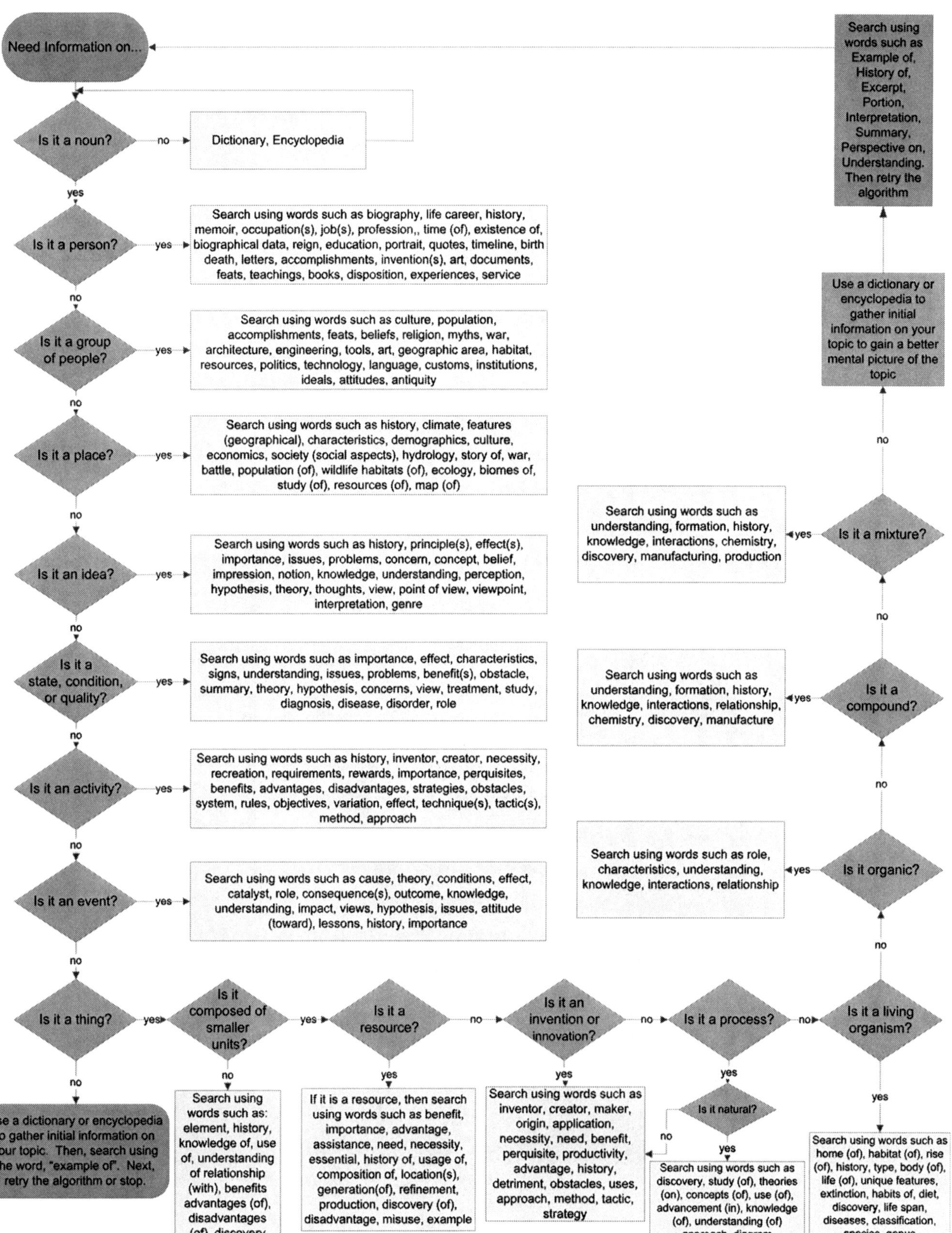

Search Term #42

"Wave", in terms of Physics, is the next term to examine with *The Imaginary Research Algorithm.* "Wave" is a very interesting subject. As we pass through decision shapes (diamonds), we note that "Wave" is not a person, a group of people, or a place. So what is a "Wave"? Since, we do not know how to define it. We are forced to go to a dictionary or encyclopedia. Since it is an observable phenomenon and has a name, it can be seen as an idea/ concept. It is an activity as well as a process. Moreover, "Waves" have been used as a resource for energy. Here are a few research possibilities to try

- explanation of wave
- discovery of wave
- study of wave
- application of wave
- requirements of a wave
- theories on waves
- importance of wave

Exercise #42

Choose four research terms. Then, use the Algorithm on these research terms.

Search Term #43

"Heat" is the next term to research. "Heat" is another interesting subject. What actually is "Heat"? How would you define "Heat"? There are so many possible definitions. This is why you must identify a research focal point. For example, "Heat" can be used as a verb.
"Heat" is a resource that humans use to do many things like cook food or stay warm. There is also "Heat" from a Physics perspective.
Here are a few research possibilities to examine

- explanation of heat
- study of heat
- concepts of heat
- advantages of heat
- theories on heat
- requirements of heat
- importance for heat
- effect of heat

Exercise #43

Choose four research terms. Then, use the Algorithm on these research terms.

Imaginary Research Algorithm

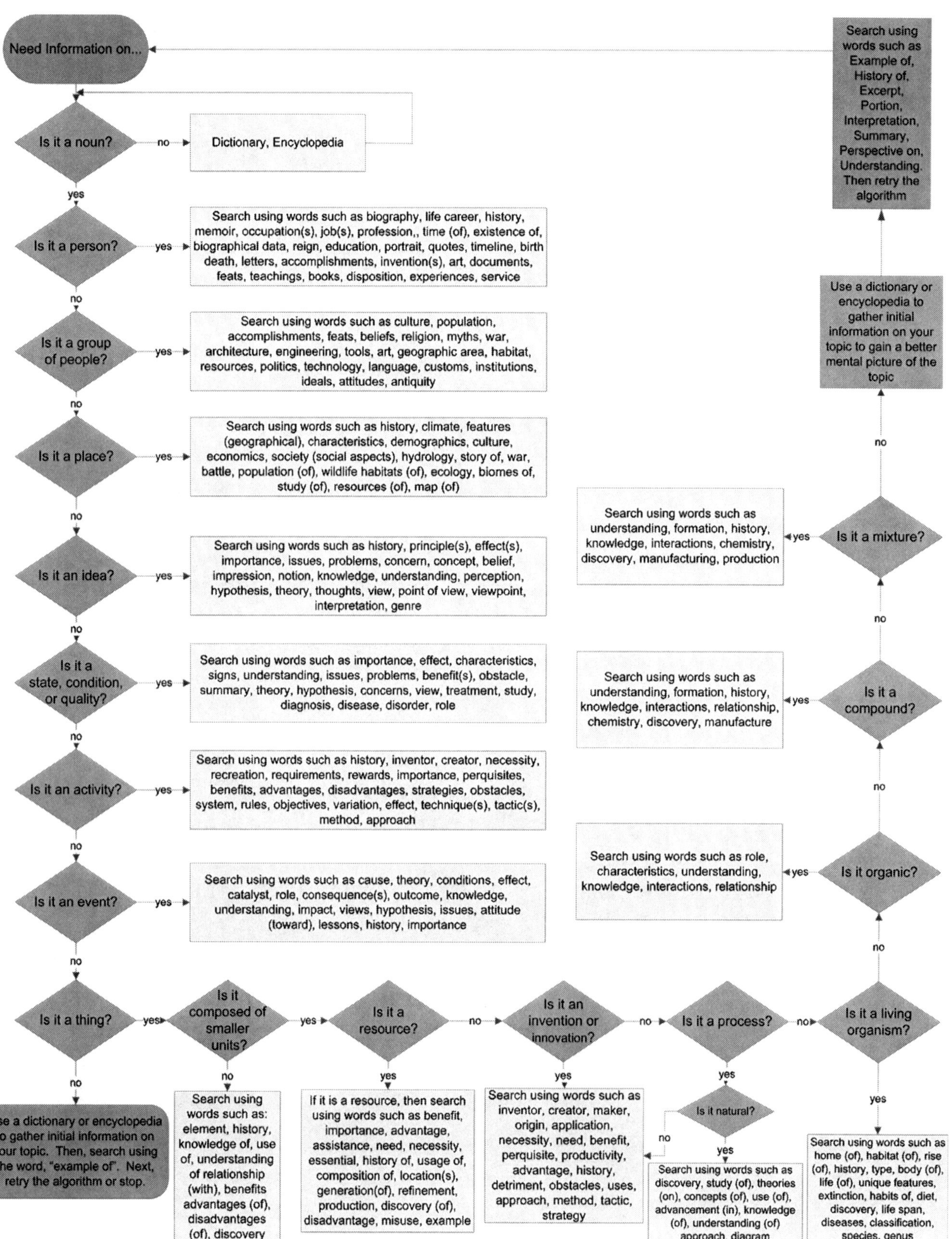

Search Term #44

"Polymerization". You do not know that "Polymerization" is a process or activity. Even though, the "tion" in "Polymerization" is a clue. Therefore, you must go to a dictionary or encyclopedia to discover the nature of "Polymerization". "Polymerization" is an activity that can occur in nature or industry. It is also a process. Here are a few research possibilities to examine

- history of polymerization
- inventor of polymerization
- discovery of polymerization
- techniques for polymerization
- advantages for polymerization
- disadvantages of polymerization
- study of polymerization
- explanation of polymerization
- concepts of polymerization

Exercise #44

Choose four research terms. Then, use the Algorithm on these research terms.

Search Term #45

A "Vacuum" as in vacuum of space is space without matter. In some eyes, "Vacuum" (of space) is a thing because it has a name and can be described as nothing. Going through the Algorithm, we would stop at **"Is it a state, condition, or quality?"** You could also go through the Algorithm, make a right turn at **"Is it a thing?"** Since a "Vacuum" is composed of nothing. You would answer no to the decision point, **"Is it composed of smaller units"**. A "Vacuum" could be used in industry, as well. So, a "Vacuum" is a useable resource. Here are a few research possibilities to examine

- discovery of vacuums
- example of vacuum
- summary of vacuum
- understanding of vacuums
- knowledge of vaucums

Exercise #45

Choose four research terms. Then, use the Algorithm on these research terms.

Imaginary Research Algorithm

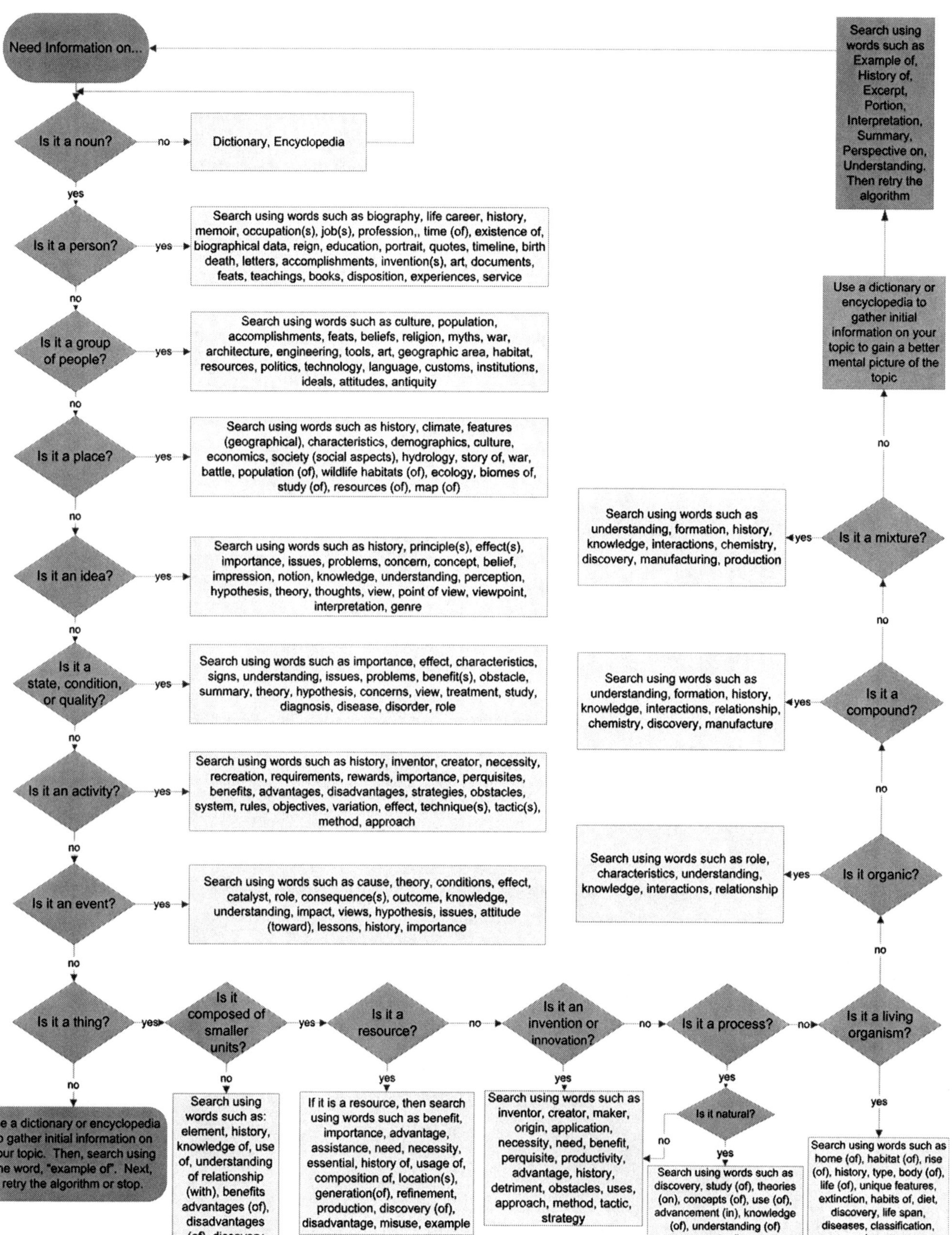

Search Term #46

What is a "Virus"? Even though, you know about computer viruses and biological viruses. Let's say, you have narrowed it down to biological viruses, but you still may not know how to classify it. Therefore, it seems that a dictionary or encyclopedia may be a great starting point. "Viruses" are not a person, group of people, place, state, condition or quality. Are "viruses" living organisms or organic machines dependent on other organism? Here are a few research possibilities to consider

- characteristics of viruses
- body of viruses
- knowledge of viruses
- understanding viruses
- relationship of virus

Exercise #46

Choose four research terms. Then, use the Algorithm on these research terms.

Lastly, for this section, I will cover the **"last resort rectangle"** found in the upper right corner of the Algorithm. The **"last resort rectangle"** provides words to discover the meaning of your search terms. For example, some words are very complex and difficult to understand even when you have a dictionary, encyclopedia or specialty dictionary. To give a boost to understanding a "complex" word, the **"last resort rectangle"** offers words that can help. For instance, the word "carcinogenesis" may lead you to a dictionary and encyclopedia. Let's say you don't understand the definition or don't find the term. If not, you can use words such as

- examples of carcinogenesis
- interpretations of carcinogenesis
- perspectives on carcinogenesis

SECTION
II

Chapter

7

Congratulations. You are almost a master at *The Imaginary Research Algorithm*. At this point, I would like to introduce nine visual analogies:

- A number keypad/Calculator
- A dial control (circular)
- A thermostat
- A thermometer
- A keyboard interface/tabs
- A pushbutton interface
- A ruler (measurement)
- A wave model
- A mountain range model

In this chapter, we will cover ways to apply the visual analogies to research. These visual analogies demonstrate optional ways to approach *The Imaginary Research Algorithm*. Furthermore, the analogies will deliver various perspectives on the Algorithm. If you skipped chapters 1-6, there is a glossary on page 209 to assist you with understanding this chapter better.

Becoming familiar with *The Imaginary Research Algorithm* is simple. However, if you are having trouble with the Algorithm, whether it is difficult to remember or tough to grasp. A simple visual strategy is a number keypad/calculator.

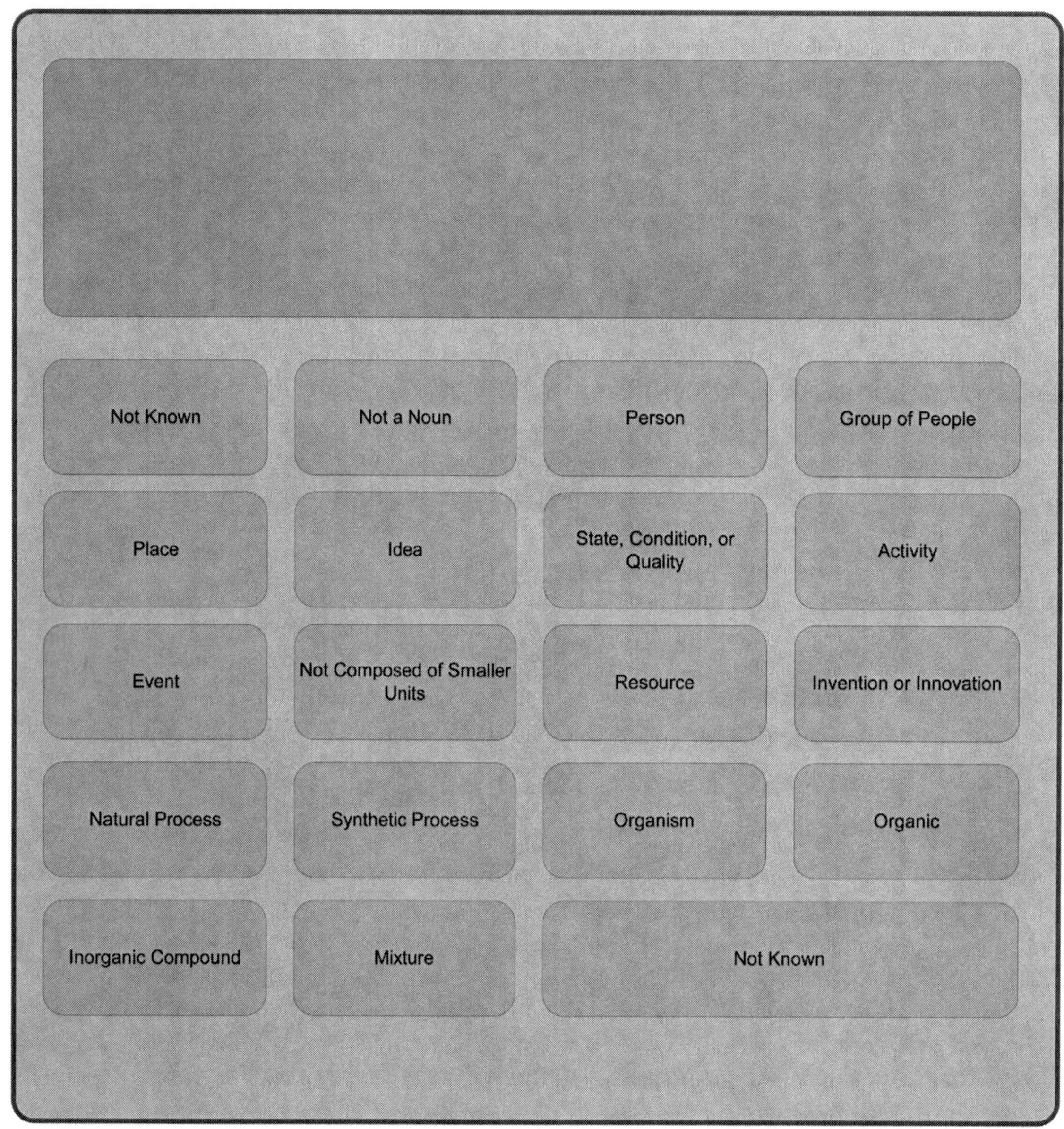

A number keypad such as the ones on digital phone can be analogous to The Imaginary Research Algorithm's flowchart representation. Starting at "Not Known", identify only the buttons that represent your research term. For instance, the word "leopard" is your research term. Simply, scan through each button that represents the word "leopard". In this case, we would select organism. Take a moment to think about the first time you operated a telephone. Did you memorize the telephone keypad layout?

Most likely, you did not. Keyboards, calculators, microwaves, VCRs, DVD players, alarm clocks or other mechanical or technological objects that have interfaces do not necessarily require initial memorization to operate. With practice, a person can operate a keyboard or a calculator effectively. Practice is the key word. The more buttons, levers, or switches a device has the more a person will most likely have to practice to become skillful. The remaining analogies are designed to add perspective to the different interfaces you have probably become good at such as televisions, remote controls, microwaves, calculators, car controls, etc. Therefore, it is perfectly normal if you have not memorized every decision point in the Algorithm. With time and practice, *The Imaginary Research Algorithm* will become second nature.

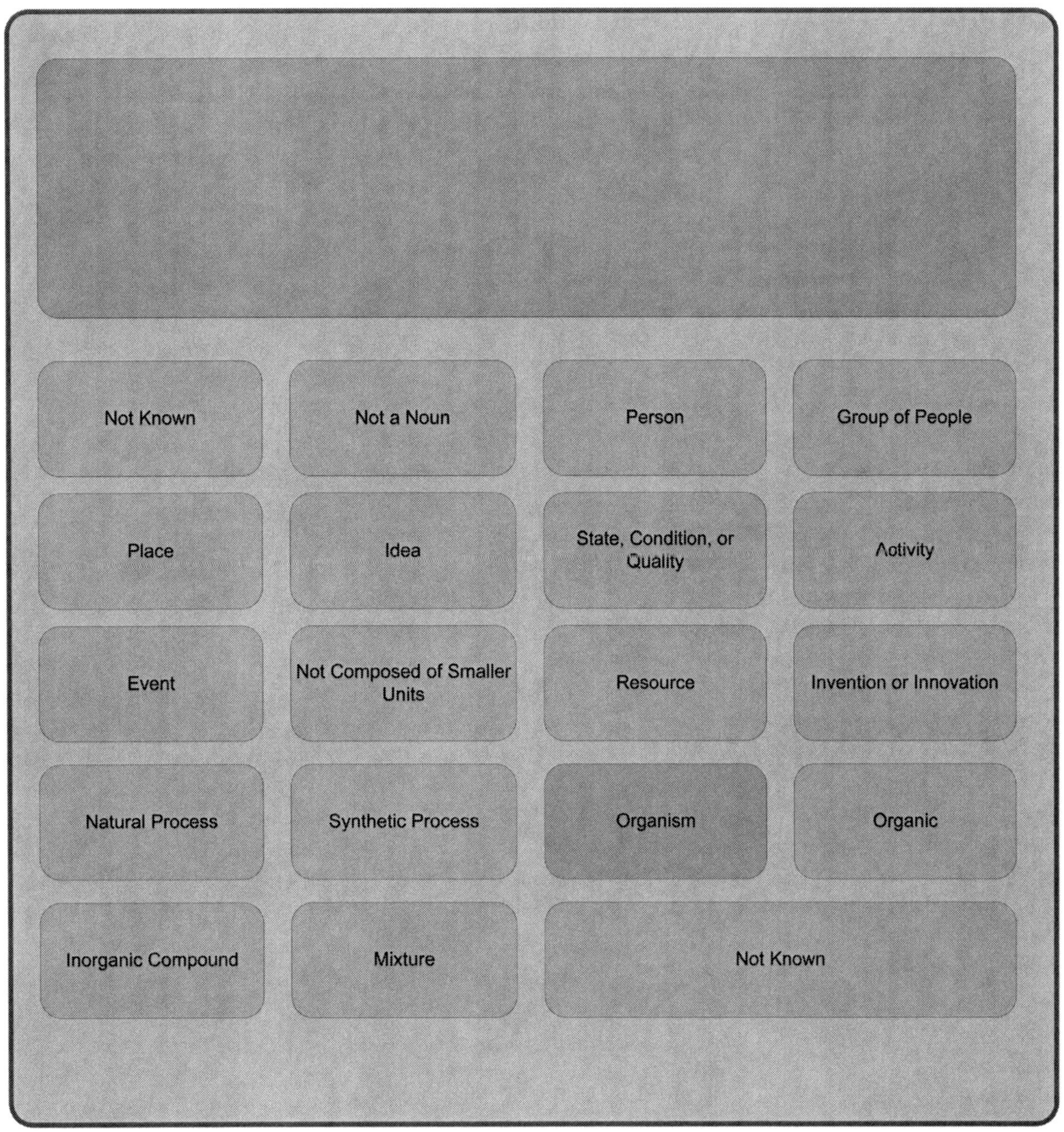

A dial control is another visual anology that can be applied to learning or processing *The Imaginary Research Algorithm*. Dial controls can be found on many different devices from ovens to timers. An Imaginary Research Algorithm user would simply move the dial clockwise and stop at applicable categories. At each applicable stop, the user will see additional information on the display screen such as beneficial keywords that stimulate the search process.

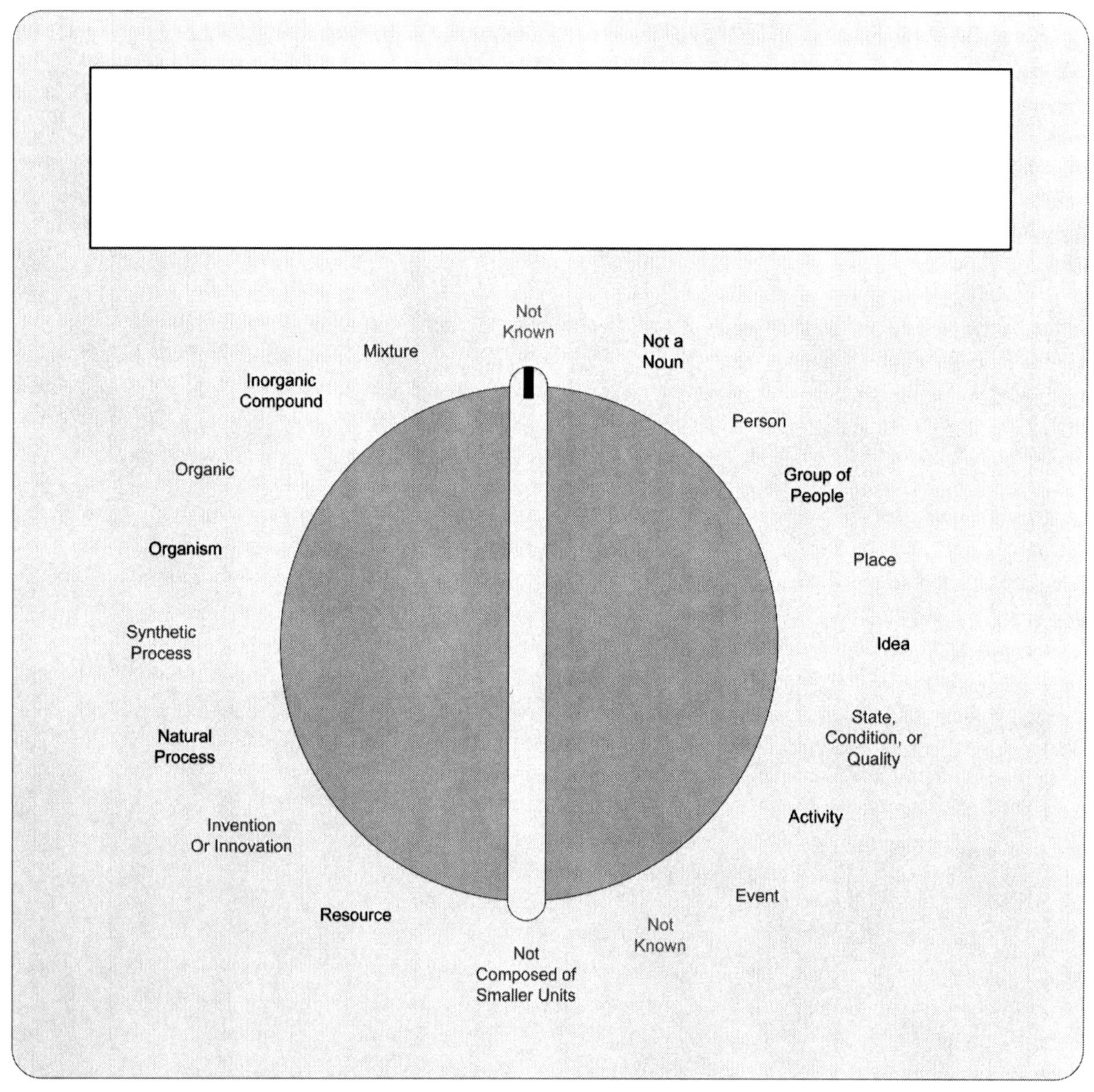

A thermostat is one more visual analogy that can be applied to digesting *The Imaginary Research Algorithm*. A thermostat can have buttons, dials, or levers. We will focus on the lever version. Look at the image below, picture the orange lever sliding to the right. The lever should stop at applicable categories.

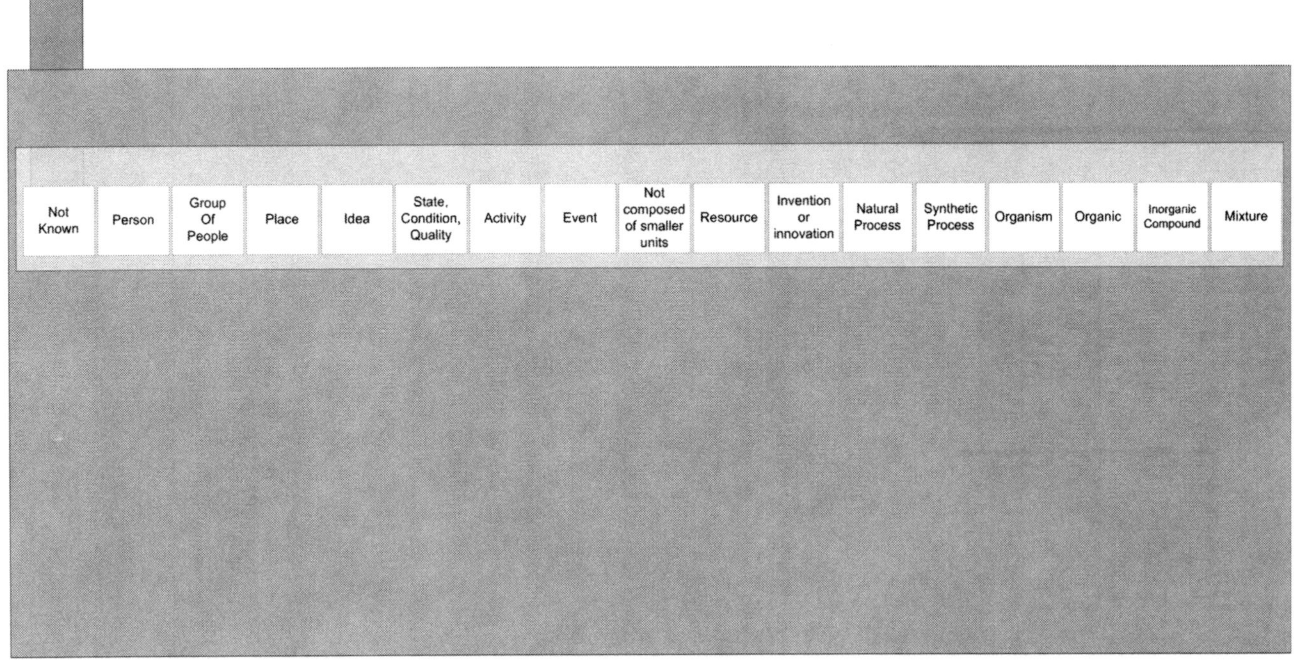

For example, the research term is "lunar landings". Even though, this information is vague, you can start off using the words provided by the "event" category.

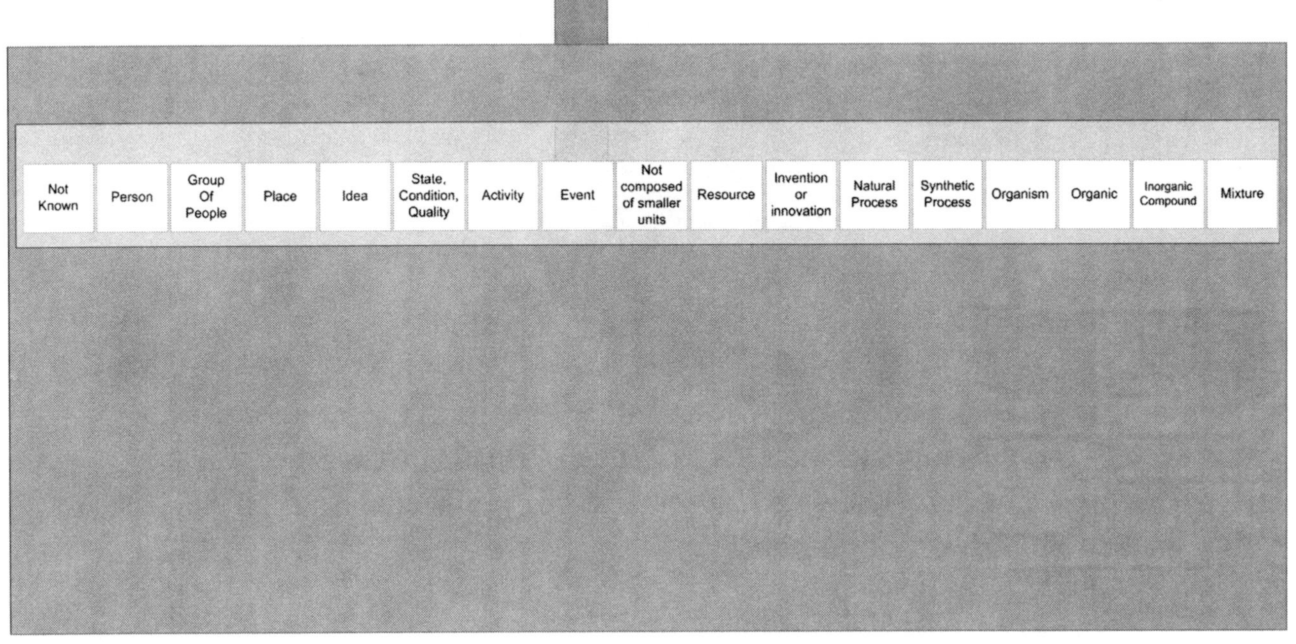

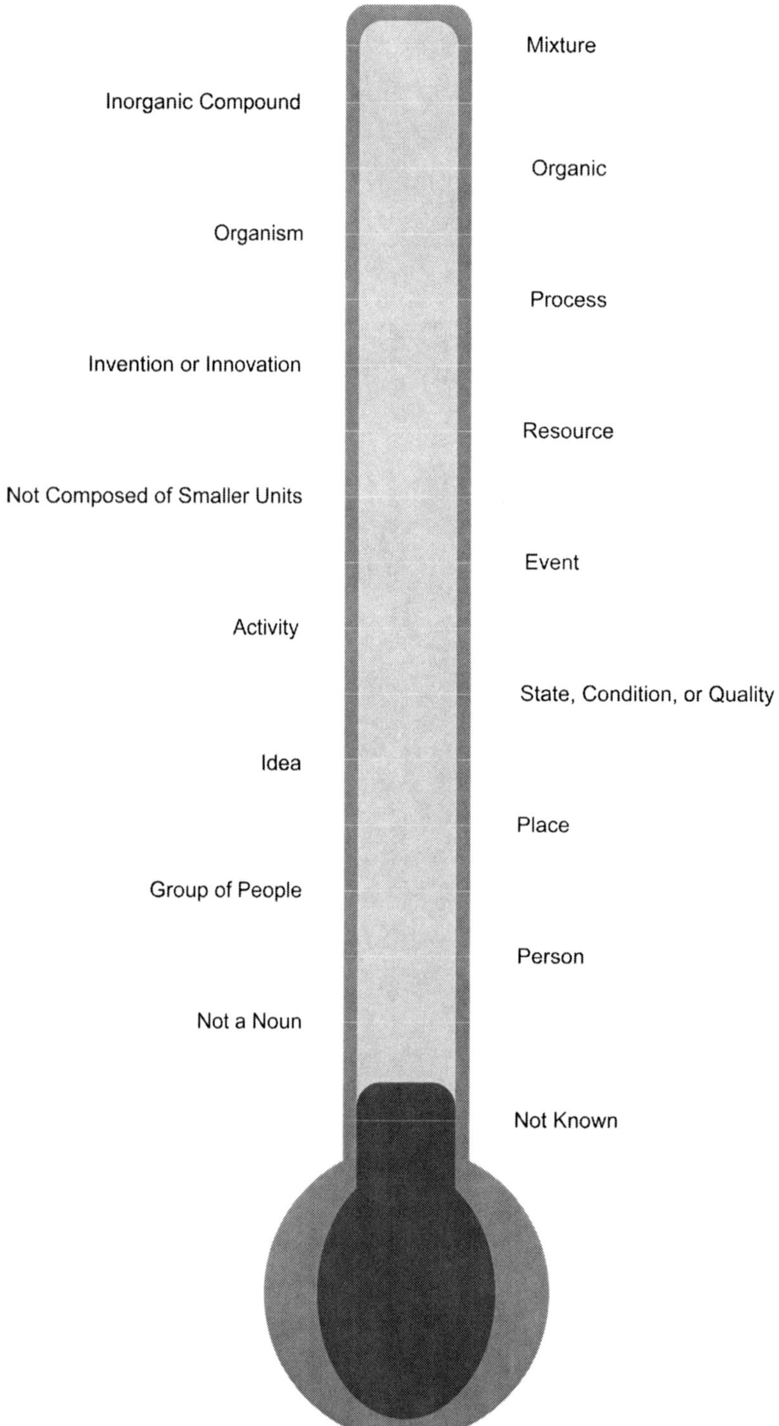

Thermometers and/or gauges can be found all around us in the modern world from battery life indicators to vehicle gas gauges. This is just another way to look at the Algorithm. Except when you use this visual analogy, you start from the bottom and work upward.

The keyboard interface is a straightforward visual approach to stimulating the research process. Starting from "Not Known", users can scan and seek out the applicable reference points from left to right. The keyboard interface or tabs analogy operates very similar to the calculator analogy.

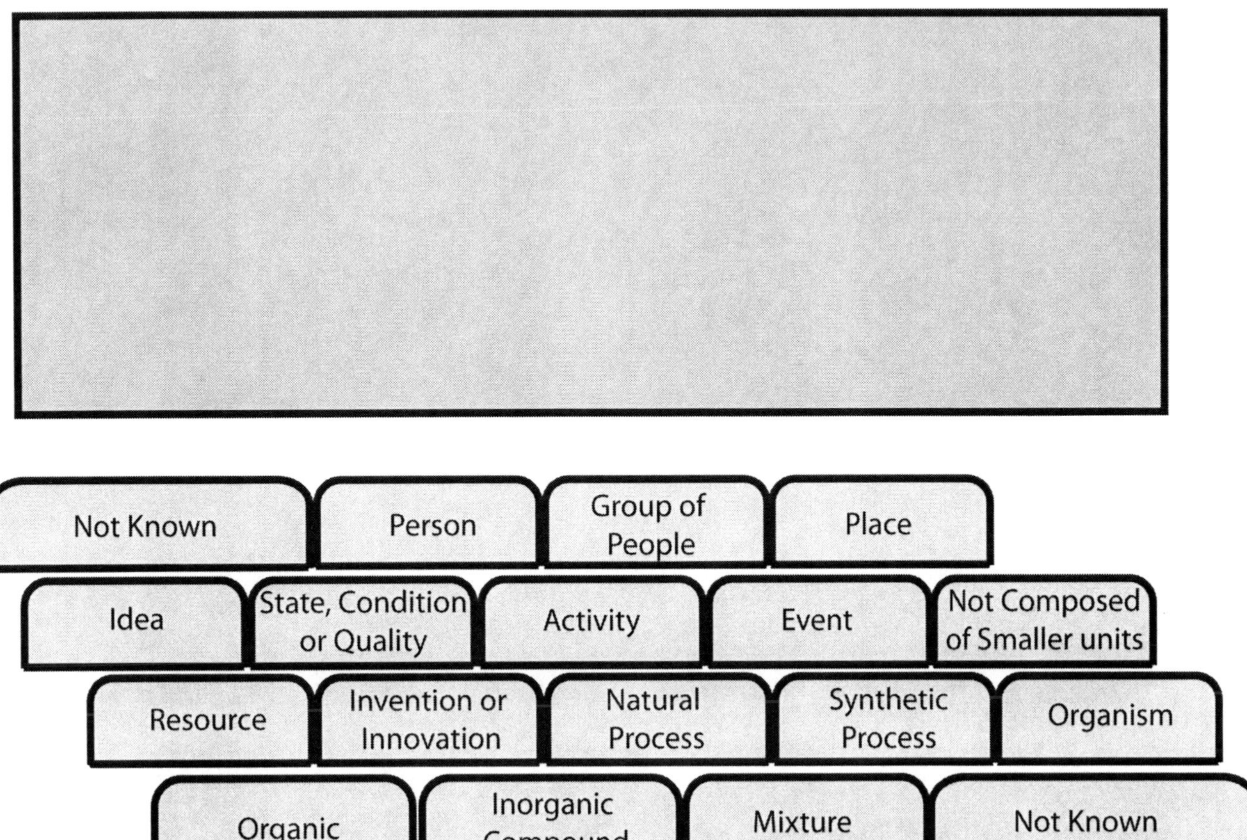

The pushbutton analogy is similar to the calculator and tabs analogy. Imagine pushing each button that applies to the research term. You can do the same thing with the calculator analogy, as well. The interface on many types of elevators allows you to pick more than one floor. This is one way you can visualize *The Imaginary Research Algorithm*.

With the ruler analogy of *The Imaginary Research Algorithm*, users will simply move from left to right and identify points that are related to the research term.

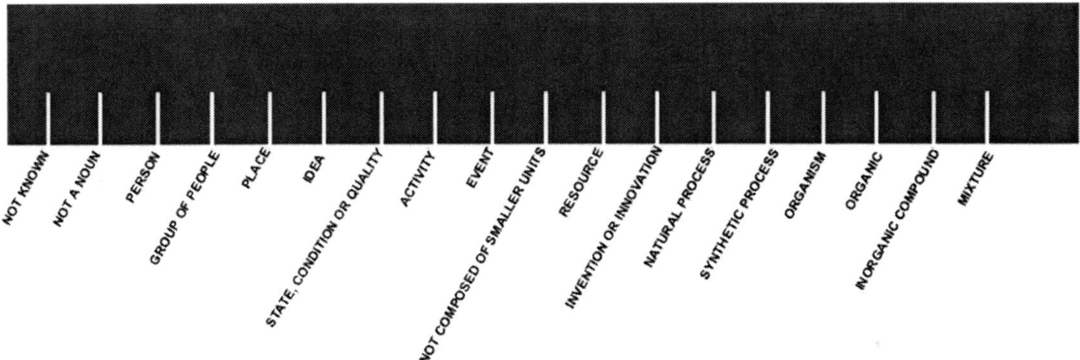

The wave analogy is similar to the ruler analogy from the perspective that you move left to right. However, you move up and down with the crests and troughs of the visual analogy.

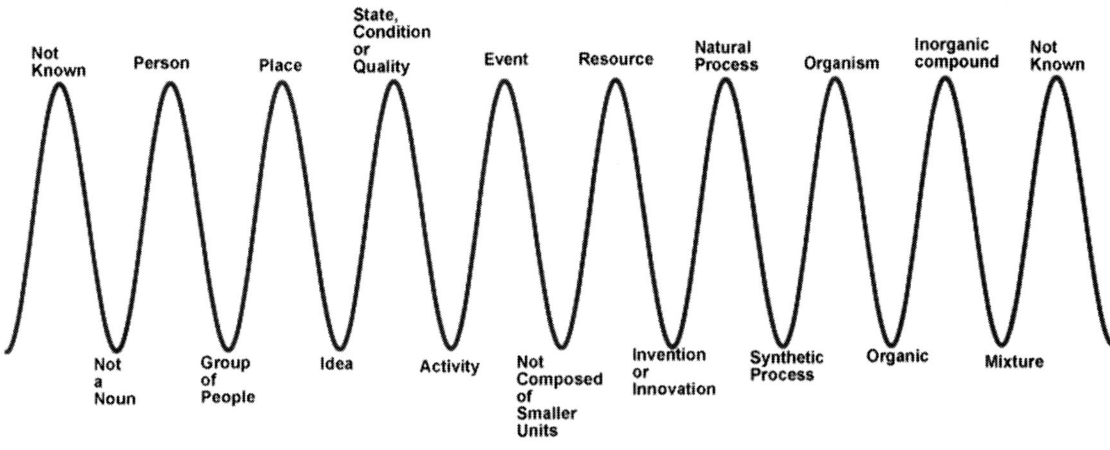

Lastly, we will examine the mountain range analogy. You have mountains(ups) and valleys(down). Using the visual analogy, you will move from left to right to identify research categories that relate to your terms.

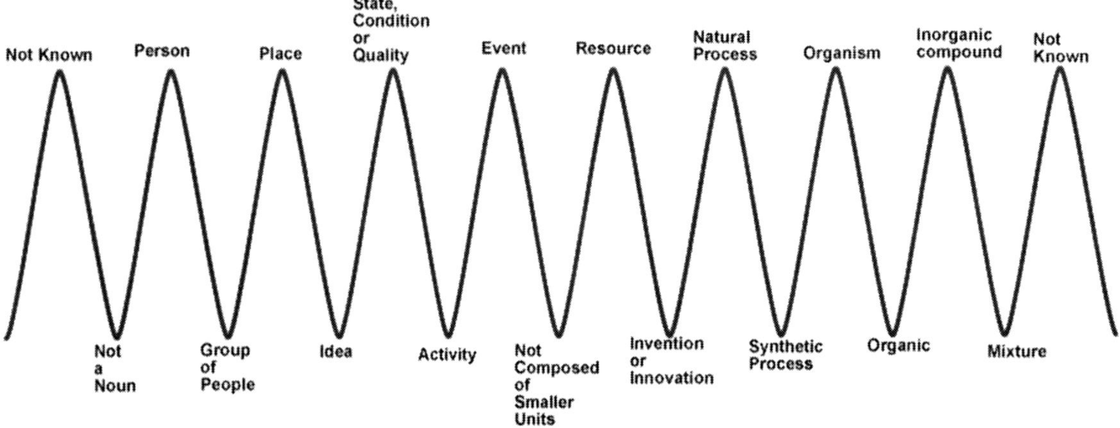

We have gone through nine visual analogies that relate to *The Imaginary Research Algorithm*. These visual expressions provide a different way of looking at the Algorithm. You may have noticed two things about the visual analogies. One, the visual expressions are less bloated with words. The analogies are straight to the point. Two, the words that connect to each decision point or category are missing. For demonstration purposes, the supplemental words that stimulate the research thought process were left out. At this point, you have mostly gained advanced skills in using *The Imaginary Research Algorithm*, so the visual analogies were provided to demonstrate other perspectives on using the Algorithm.

Chapter

8

The remaining chapters revolve around the practice and application of *The Imaginary Research Algorithm*. You have learned the mechanics of the Algorithm. At this point, you should be very comfortable with the Algorithm. Remember, thinking about your research topic is a prime requirement. Identifying decision points on *The Imaginary Research Algorithm* will guide you to valuable words that stimulate the research process. In section one of this book, you were guided to relevant decision points on the Algorithm. Now, it is your turn to focus and identify the various research possibilities of the following words, which may possibly challenge the way you perceive things. You will also be required to defend your research statements in the upcoming activities. These remaining chapters are dedicated to highlighting the exploration of research options when initiating a search at a library or web site.

Imaginary Research Algorithm

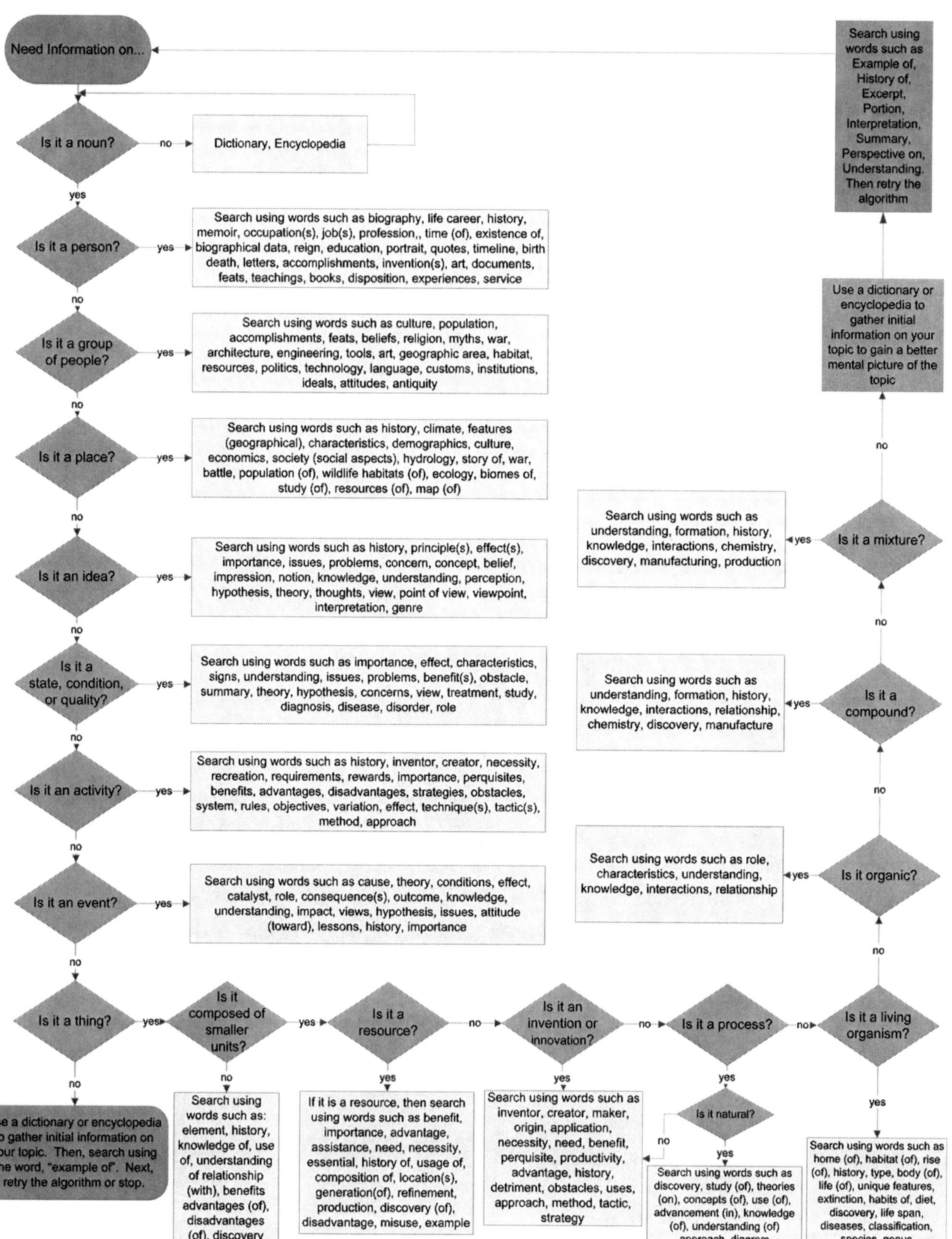

Day
1

For each research term, identify the research category based on *The Imaginary Research Algorithm*. Next, defend your choice(s) with a sentence that reflects each choice.

For example:

> Mirror: verb, idea, resource, invention or innovation

> The sad songs mirror the listener's feelings.
> (verb)(not noun)

> The mirror was most likely inspired by water.
> (idea)

> The mirror is an important tool for barbers.
> (resource)

> The ancient Greeks usually receive credit for the creation of the modern mirror.
> (invention or innovation)

Group 1	Group 2	Group 3
1. Baking Soda	6. Quartz	11. Legumes
2. Motivation	7. Quarks	12. Punic Wars
3. Attention	8. Quicksand	13. Fuel
4. Association	9. Hydroponics	14. Carbonation
5. Syndrome	10. Berries	15. Squirrel

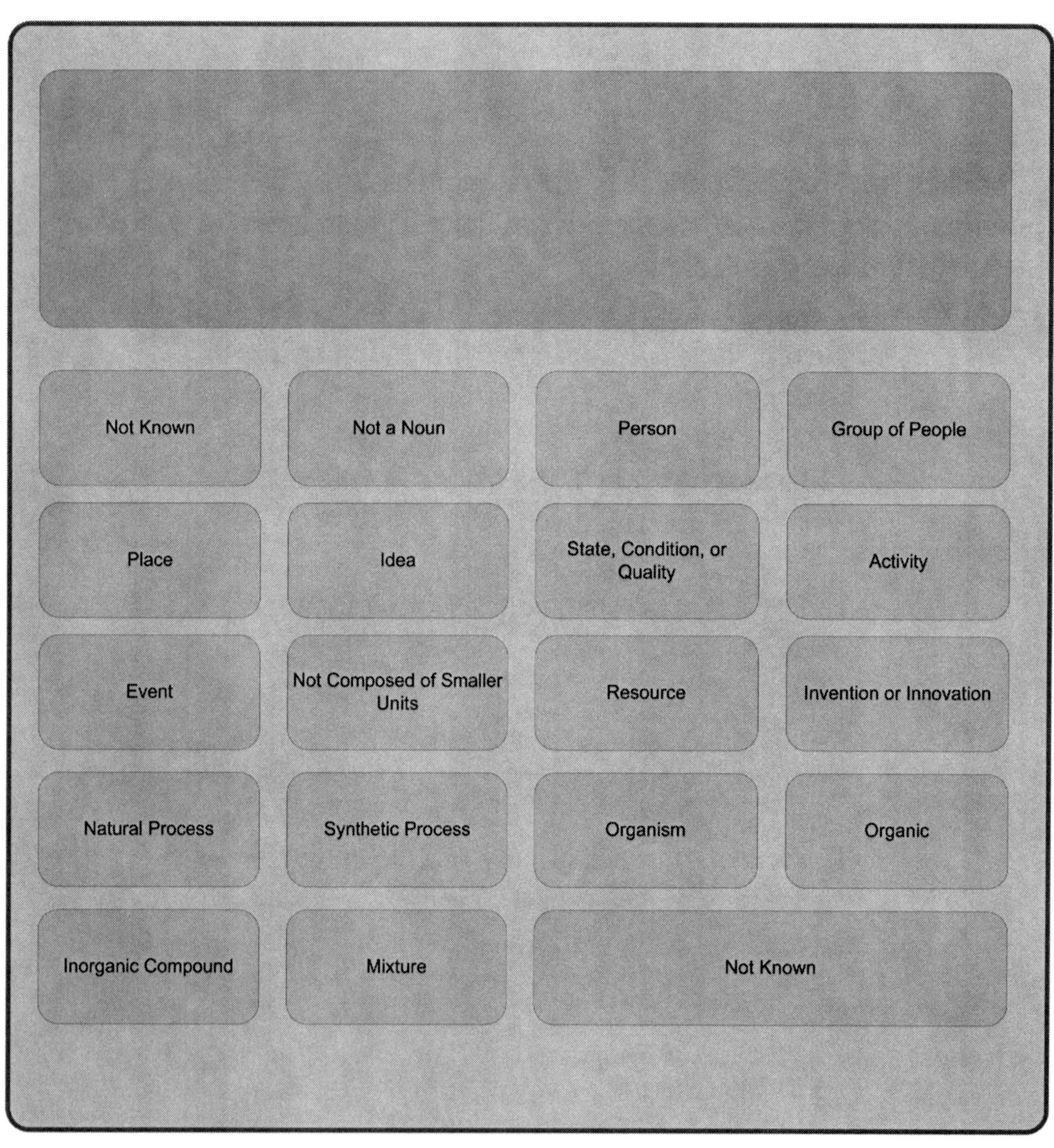

Not Known
Not a Noun
Person
Group of People
Place
Idea
State, Condition, or Quality
Activity
Event
Not Composed of Smaller Units
Resource
Invention or Innovation
Natural Process
Synthetic Process
Organism
Organic
Inorganic Compound
Mixture
Not Known

Day
2

For each research term, identify the research category based on *The Imaginary Research Algorithm*. Next, defend your choice(s) with a sentence that reflects each choice.

For example:

> Mirror: verb, idea, resource, invention or innovation

> The sad songs mirror the listener's feelings.
> (verb)(not noun)

> The mirror was most likely inspired by water.
> (idea)

> The mirror is an important tool for barbers.
> (resource)

> The ancient Greeks usually receive credit for the creation of the modern mirror.
> (invention or innovation)

Group 1	Group 2	Group 3
1. Dinosaur	6. Appendix	11. Hermes
2. Allosaur	7. Propane	12. Anu
3. Finger	8. Spinach	13. Horus
4. Eyes	9. Soap	14. Property
5. Tongue	10. Seawater	15. Infinity

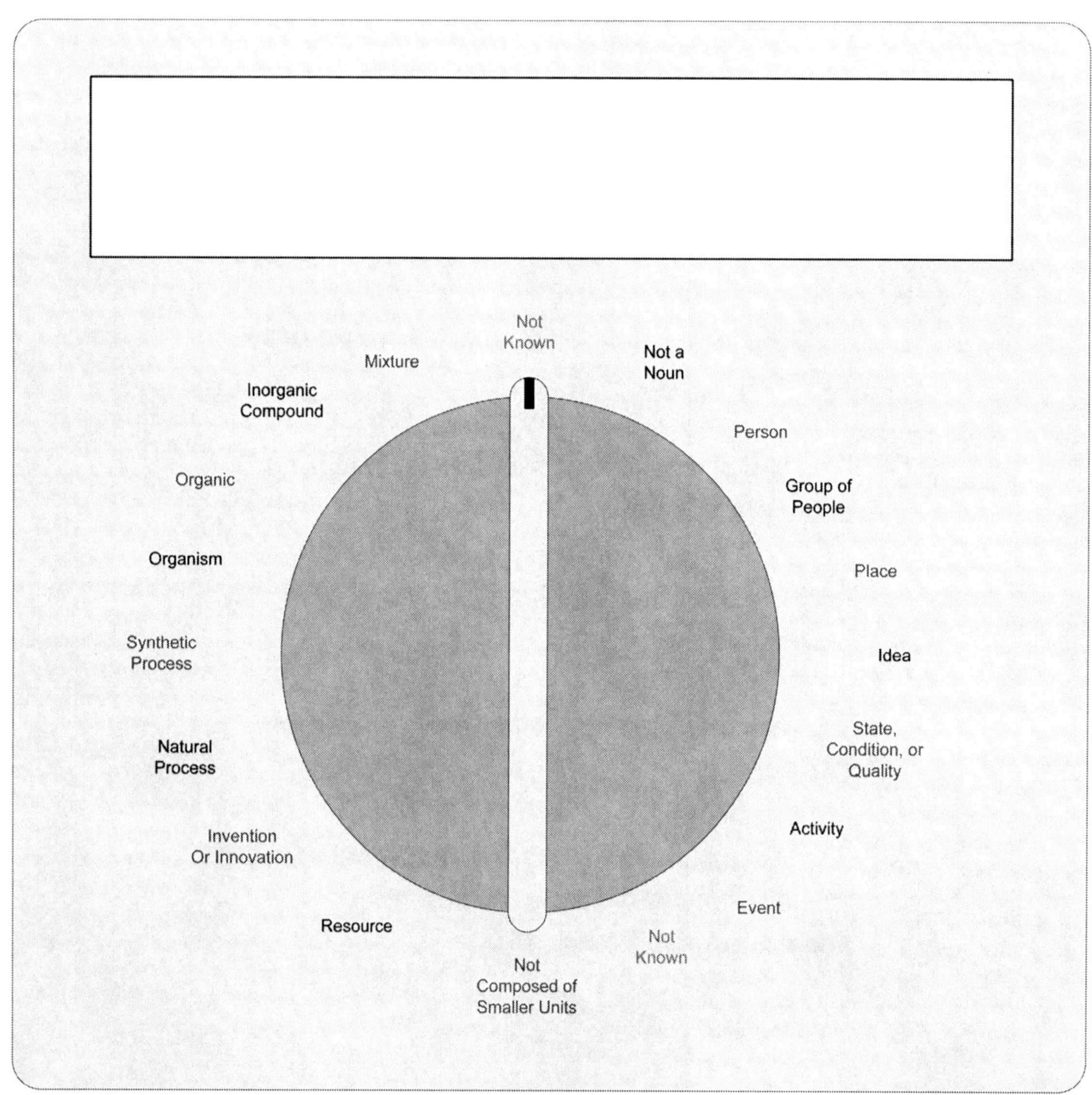
Not
Known
Mixture
Not a
Noun
Inorganic
Compound
Person
Organic
Group of
People
Organism
Place
Synthetic
Process
Idea
State,
Condition, or
Quality
Natural
Process
Activity
Invention
Or Innovation
Event
Resource
Not
Known
Not
Composed of
Smaller Units

Day
3

For each research term, identify the research category based on *The Imaginary Research Algorithm*. Next, defend your choice(s) with a sentence that reflects each choice.

For example:

>Mirror: verb, idea, resource, invention or innovation

>The sad songs mirror the listener's feelings.
>(verb)(not noun)

>The mirror was most likely inspired by water.
>(idea)

>The mirror is an important tool for barbers.
>(resource)

>The ancient Greeks usually receive credit for the creation of the modern mirror.
>(invention or innovation)

Group 1	Group 2	Group 3
1. Acceleration	6. Recombination	11. Learning
2. Velocity	7. Bohrs	12. George Washington Carver
3. Pi	8. Balloon	13. Uranium
4. Nile	9. Joseph Lister	14. Al-Jazari
5. Calorie	10. Aristole	15. Colchis

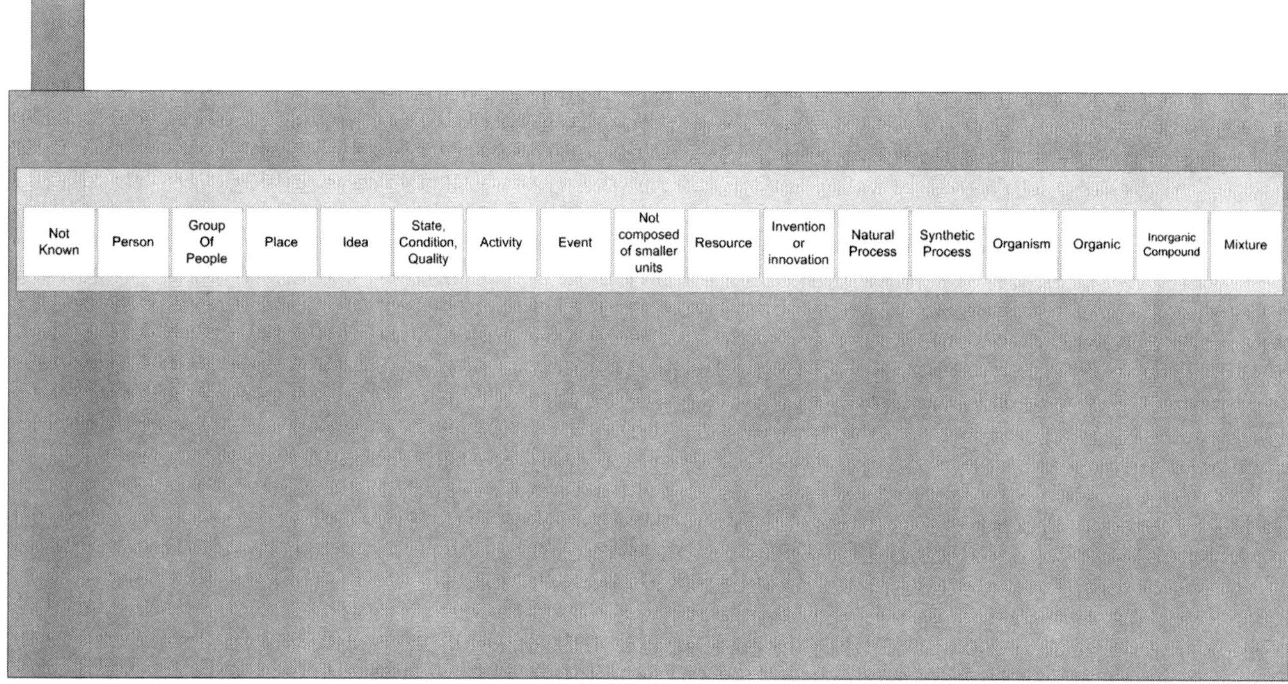

Not Known
Person
Group Of People
Place
Idea
State, Condition, Quality
Activity
Event
Not composed of smaller units
Resource
Invention or innovation
Natural Process
Synthetic Process
Organism
Organic
Inorganic Compound
Mixture

Day
4

For each research term, identify the research category based on *The Imaginary Research Algorithm.* Next, defend your choice(s) with a sentence that reflects each choice.

For example:

> Mirror: verb, idea, resource, invention or innovation
>
> The sad songs mirror the listener's feelings.
> (verb)(not noun)
>
> The mirror was most likely inspired by water.
> (idea)
>
> The mirror is an important tool for barbers.
> (resource)
>
> The ancient Greeks usually receive credit for the creation of the modern mirror.
> (invention or innovation)

Group 1	Group 2	Group 3
1. Colchians	6. Huckleberry	11. Balsam
2. Physiology	7. Vulcanization	12. Paris
3. Temperment	8. Honey	13. Humus
4. Guitar	9. Beeswax	14. Sucrose
5. Oncology	10. Beagle	15. Frutose

Imaginary Research Algorithm

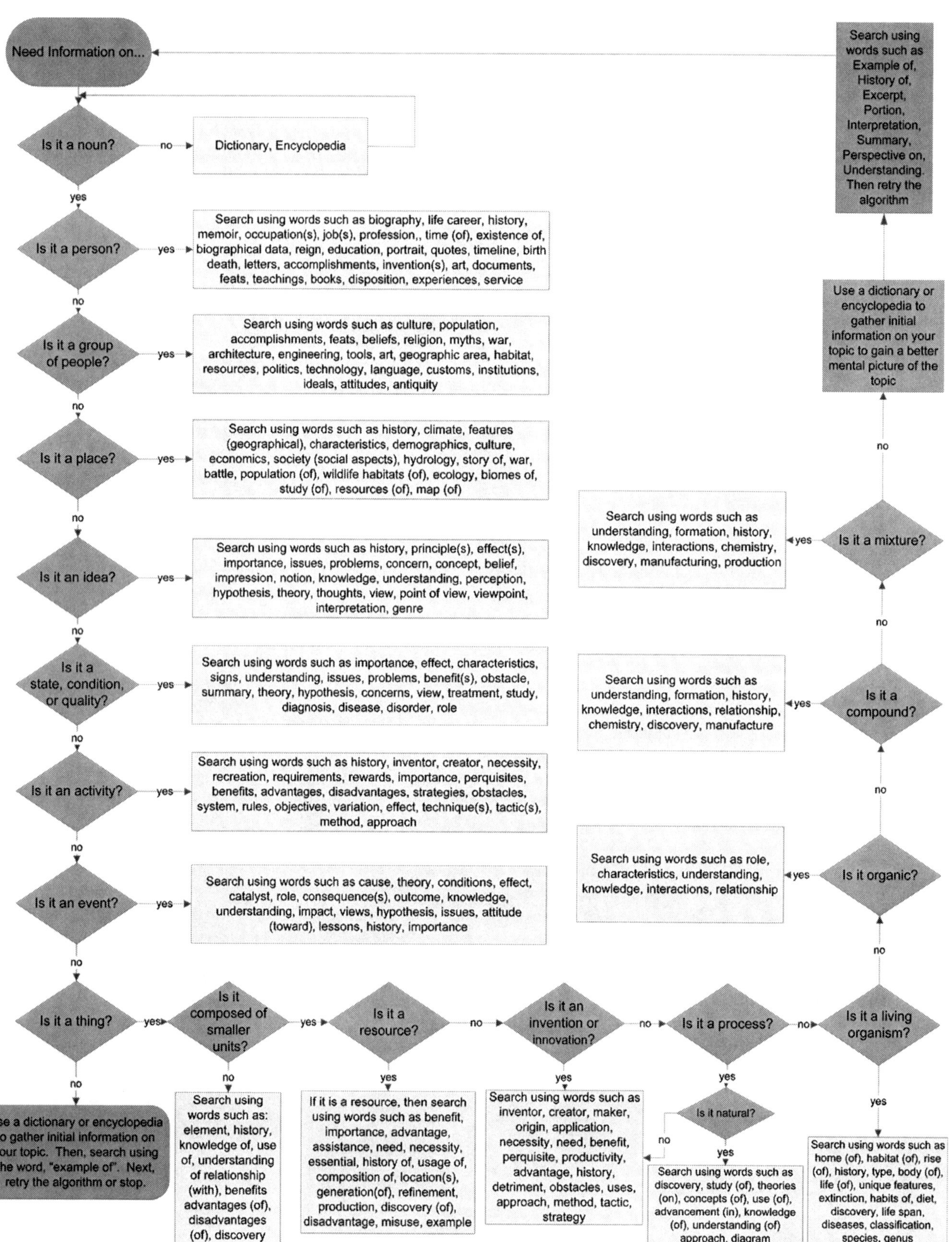

Day
5

For each research term, identify the research category based on *The Imaginary Research Algorithm*. Next, defend your choice(s) with a sentence that reflects each choice.

For example:

>Mirror: verb, idea, resource, invention or innovation

>The sad songs mirror the listener's feelings.
>(verb)(not noun)

>The mirror was most likely inspired by water.
>(idea)

>The mirror is an important tool for barbers.
>(resource)

>The ancient Greeks usually receive credit for the creation of the modern mirror.
>(invention or innovation)

Group 1	Group 2	Group 3
1. Glucose	6. Boston Tea Party	11. Revolution
2. Lactose	7. Factorial	12. American Revolution
3. Carbohydrates	8. Solstice	13. Tea Act
4. Fat	9. Equinox	14. Manifest Destiny
5. Butter	10. Shay's Rebellion	15. Spice

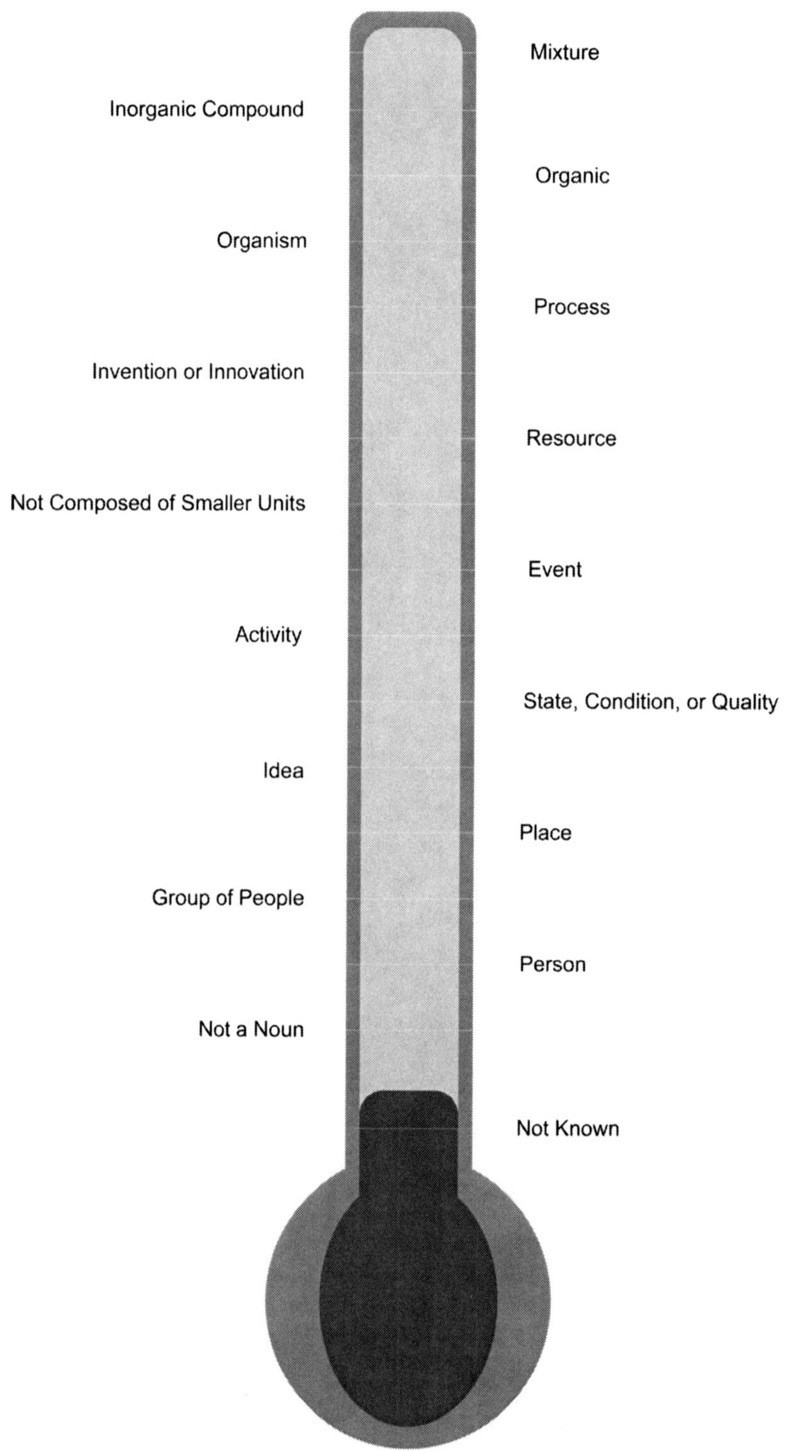
Mixture
Inorganic Compound
Organic
Organism
Process
Invention or Innovation
Resource
Not Composed of Smaller Units
Event
Activity
State, Condition, or Quality
Idea
Place
Group of People
Person
Not a Noun
Not Known

Day
6

For each research term, identify the research category based on *The Imaginary Research Algorithm*. Next, defend your choice(s) with a sentence that reflects each choice.

For example:

> Mirror: verb, idea, resource, invention or innovation

> The sad songs mirror the listener's feelings.
> (verb)(not noun)

> The mirror was most likely inspired by water.
> (idea)

> The mirror is an important tool for barbers.
> (resource)

> The ancient Greeks usually receive credit for the creation of the modern mirror.
> (invention or innovation)

Group 1	Group 2	Group 3
1. Avanti	6. Pigment	11. Taoism
2. Black Pepper	7. Timbuktu	12. Pearl
3. Mercantilism	8. Great Wall of China	13. Tofu
4. Dye	9. Guan Yu	14. Sirocco
5. Indigo	10. Confucius	15. Animism

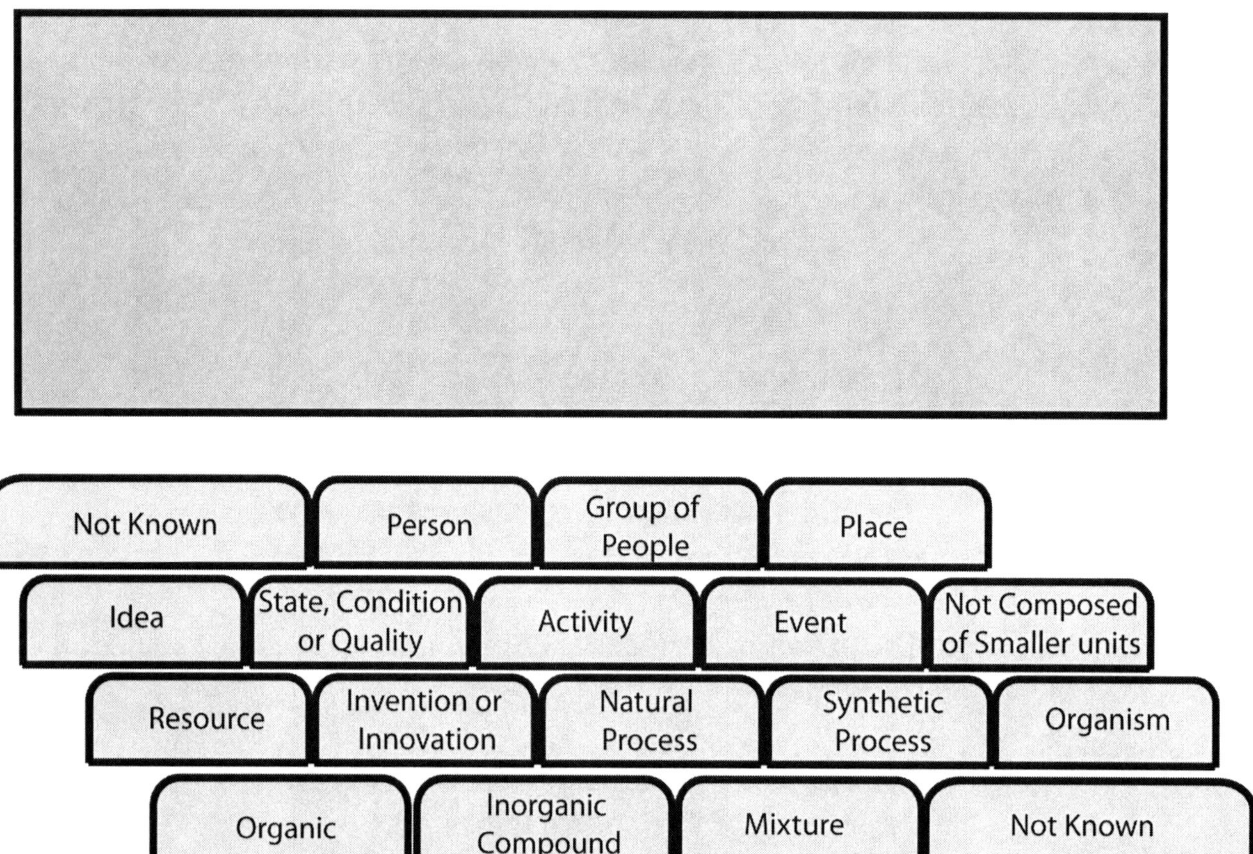
Not Known
Person
Group of People
Place
Idea
State, Condition or Quality
Activity
Event
Not Composed of Smaller units
Resource
Invention or Innovation
Natural Process
Synthetic Process
Organism
Organic
Inorganic Compound
Mixture
Not Known

Day 7

For each research term, identify the research category based on *The Imaginary Research Algorithm*. Next, defend your choice(s) with a sentence that reflects each choice.

For example:

> Mirror: verb, idea, resource, invention or innovation

> The sad songs mirror the listener's feelings.
> (verb)(not noun)

> The mirror was most likely inspired by water.
> (idea)

> The mirror is an important tool for barbers.
> (resource)

> The ancient Greeks usually receive credit for the creation of the modern mirror.
> (invention or innovation)

Group 1	Group 2	Group 3
1. Sundiata	6. Turquoise	11. Agriculture
2. Marshmallow	7. Ibn Khaldun	12. Sicily
3. Shadow	8. Herodotus	13. Sahara
4. Alphabet	9. Tripolitan	14. Egypt
5. Phoenicians	10. Company	15. World War I

Not Known
Not A Noun
Person
Group of People
Place
Idea
State, Condition, Or Quality
Activity
Event
Not Composed of Smaller Units
Resource
Invention or Innovation
Natural Process
Synthetic Process
Organism
Organic
Inorganic Compound
Mixture

Day
8

For each research term, identify the research category based on *The Imaginary Research Algorithm*. Next, defend your choice(s) with a sentence that reflects each choice.
For example:

> Mirror: verb, idea, resource, invention or innovation

> The sad songs mirror the listener's feelings.
> (verb)(not noun)

> The mirror was most likely inspired by water.
> (idea)

> The mirror is an important tool for barbers.
> (resource)

> The ancient Greeks usually receive credit for
> the creation of the modern mirror.
> (invention or innovation)

Group 1	Group 2	Group 3
1. Shinto	6. Axiom	11. Variable
2. Silk	7. Brahmagupta	12. Saracens
3. Nylon	8. Algebra	13. Flag
4. Theater	9. Polynomials	14. Templars
5. Theatrics	10. Al-Khwarizmi	15. Chivalry

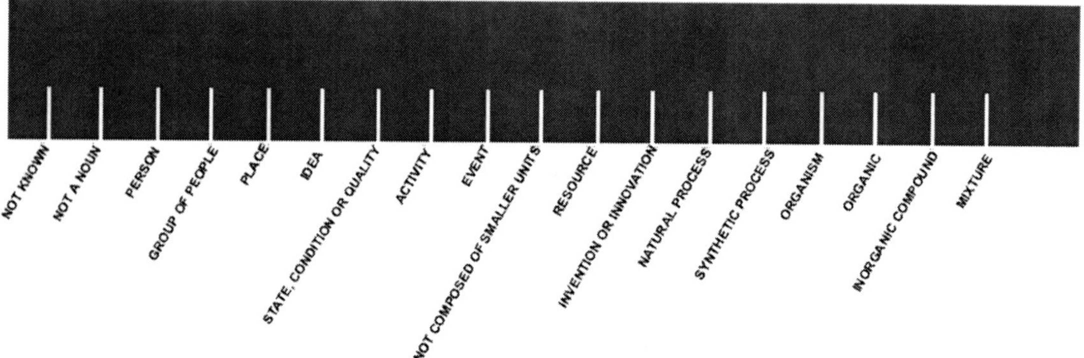

NOT KNOWN
NOT A NOUN
PERSON
GROUP OF PEOPLE
PLACE
IDEA
STATE, CONDITION OR QUALITY
ACTIVITY
EVENT
NOT COMPOSED OF SMALLER UNITS
RESOURCE
INVENTION OR INNOVATION
NATURAL PROCESS
SYNTHETIC PROCESS
ORGANISM
ORGANIC
INORGANIC COMPOUND
MIXTURE

Day 9

For each research term, identify the research category based on *The Imaginary Research Algorithm*. Next, defend your choice(s) with a sentence that reflects each choice.

For example:

> Mirror: verb, idea, resource, invention or innovation

> The sad songs mirror the listener's feelings.
> (verb)(not noun)

> The mirror was most likely inspired by water.
> (idea)

> The mirror is an important tool for barbers.
> (resource)

> The ancient Greeks usually receive credit for the creation of the modern mirror.
> (invention or innovation)

Group 1	Group 2	Group 3
1. Force	6. Altruism	11. Papyrus
2. Friction	7. Vertigo	12. Infantry
3. Ronin	8. Shame	13. Symposium
4. Eukaryote	9. Mencius	14. Armor
5. Haiku	10. Epigram	15. Genghis Khan

Imaginary Research Algorithm

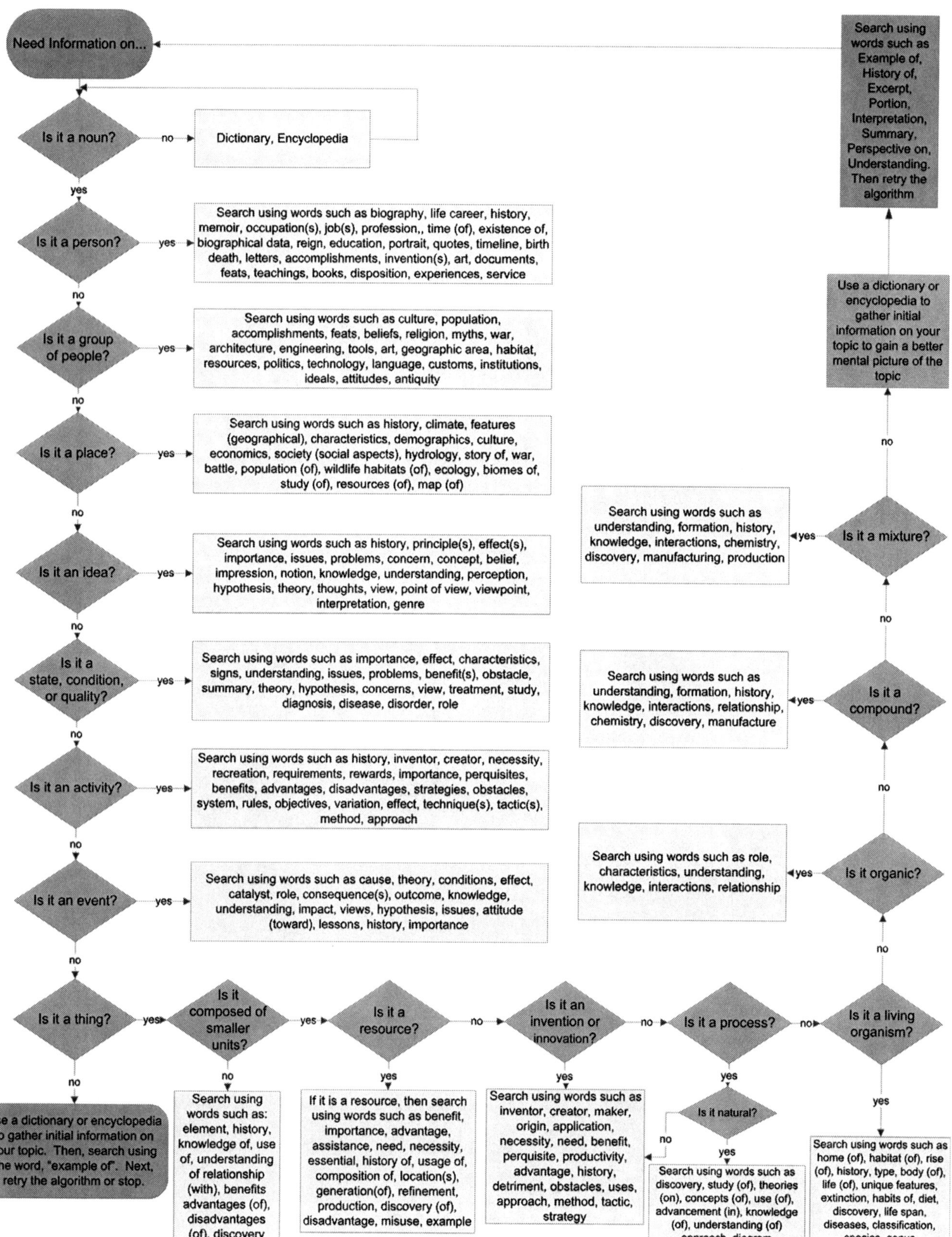

Day
10

For each research term, identify the research category based on *The Imaginary Research Algorithm.* Next, defend your choice(s) with a sentence that reflects each choice.
For example:

Mirror: verb, idea, resource, invention or innovation

The sad songs mirror the listener's feelings.
(verb)(not noun)

The mirror was most likely inspired by water.
(idea)

The mirror is an important tool for barbers.
(resource)

The ancient Greeks usually receive credit for the creation of the modern mirror.
(invention or innovation)

Group 1	Group 2	Group 3
1. Huns	6. Potash	11. Epinephrine
2. Funny	7. Vinegar	12. Calculator
3. Idiom	8. Hydrogen Peroxide	13. Abacus
4. Pirates	9. Hay Fever	14. Calendar
5. Alum	10. Ibuprofen	15. Telephone

This concludes the first ten days of practice and application of *The Imaginary Research Algorithm.*

Chapter

9

In this chapter, we will cover days 11 - 20. Take time to think about each research term. Do not forget to defend your decision point selections.

Imaginary Research Algorithm

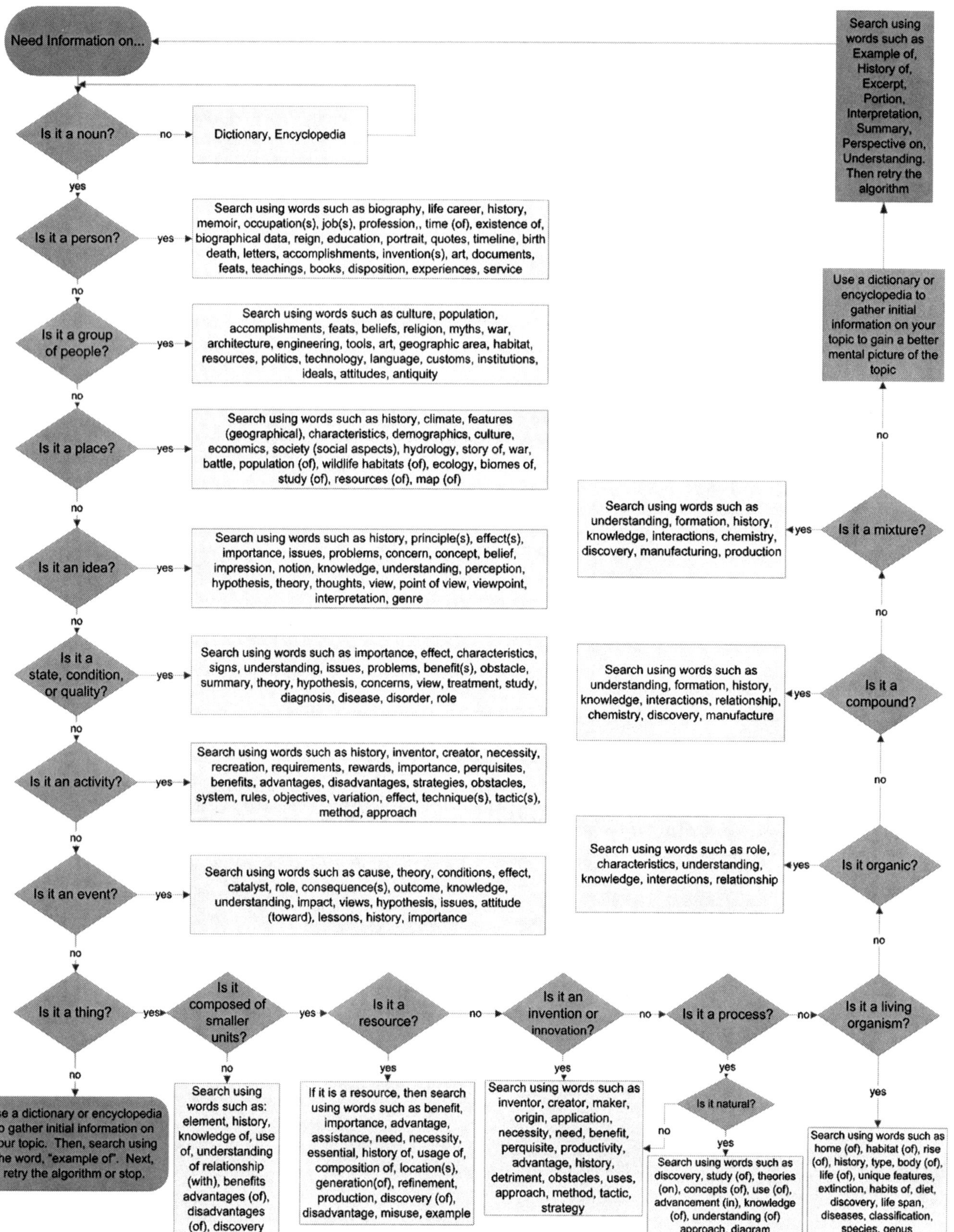

Day
11

For each research term, identify the research category based on *The Imaginary Research Algorithm.* Next, defend your choice(s) with a sentence that reflects each choice.
For example:

> Mirror: verb, idea, resource, invention or innovation

> The sad songs mirror the listener's feelings.
> (verb)(not noun)

> The mirror was most likely inspired by water.
> (idea)

> The mirror is an important tool for barbers.
> (resource)

> The ancient Greeks usually receive credit for the creation of the modern mirror.
> (invention or innovation)

Group 1	Group 2	Group 3
1. Cartography	6. Militia	11. Silk Road
2. Great Zimbabwe	7. Violin	12. Marco Polo
3. Steel	8. Great Depression	13. Dust Bowl
4. Sundial	9. Mojave Desert	14. Plutarch
5. Suez Canal	10. Mansa Musa	15. Canterbury Tales

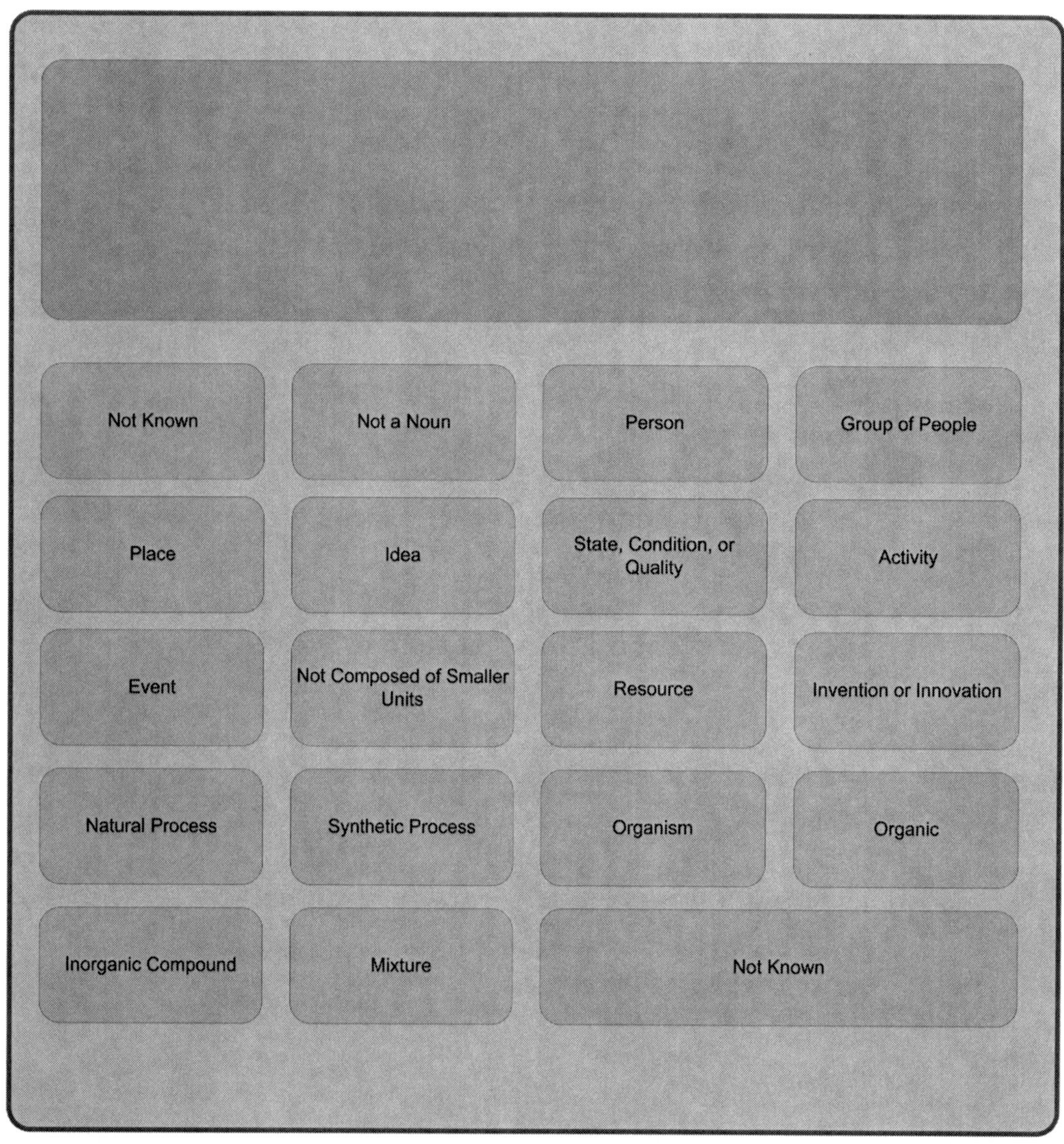

Not Known
Not a Noun
Person
Group of People
Place
Idea
State, Condition, or Quality
Activity
Event
Not Composed of Smaller Units
Resource
Invention or Innovation
Natural Process
Synthetic Process
Organism
Organic
Inorganic Compound
Mixture
Not Known

Day
12

For each research term, identify the research category based on *The Imaginary Research Algorithm*. Next, defend your choice(s) with a sentence that reflects each choice.

For example:

Mirror: verb, idea, resource, invention or innovation

The sad songs mirror the listener's feelings.
(verb)(not noun)

The mirror was most likely inspired by water.
(idea)

The mirror is an important tool for barbers.
(resource)

The ancient Greeks usually receive credit for the creation of the modern mirror.
(invention or innovation)

Group 1	Group 2	Group 3
1. Niagra Falls	6. Saturn	11. Sodium Chloride
2. Hieroglyphics	7. Textile	12. Supercomputer
3. Pictograph	8. Protectionism	13. Internet
4. Spanish Armada	9. Capitalism	14. Consciousness
5. Isolationism	10. Laissez-faire	15. Skin

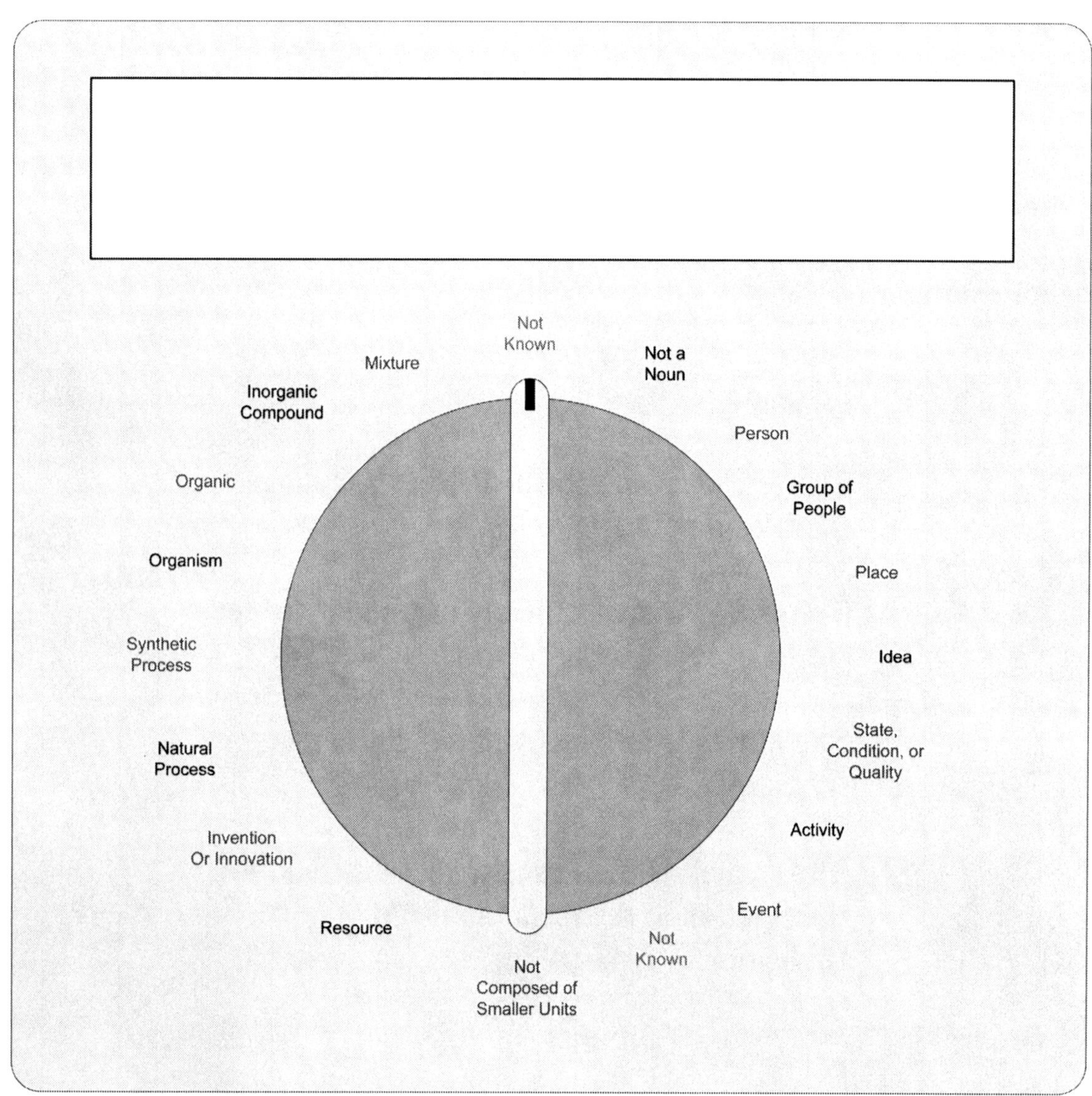

Not Known
Mixture
Not a Noun
Inorganic Compound
Person
Organic
Group of People
Organism
Place
Synthetic Process
Idea
State, Condition, or Quality
Natural Process
Activity
Invention Or Innovation
Event
Resource
Not Known
Not Composed of Smaller Units

Day
13

For each research term, identify the research category based on *The Imaginary Research Algorithm*. Next, defend your choice(s) with a sentence that reflects each choice.

For example:

> Mirror: verb, idea, resource, invention or innovation

> The sad songs mirror the listener's feelings.
> (verb)(not noun)

> The mirror was most likely inspired by water.
> (idea)

> The mirror is an important tool for barbers.
> (resource)

> The ancient Greeks usually receive credit for
> the creation of the modern mirror.
> (invention or innovation)

Group 1	Group 2	Group 3
1. Epidermis	6. Biodegradability	11. Perspiration
2. Bean	7. Greenhouse Effect	12. Aquaculture
3. Water	8. Equilibrium	13. Electroencephalograpy
4. Insolvency	9. Semantics	14. Foundry
5. Krypton	10. Insomnia	15. Founding

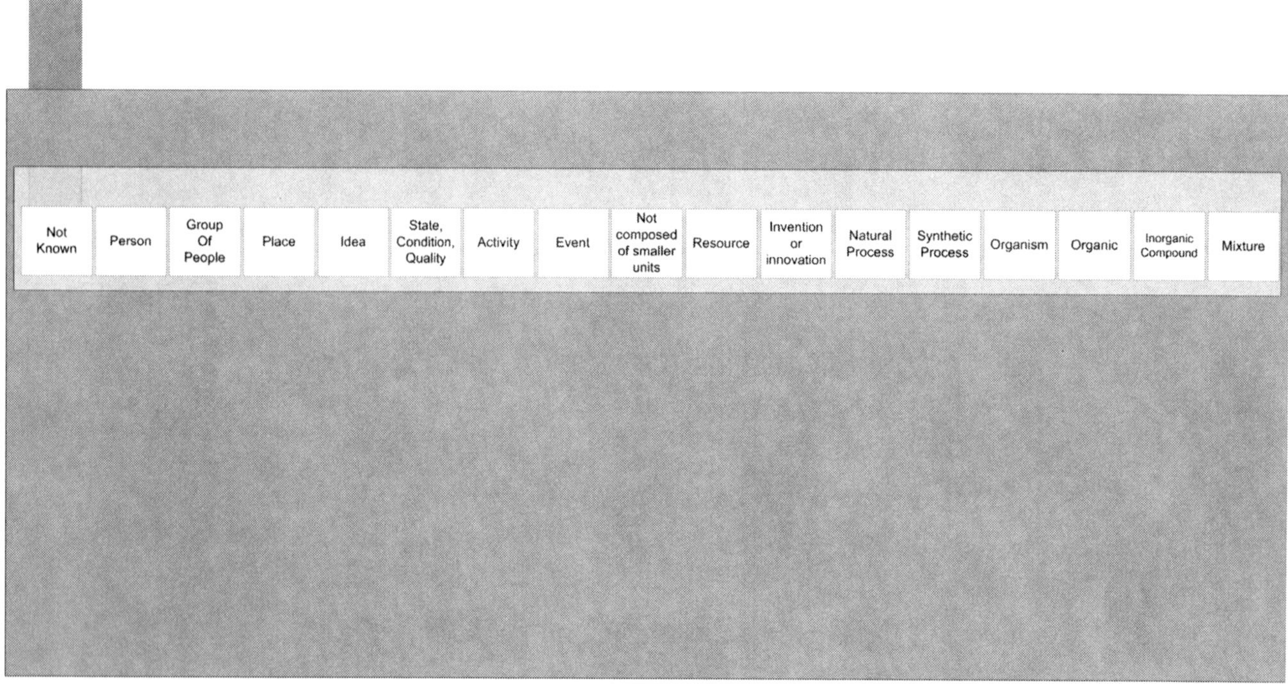

Not Known
Person
Group Of People
Place
Idea
State, Condition, Quality
Activity
Event
Not composed of smaller units
Resource
Invention or innovation
Natural Process
Synthetic Process
Organism
Organic
Inorganic Compound
Mixture

Day 14

For each research term, identify the research category based on *The Imaginary Research Algorithm*. Next, defend your choice(s) with a sentence that reflects each choice.

For example:

Mirror: verb, idea, resource, invention or innovation

The sad songs mirror the listener's feelings.
(verb)(not noun)

The mirror was most likely inspired by water.
(idea)

The mirror is an important tool for barbers.
(resource)

The ancient Greeks usually receive credit for the creation of the modern mirror.
(invention or innovation)

Group 1	Group 2	Group 3
1. Tryptophan	6. Blight	11. Fascism
2. Spore	7. Bronchitis	12. Serfdom
3. Peat	8. Boycott	13. Lightning
4. Interferon	9. Crystal	14. Rain Forest
5. Prion	10. Famine	15. Colosseum

Imaginary Research Algorithm

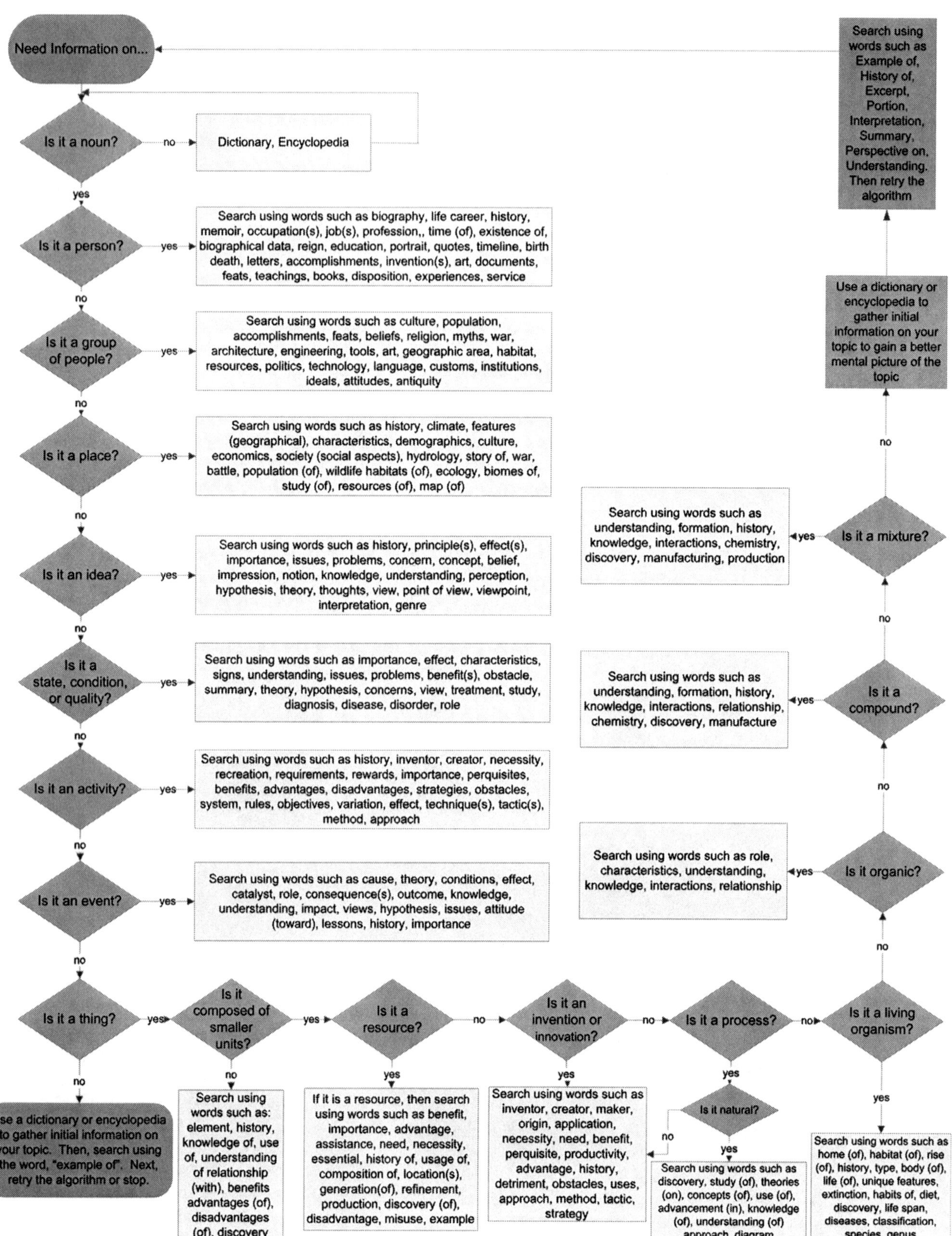

Day 15

For each research term, identify the research category based on *The Imaginary Research Algorithm.* Next, defend your choice(s) with a sentence that reflects each choice.
For example:

Mirror: verb, idea, resource, invention or innovation

The sad songs mirror the listener's feelings.
(verb)(not noun)

The mirror was most likely inspired by water.
(idea)

The mirror is an important tool for barbers.
(resource)

The ancient Greeks usually receive credit for the creation of the modern mirror.
(invention or innovation)

Group 1	Group 2	Group 3
1. Cartoon	6. Skydiving	11. Hydrogen
2. Tapestry	7. Skiing	12. Calcium
3. Drawing	8. Night	13. Sodium
4. Instinct	9. Enzyme	14. Chlorine
5. Corporation	10. Camping	15. Argon

Imaginary Research Algorithm

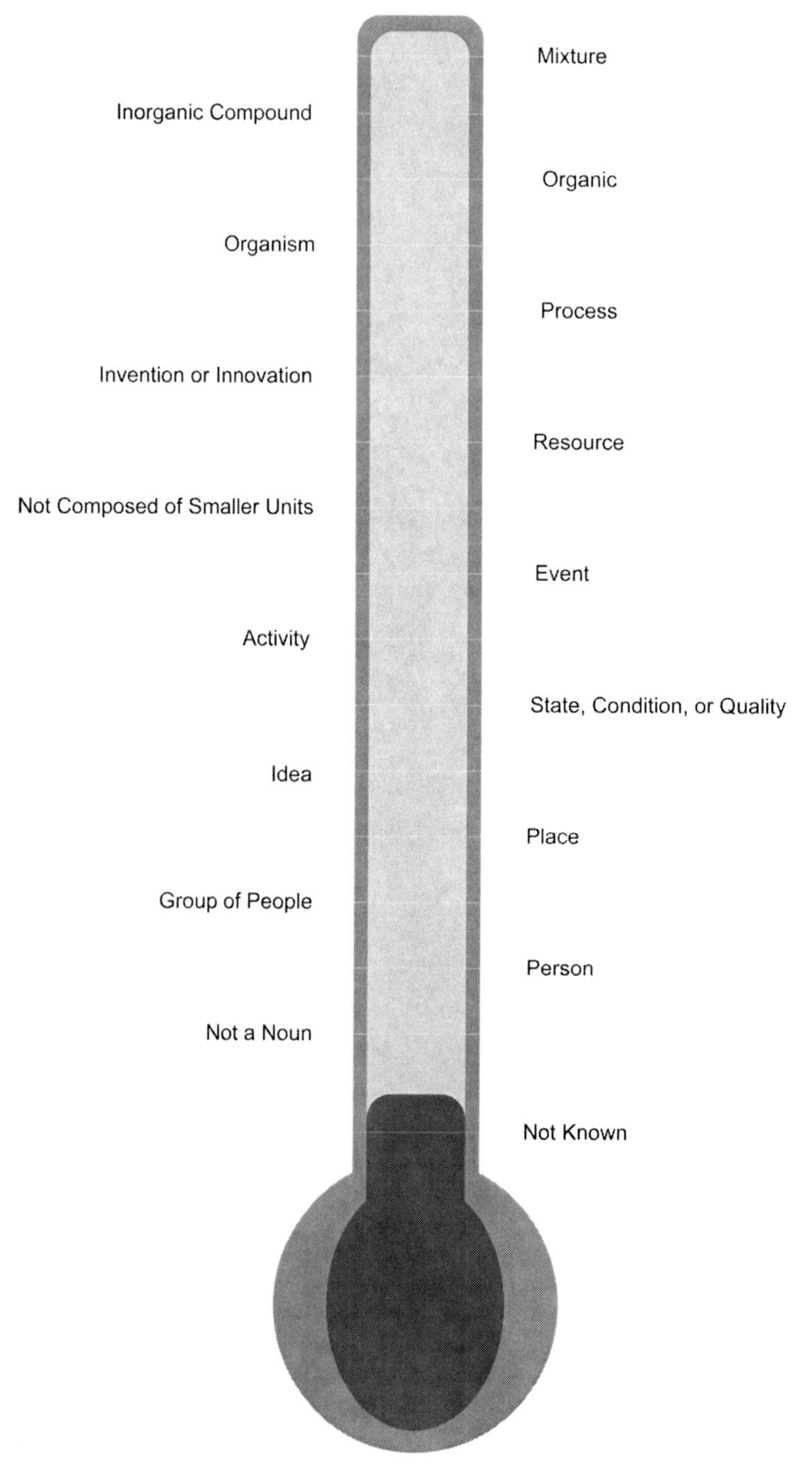

Day 16

For each research term, identify the research category based on *The Imaginary Research Algorithm*. Next, defend your choice(s) with a sentence that reflects each choice.

For example:

> Mirror: verb, idea, resource, invention or innovation
>
> The sad songs mirror the listener's feelings.
> (verb)(not noun)
>
> The mirror was most likely inspired by water.
> (idea)
>
> The mirror is an important tool for barbers.
> (resource)
>
> The ancient Greeks usually receive credit for the creation of the modern mirror.
> (invention or innovation)

Group 1	Group 2	Group 3
1. Silicon	6. Scientific Method	11. Embargo
2. Stress	7. Drill	12. Shaman
3. Rubric	8. Beekeeping	13. Telescope
4. Ruler	9. Iconoclast	14. Cobalt
5. Scissors	10. Hammer	15. Folklore

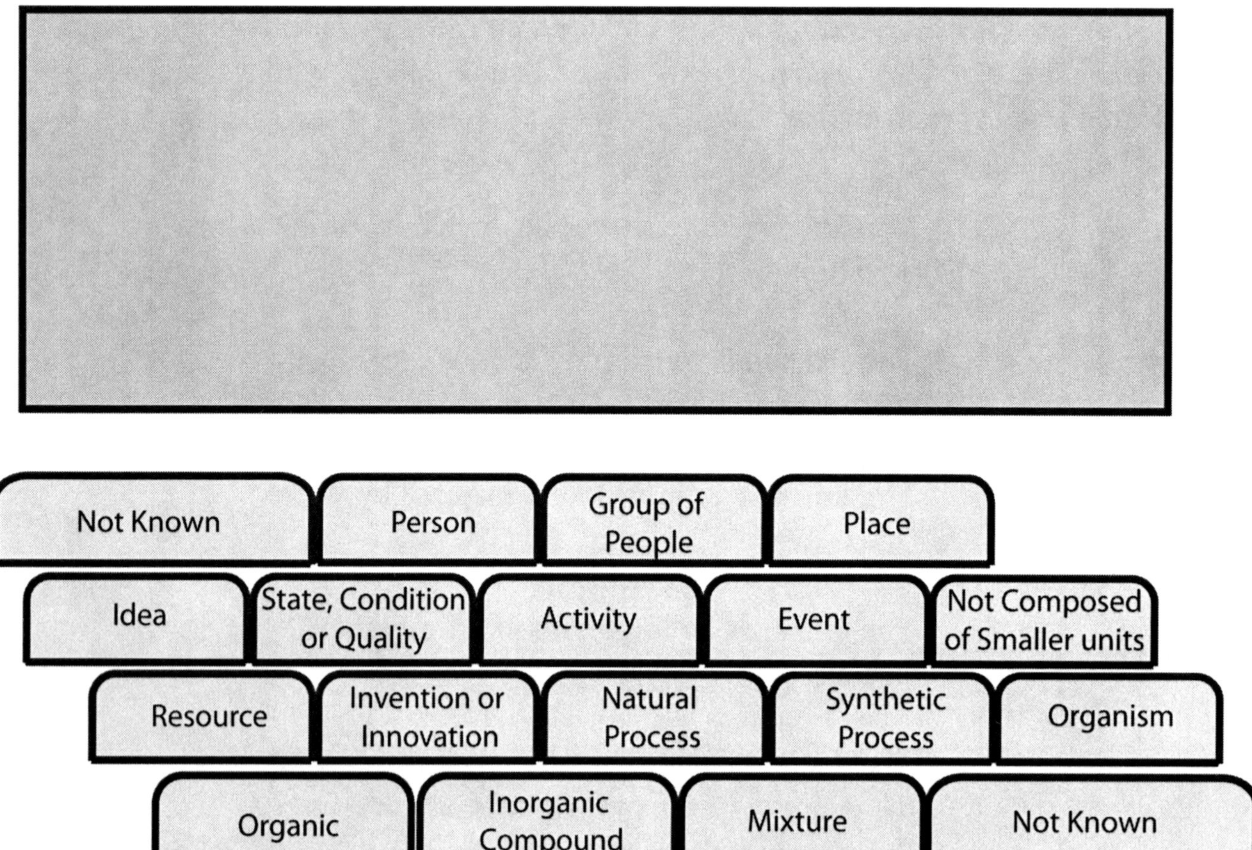

Not Known
Person
Group of People
Place
Idea
State, Condition or Quality
Activity
Event
Not Composed of Smaller units
Resource
Invention or Innovation
Natural Process
Synthetic Process
Organism
Organic
Inorganic Compound
Mixture
Not Known

Day
17

For each research term, identify the research category based on *The Imaginary Research Algorithm*. Next, defend your choice(s) with a sentence that reflects each choice.

For example:

Mirror: verb, idea, resource, invention or innovation

The sad songs mirror the listener's feelings.
(verb)(not noun)

The mirror was most likely inspired by water.
(idea)

The mirror is an important tool for barbers.
(resource)

The ancient Greeks usually receive credit for the creation of the modern mirror.
(invention or innovation)

Group 1	Group 2	Group 3
1. Bacteriophage	6. Pyrometer	11. Protractor
2. Astrolabe	7. Oboe	12. Periscope
3. Gyroscope	8. Flute	13. Promissory Note
4. Thermocouple	9. Piccolo	14. Planeterium
5. Lute	10. Binoculars	15. Galvanometer

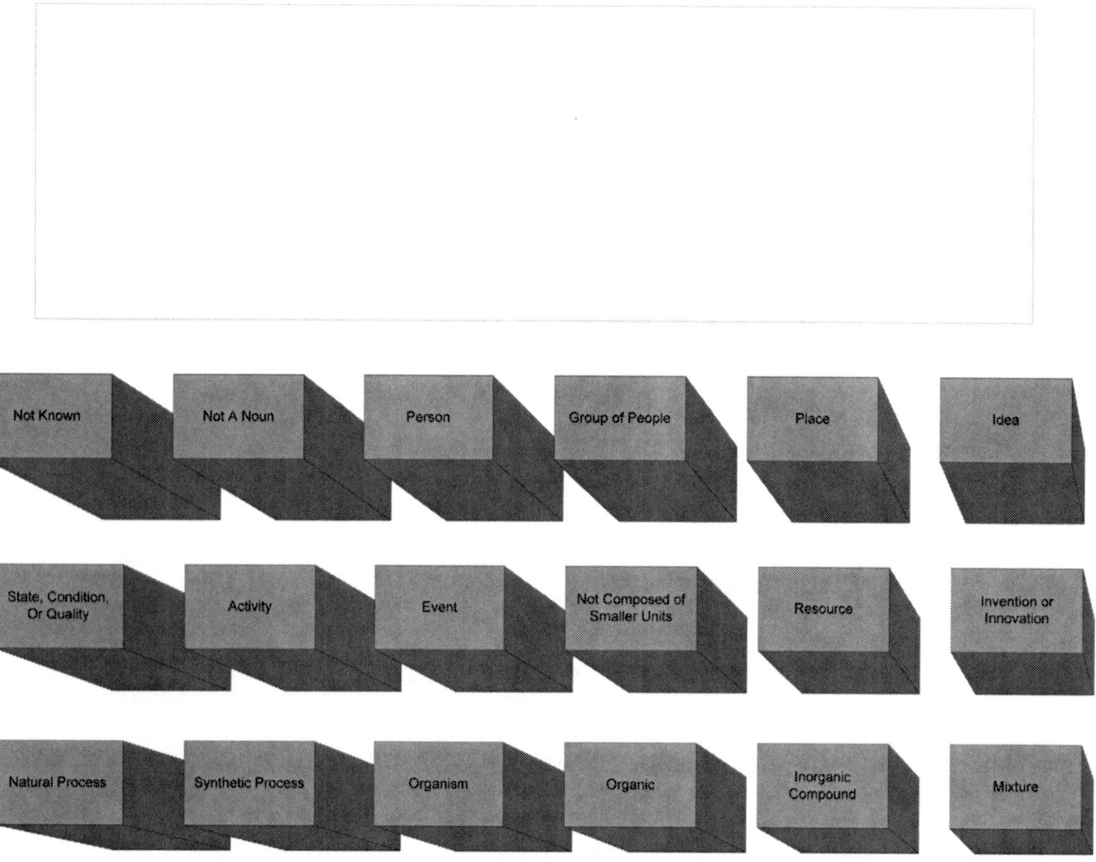

Not Known
Not A Noun
Person
Group of People
Place
Idea
State, Condition, Or Quality
Activity
Event
Not Composed of Smaller Units
Resource
Invention or Innovation
Natural Process
Synthetic Process
Organism
Organic
Inorganic Compound
Mixture

Day
18

For each research term, identify the research category based on *The Imaginary Research Algorithm*. Next, defend your choice(s) with a sentence that reflects each choice.

For example:

Mirror: verb, idea, resource, invention or innovation

The sad songs mirror the listener's feelings.
(verb)(not noun)

The mirror was most likely inspired by water.
(idea)

The mirror is an important tool for barbers.
(resource)

The ancient Greeks usually receive credit for the creation of the modern mirror.
(invention or innovation)

Group 1

1. Electric Current
2. Test tube
3. Treaty
4. Xylophone
5. Chromosphere

Group 2

6. Refraction
7. Magnetism
8. Photoelectric effect
9. Jet Lag
10. Aurora

Group 3

11. Chips
12. Stomata
13. Transpiration
14. Inflation
15. Deflation

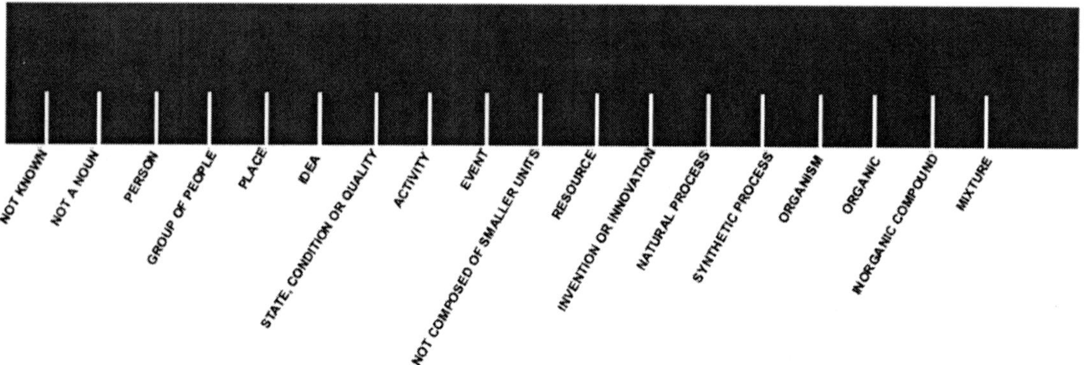

NOT KNOWN
NOT A NOUN
PERSON
GROUP OF PEOPLE
PLACE
IDEA
STATE, CONDITION OR QUALITY
ACTIVITY
EVENT
NOT COMPOSED OF SMALLER UNITS
RESOURCE
INVENTION OR INNOVATION
NATURAL PROCESS
SYNTHETIC PROCESS
ORGANISM
ORGANIC
INORGANIC COMPOUND
MIXTURE

Day
19

For each research term, identify the research category based on *The Imaginary Research Algorithm*. Next, defend your choice(s) with a sentence that reflects each choice.

For example:

> Mirror: verb, idea, resource, invention or innovation

> The sad songs mirror the listener's feelings.
> (verb)(not noun)

> The mirror was most likely inspired by water.
> (idea)

> The mirror is an important tool for barbers.
> (resource)

> The ancient Greeks usually receive credit for the creation of the modern mirror.
> (invention or innovation)

Group 1	Group 2	Group 3
1. Stagnation	6. Inch	11. Luddite
2. Blackbeard	7. Barometer	12. Virulent
3. Altimeter	8. Entropy	13. Patrician
4. Inertia	9. Heterosis	14. Maser
5. Meter	10. Temperature	15. Mantle

Imaginary Research Algorithm

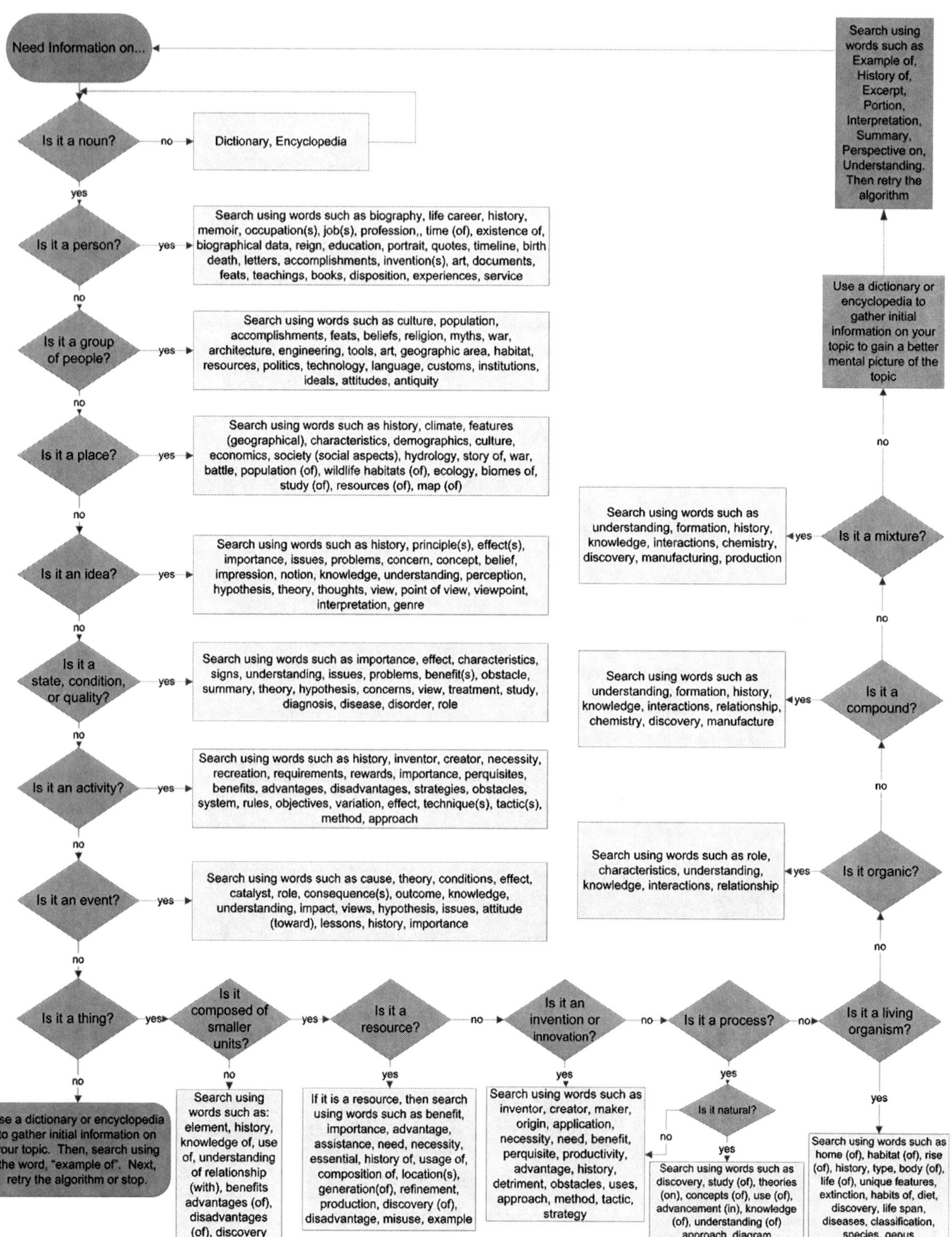

Day 20

For each research term, identify the research category based on *The Imaginary Research Algorithm.* Next, defend your choice(s) with a sentence that reflects each choice.

For example:

Mirror: verb, idea, resource, invention or innovation

The sad songs mirror the listener's feelings.
(verb)(not noun)

The mirror was most likely inspired by water.
(idea)

The mirror is an important tool for barbers.
(resource)

The ancient Greeks usually receive credit for the creation of the modern mirror.
(invention or innovation)

Group 1	Group 2	Group 3
1. Bebop	6. Herophilus	11. Iridium
2. Photovoltaic Effect	7. Richter Scale	12. Observatory
3. Investment	8. Bicameral System	13. Dowry
4. CD	9. Populist	14. Enlightenment
5. Filibuster	10. Methane	15. Martin Van Buren

At this point and time, if you have completed each research term from day one to day twenty, then you have completed three hundred research terms. Some words you knew. Some words you might not have known. Creating sentences to prove and validate your selected decision points or categories may have seemed difficult at first. But, as you continue to work, think, and reflect on various research terms. Your research skills should become faster in conjunction with *The Imaginary Research Algorithm*.

Chapter

10

Congratulations. You have reached the final chapter. In this chapter, you will continue with the reflective exercises listed under Day 21 through Day 30. These exercises are designed to assist Imaginary Research Algorithm users with selecting decision points that relate to the research topic. Once an algorithm user excels at selecting decision points, then a user can focus their search to the appropriate topic within *The Imaginary Research Algorithm*. For instance, when you research the word "mirror". You can identify it as a verb, a past idea, an invention or innovation or a resource. Then, as a user, you can focus your research on the word "mirror" as a resource. From there, you can use key words from the Algorithm under the decision point for "Is it a Resource?". *The Imaginary Research Algorithm* was developed to stimulate the internal mental machinery when engaged in research. It is designed to be a performance support system that augments a users search skills through direction and cognition.

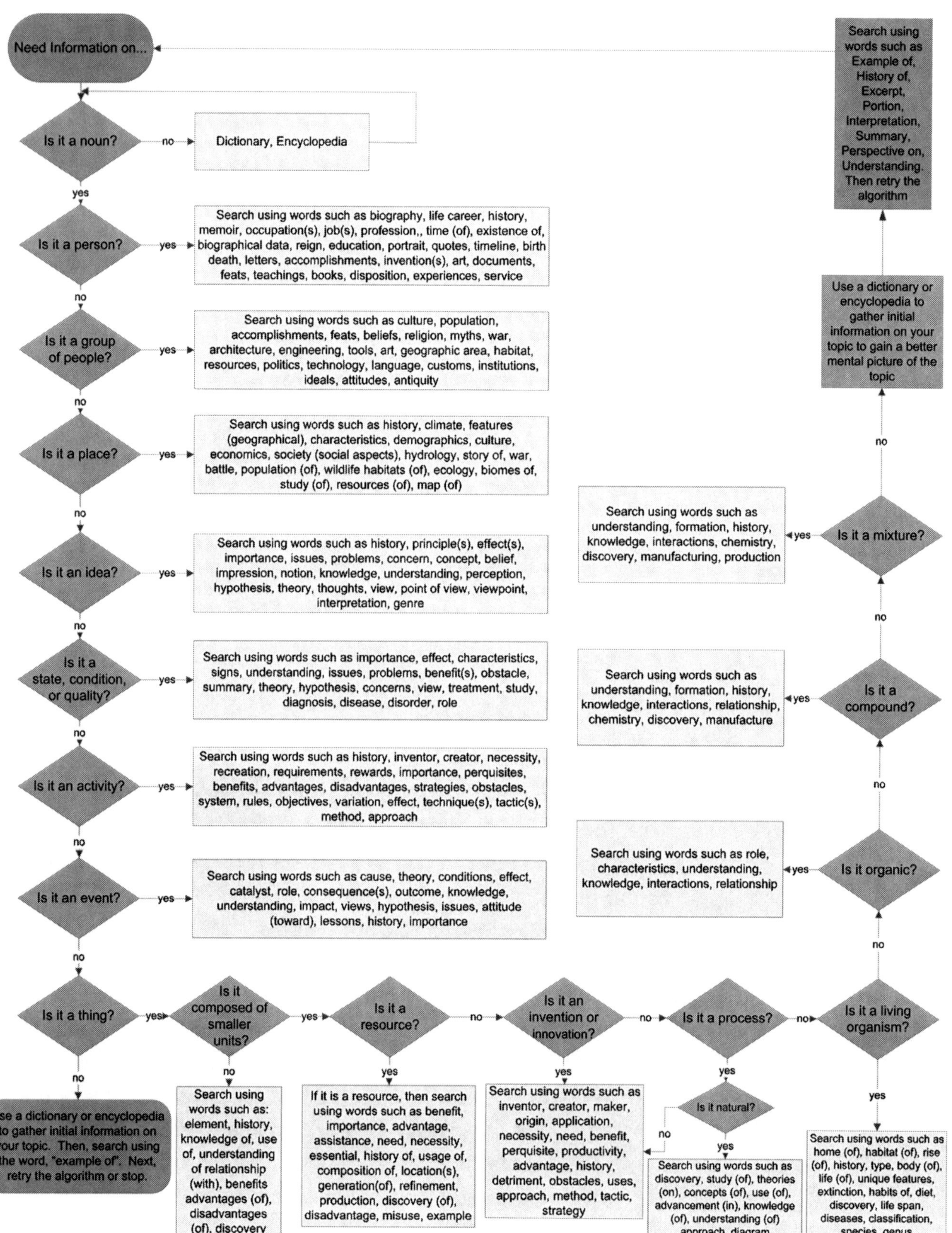

Need Information on...
Is it a noun?
no
Dictionary, Encyclopedia
yes
Is it a person?
yes
Search using words such as biography, life career, history, memoir, occupation(s), job(s), profession,, time (of), existence of, biographical data, reign, education, portrait, quotes, timeline, birth death, letters, accomplishments, invention(s), art, documents, feats, teachings, books, disposition, experiences, service
no
Is it a group of people?
yes
Search using words such as culture, population, accomplishments, feats, beliefs, religion, myths, war, architecture, engineering, tools, art, geographic area, habitat, resources, politics, technology, language, customs, institutions, ideals, attitudes, antiquity
no
Is it a place?
yes
Search using words such as history, climate, features (geographical), characteristics, demographics, culture, economics, society (social aspects), hydrology, story of, war, battle, population (of), wildlife habitats (of), ecology, biomes of, study (of), resources (of), map (of)
no
Is it an idea?
yes
Search using words such as history, principle(s), effect(s), importance, issues, problems, concern, concept, belief, impression, notion, knowledge, understanding, perception, hypothesis, theory, thoughts, view, point of view, viewpoint, interpretation, genre
no
Is it a state, condition, or quality?
yes
Search using words such as importance, effect, characteristics, signs, understanding, issues, problems, benefit(s), obstacle, summary, theory, hypothesis, concerns, view, treatment, study, diagnosis, disease, disorder, role
no
Is it an activity?
yes
Search using words such as history, inventor, creator, necessity, recreation, requirements, rewards, importance, perquisites, benefits, advantages, disadvantages, strategies, obstacles, system, rules, objectives, variation, effect, technique(s), tactic(s), method, approach
no
Is it an event?
yes
Search using words such as cause, theory, conditions, effect, catalyst, role, consequence(s), outcome, knowledge, understanding, impact, views, hypothesis, issues, attitude (toward), lessons, history, importance
no
Is it a thing?
yes
Is it composed of smaller units?
yes
Is it a resource?
no
Is it an invention or innovation?
no
Is it a process?
no
Is it a living organism?
no
Use a dictionary or encyclopedia to gather initial information on your topic. Then, search using the word, "example of". Next, retry the algorithm or stop.
no
Search using words such as: element, history, knowledge of, use of, understanding of relationship (with), benefits advantages (of), disadvantages (of), discovery
yes
If it is a resource, then search using words such as benefit, importance, advantage, assistance, need, necessity, essential, history of, usage of, composition of, location(s), generation(of), refinement, production, discovery (of), disadvantage, misuse, example
yes
Search using words such as inventor, creator, maker, origin, application, necessity, need, benefit, perquisite, productivity, advantage, history, detriment, obstacles, uses, approach, method, tactic, strategy
yes
Is it natural?
no
yes
Search using words such as discovery, study (of), theories (on), concepts (of), use (of), advancement (in), knowledge (of), understanding (of) approach, diagram
yes
Search using words such as home (of), habitat (of), rise (of), history, type, body (of), life (of), unique features, extinction, habits of, diet, discovery, life span, diseases, classification, species, genus
Is it organic?
yes
Search using words such as role, characteristics, understanding, knowledge, interactions, relationship
no
Is it a compound?
yes
Search using words such as understanding, formation, history, knowledge, interactions, relationship, chemistry, discovery, manufacture
no
Is it a mixture?
yes
Search using words such as understanding, formation, history, knowledge, interactions, chemistry, discovery, manufacturing, production
no
Use a dictionary or encyclopedia to gather initial information on your topic to gain a better mental picture of the topic
no
Search using words such as Example of, History of, Excerpt, Portion, Interpretation, Summary, Perspective on, Understanding. Then retry the algorithm

Day 21

For each research term, identify the research category based on *The Imaginary Research Algorithm*. Next, defend your choice(s) with a sentence that reflects each choice.

For example:

> Mirror: verb, idea, resource, invention or innovation
>
> The sad songs mirror the listener's feelings.
> (verb)(not noun)
>
> The mirror was most likely inspired by water.
> (idea)
>
> The mirror is an important tool for barbers.
> (resource)
>
> The ancient Greeks usually receive credit for the creation of the modern mirror.
> (invention or innovation)

Group 1	Group 2	Group 3
1. Singapore	6. Prokaryotes	11. Lobbying
2. Theodore Roosevelt	7. Nucleotides	12. Cash Flow
3. Caste	8. Coxey's Army	13. Ribose
4. Hemoglobin	9. Dolphin	14. Caravan
5. Blood Transfusion	10. Chicken Pox	15. Astronauts

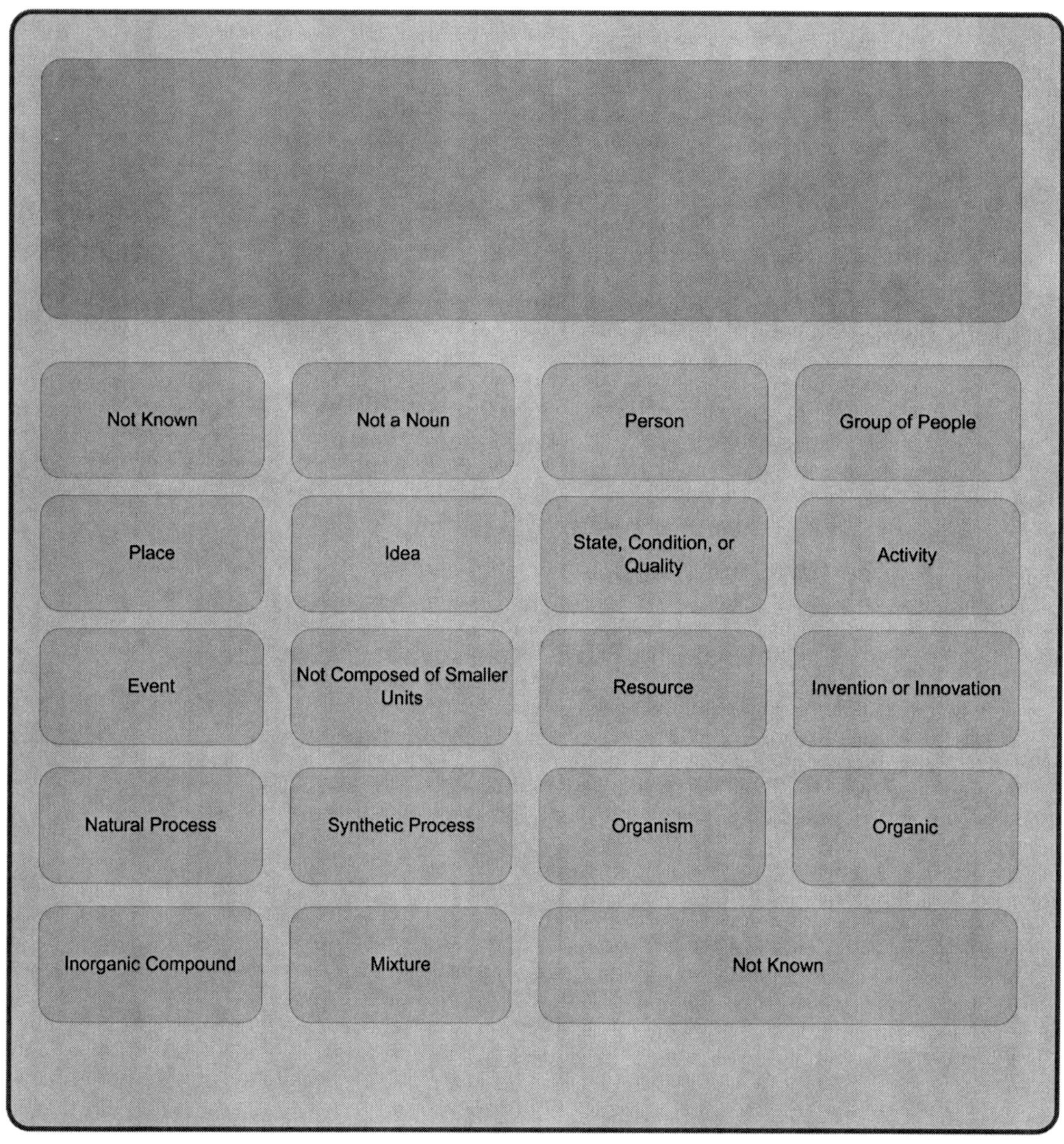

Not Known
Not a Noun
Person
Group of People
Place
Idea
State, Condition, or Quality
Activity
Event
Not Composed of Smaller Units
Resource
Invention or Innovation
Natural Process
Synthetic Process
Organism
Organic
Inorganic Compound
Mixture
Not Known

Day
22

For each research term, identify the research category based on *The Imaginary Research Algorithm.* Next, defend your choice(s) with a sentence that reflects each choice.

For example:

> Mirror: verb, idea, resource, invention or innovation
>
> The sad songs mirror the listener's feelings.
> (verb)(not noun)
>
> The mirror was most likely inspired by water.
> (idea)
>
> The mirror is an important tool for barbers.
> (resource)
>
> The ancient Greeks usually receive credit for the creation of the modern mirror.
> (invention or innovation)

Group 1	Group 2	Group 3
1. Space Shuttle	6. Nebula	11. Federalist
2. Solar Flare	7. Pueblo Indians	12. Hyksos
3. Aristocrat	8. Galapagos Island	13. Dioxin
4. Bureaucrat	9. Histamine	14. Tornado
5. Tariff	10. Chief	15. Cottonwood

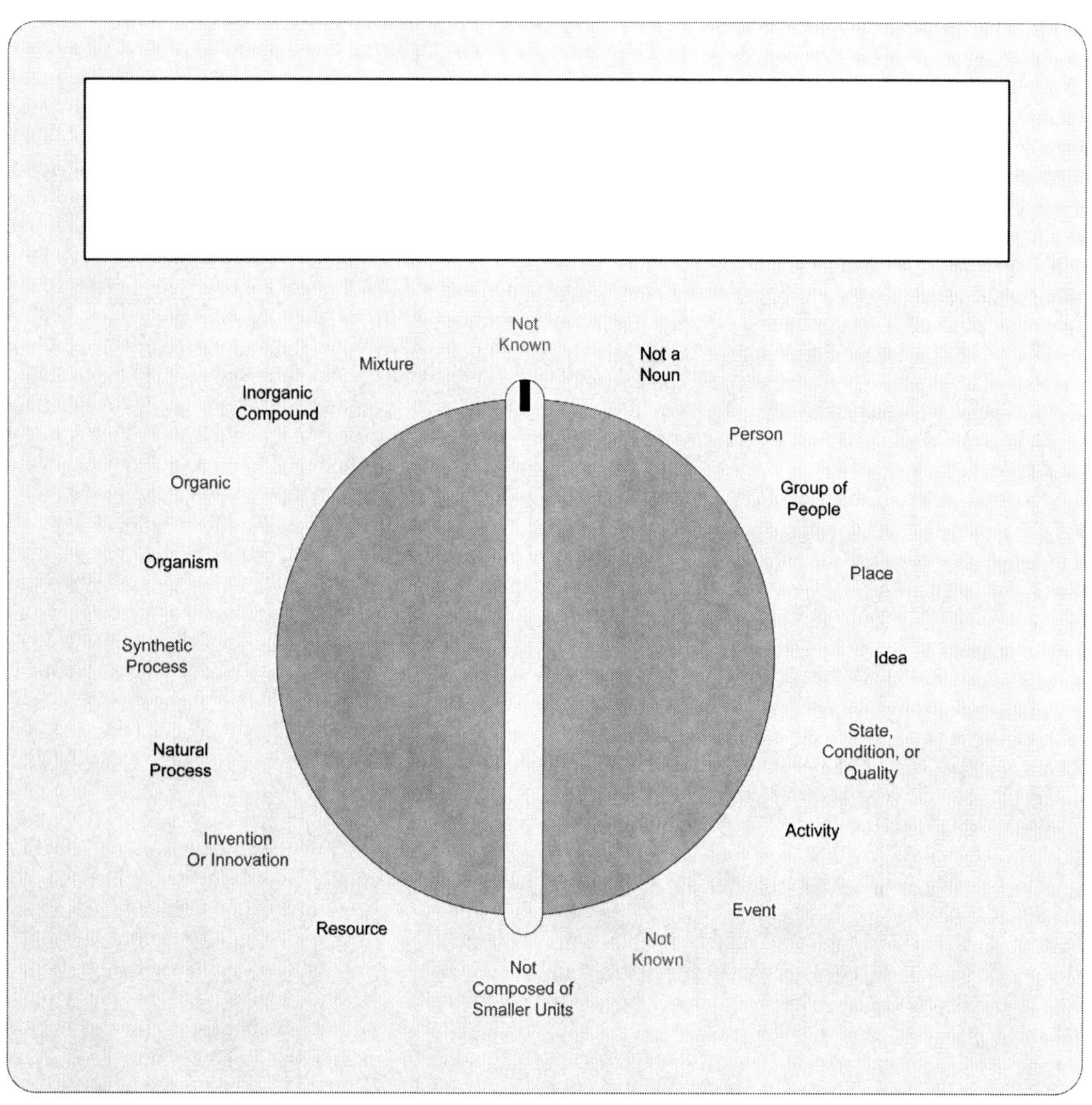

Not Known
Mixture
Not a Noun
Inorganic Compound
Person
Organic
Group of People
Organism
Place
Synthetic Process
Idea
State, Condition, or Quality
Natural Process
Activity
Invention Or Innovation
Event
Resource
Not Known
Not Composed of Smaller Units

Day 23

For each research term, identify the research category based on *The Imaginary Research Algorithm*. Next, defend your choice(s) with a sentence that reflects each choice.

For example:

Mirror: verb, idea, resource, invention or innovation

The sad songs mirror the listener's feelings. (verb)(not noun)

The mirror was most likely inspired by water. (idea)

The mirror is an important tool for barbers.(resource)

The ancient Greeks usually receive credit for the creation of the modern mirror. (invention or innovation)

Group 1	Group 2	Group 3
1. Cotton	6. Blood Pressure	11. Madeira
2. Database	7. Peasant's War	12. Sociologist
3. Salamander	8. Matterhorn	13. Mastodon
4. Nomad	9. Chameleon	14. Muse
5. Nomadism	10. Trilobite	15. Portuguese Language

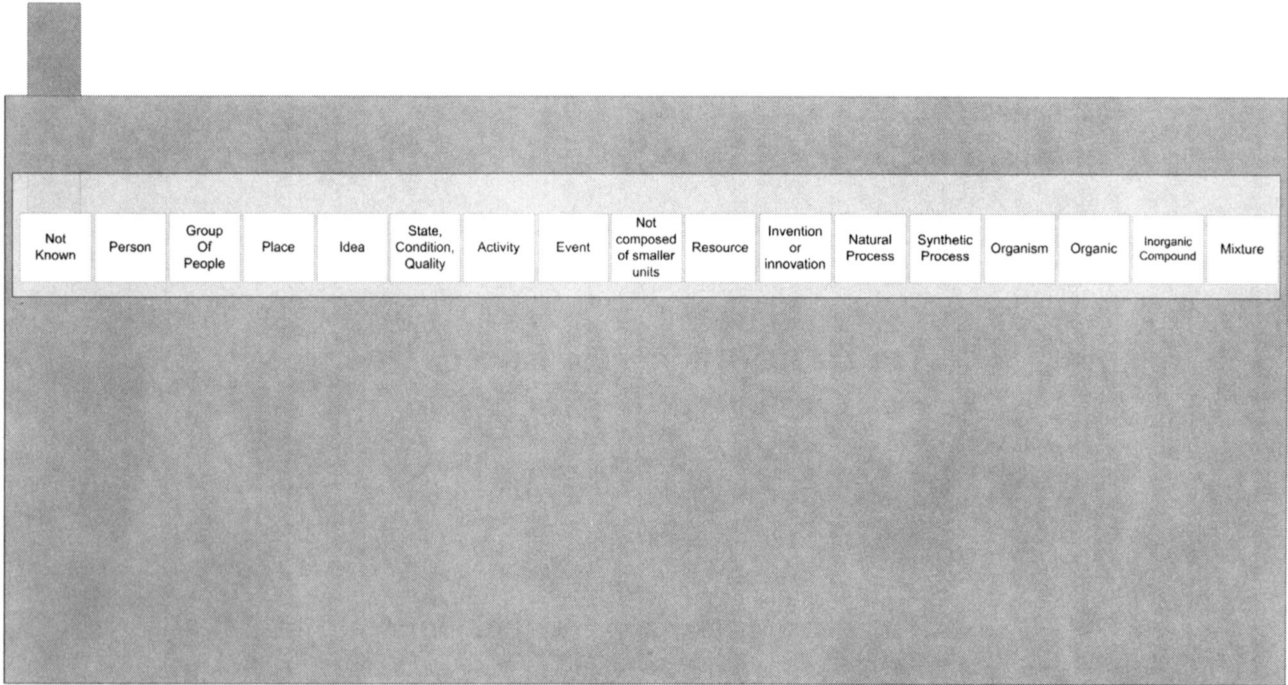

Not Known
Person
Group Of People
Place
Idea
State, Condition, Quality
Activity
Event
Not composed of smaller units
Resource
Invention or innovation
Natural Process
Synthetic Process
Organism
Organic
Inorganic Compound
Mixture

Day
24

For each research term, identify the research category based on *The Imaginary Research Algorithm*. Next, defend your choice(s) with a sentence that reflects each choice.
For example:

> Mirror: verb, idea, resource, invention or innovation

> The sad songs mirror the listener's feelings.
> (verb)(not noun)

> The mirror was most likely inspired by water.
> (idea)

> The mirror is an important tool for barbers.
> (resource)

> The ancient Greeks usually receive credit for the creation of the modern mirror.
> (invention or innovation)

Group 1	Group 2	Group 3
1. Slang	6. Gallic Wars	11. King Lear
2. Colloquialism	7. Alexander Hamilton	12. Insurance
3. New Orleans	8. Muckraker	13. Shoes
4. Ecology	9. Subsidy	14. Socks
5. Romance Languages	10. Hamlet	15. Sandals

Imaginary Research Algorithm

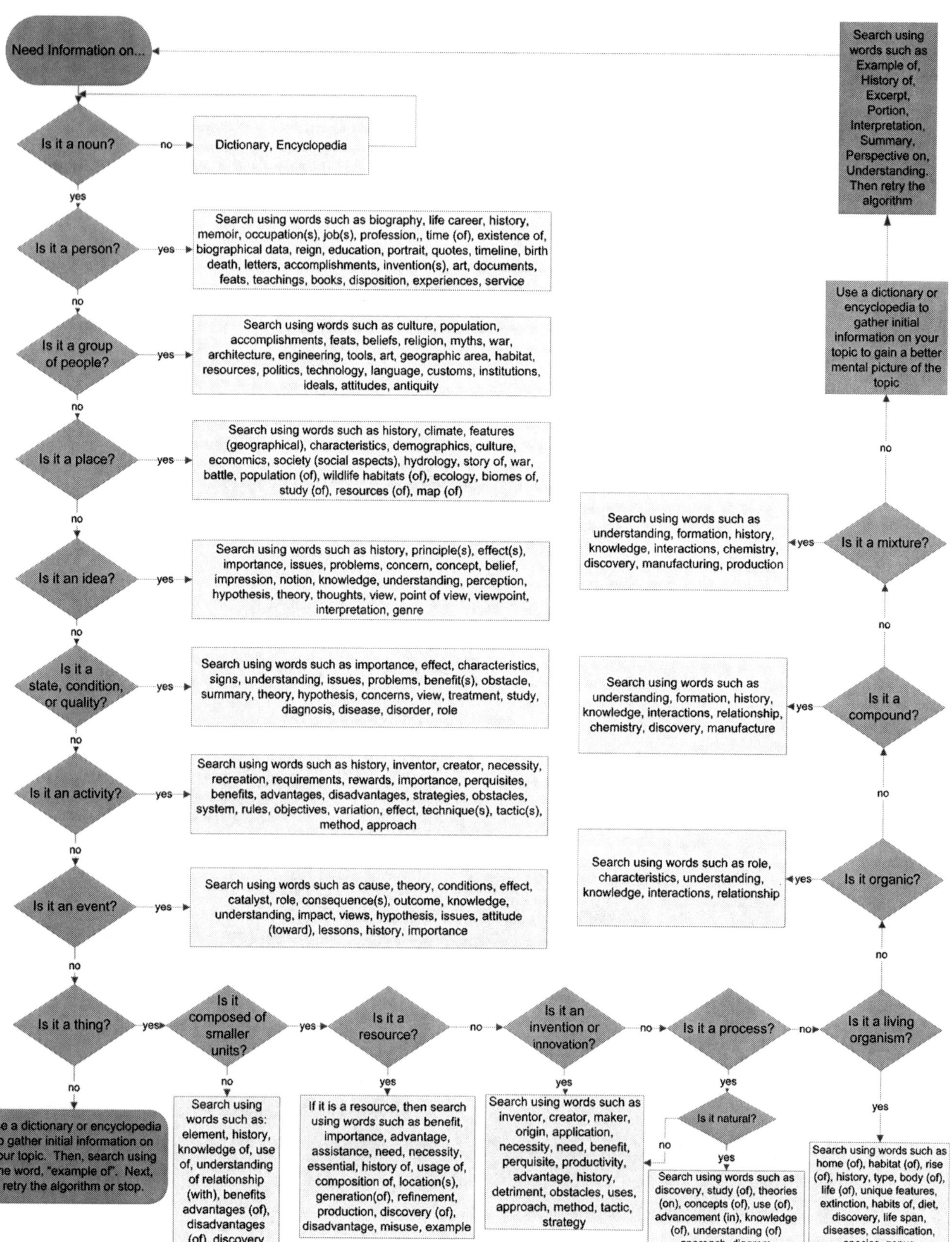

Day
25

For each research term, identify the research category based on *The Imaginary Research Algorithm*. Next, defend your choice(s) with a sentence that reflects each choice.

For example:

Mirror: verb, idea, resource, invention or innovation

The sad songs mirror the listener's feelings.
(verb)(not noun)

The mirror was most likely inspired by water.
(idea)

The mirror is an important tool for barbers.
(resource)

The ancient Greeks usually receive credit for the creation of the modern mirror.
(invention or innovation)

Group 1	Group 2	Group 3
1. Feather	6. Navajo	11. Costa Rica
2. Credit Union	7. Gnosticism	12. Running
3. Venom	8. Lumber	13. Captivate
4. Bowling	9. Montana	14. Cacophony
5. Canary Islands	10. Brazil	15. Adroit

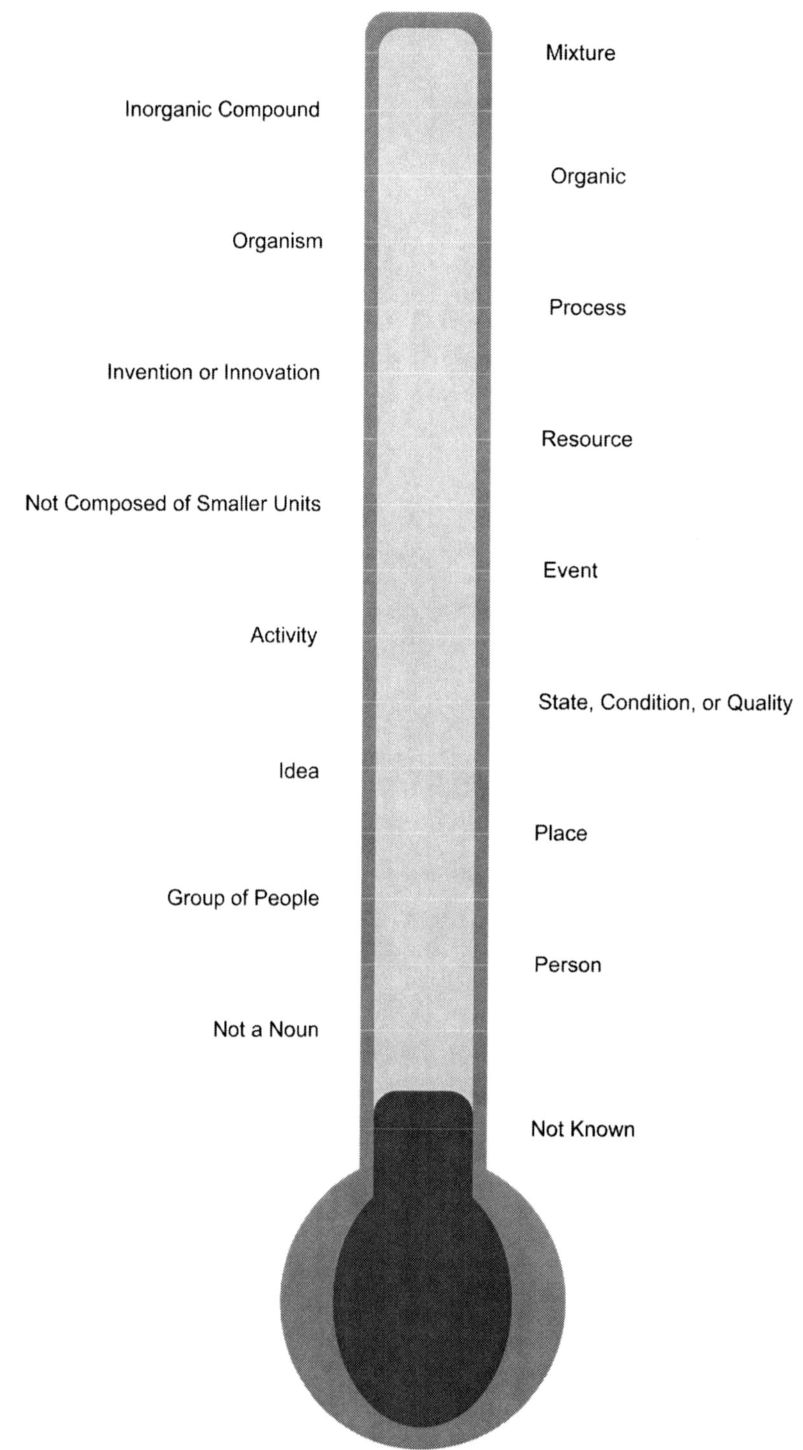

Mixture
Inorganic Compound
Organic
Organism
Process
Invention or Innovation
Resource
Not Composed of Smaller Units
Event
Activity
State, Condition, or Quality
Idea
Place
Group of People
Person
Not a Noun
Not Known

Day 26

For each research term, identify the research category based on *The Imaginary Research Algorithm*. Next, defend your choice(s) with a sentence that reflects each choice.

For example:

> Mirror: verb, idea, resource, invention or innovation

> The sad songs mirror the listener's feelings.
> (verb)(not noun)

> The mirror was most likely inspired by water.
> (idea)

> The mirror is an important tool for barbers.
> (resource)

> The ancient Greeks usually receive credit for the creation of the modern mirror.
> (invention or innovation)

Group 1	Group 2	Group 3
1. Ambidextrous	6. Demure	11. Elation
2. Gregarious	7. Clandestine	12. Embroil
3. Progressively	8. Brazen	13. Anthropomorphic
4. Viable	9. Apt	14. Indict
5. Lewis and Clark Expedition	10. Draconian	15. Grevious

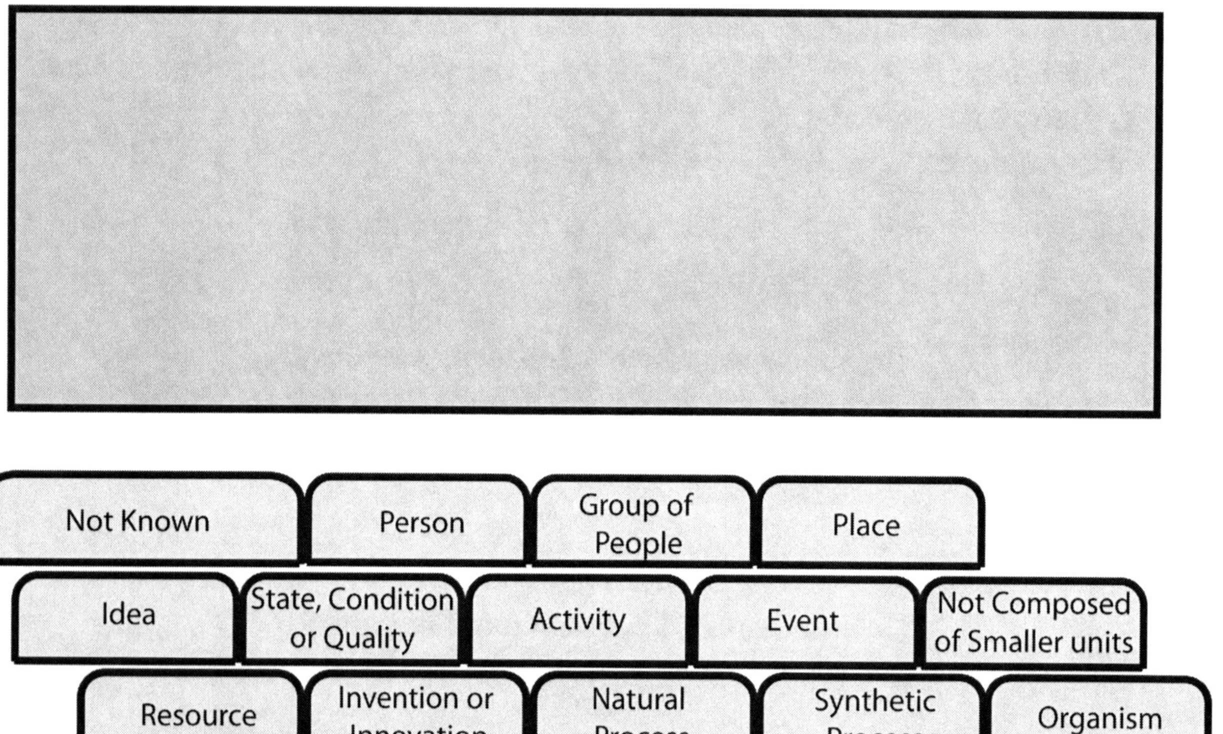

Not Known
Person
Group of People
Place
Idea
State, Condition or Quality
Activity
Event
Not Composed of Smaller units
Resource
Invention or Innovation
Natural Process
Synthetic Process
Organism
Organic
Inorganic Compound
Mixture
Not Known

Day
27

For each research term, identify the research category based on *The Imaginary Research Algorithm.* Next, defend your choice(s) with a sentence that reflects each choice.
For example:

> Mirror: verb, idea, resource, invention or innovation

> The sad songs mirror the listener's feelings.
> (verb)(not noun)

> The mirror was most likely inspired by water.
> (idea)

> The mirror is an important tool for barbers.
> (resource)

> The ancient Greeks usually receive credit for the creation of the modern mirror.
> (invention or innovation)

Group 1	Group 2	Group 3
1. Homage	6. Paranormal	11. Conjecture
2. Jargon	7. Sophomoric	12. Categorically
3. Livid	8. Vivacious	13. Caustic
4. Meticulous	9. Surmise	14. Duplicitous
5. Nullify	10. Replicate	15. Encroach

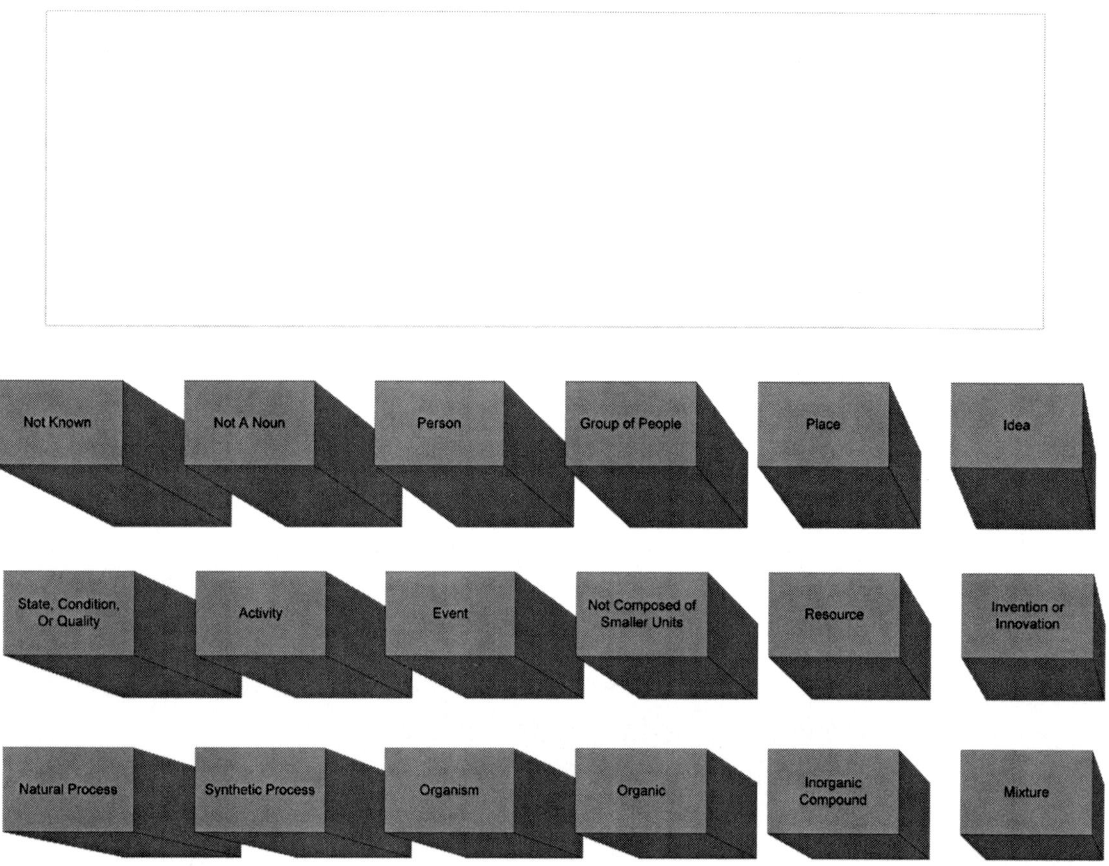
Not Known
Not A Noun
Person
Group of People
Place
Idea
State, Condition, Or Quality
Activity
Event
Not Composed of Smaller Units
Resource
Invention or Innovation
Natural Process
Synthetic Process
Organism
Organic
Inorganic Compound
Mixture

Day
28

For each research term, identify the research category based on *The Imaginary Research Algorithm*. Next, defend your choice(s) with a sentence that reflects each choice.

For example:

> Mirror: verb, idea, resource, invention or innovation

> The sad songs mirror the listener's feelings.
> (verb)(not noun)

> The mirror was most likely inspired by water.
> (idea)

> The mirror is an important tool for barbers.
> (resource)

> The ancient Greeks usually receive credit for the creation of the modern mirror.
> (invention or innovation)

Group 1	Group 2	Group 3
1. Erudite	6. Frugal	11. Ironic
2. Exhaustive	7. Hermetic	12. Machination
3. Extraneous	8. Hyperbole	13. Mercurial
4. Facetious	9. Idiosyncrasy	14. Myopic
5. Foible	10. Idyllic	15. Notorious

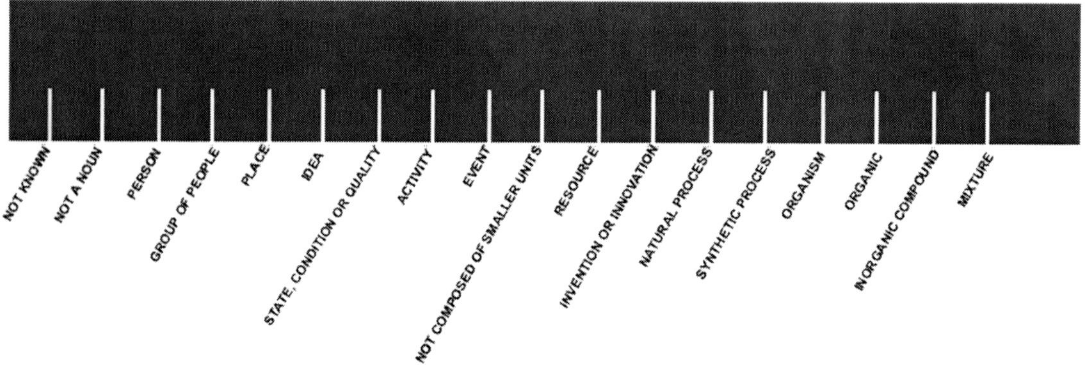

NOT KNOWN
NOT A NOUN
PERSON
GROUP OF PEOPLE
PLACE
IDEA
STATE, CONDITION OR QUALITY
ACTIVITY
EVENT
NOT COMPOSED OF SMALLER UNITS
RESOURCE
INVENTION OR INNOVATION
NATURAL PROCESS
SYNTHETIC PROCESS
ORGANISM
ORGANIC
INORGANIC COMPOUND
MIXTURE

Day 29

For each research term, identify the research category based on *The Imaginary Research Algorithm*. Next, defend your choice(s) with a sentence that reflects each choice.

For example:

> Mirror: verb, idea, resource, invention or innovation

> The sad songs mirror the listener's feelings.
> (verb)(not noun)

> The mirror was most likely inspired by water.
> (idea)

> The mirror is an important tool for barbers.
> (resource)

> The ancient Greeks usually receive credit for the creation of the modern mirror.
> (invention or innovation)

Group 1	Group 2	Group 3
1. Opulent	6. Inn	11. Of
2. Parsimonious	7. Grouse	12. Polar Bear
3. Pedantic	8. Explicit Knowledge	13. Free
4. Refute	9. Training	14. DVD
5. Tacit	10. Tetra	15. Ocelot

Imaginary Research Algorithm

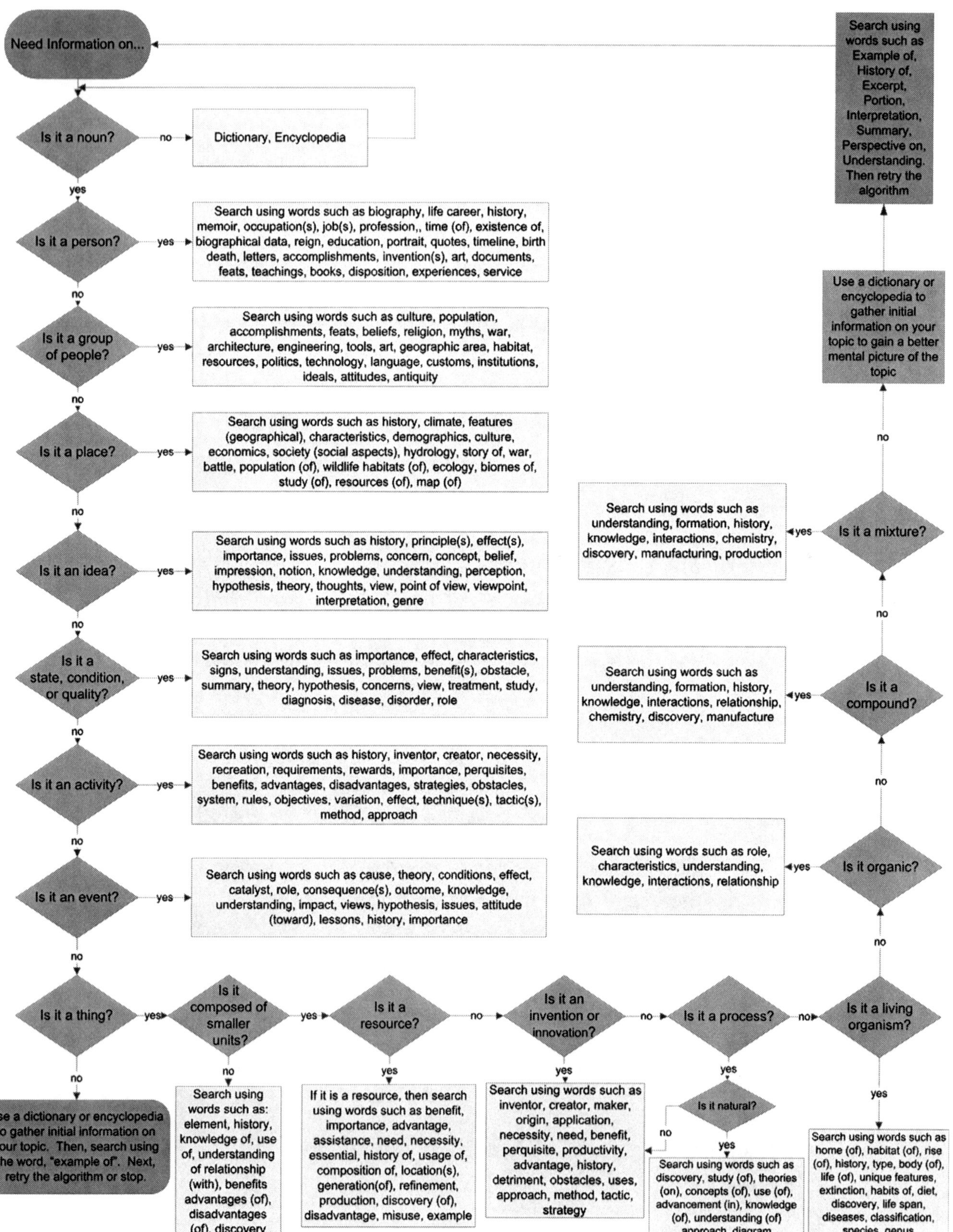

Day
30

For each research term, identify the research category based on *The Imaginary Research Algorithm*. Next, defend your choice(s) with a sentence that reflects each choice.

For example:

> Mirror: verb, idea, resource, invention or innovation

> The sad songs mirror the listener's feelings.
> (verb)(not noun)

> The mirror was most likely inspired by water.
> (idea)

> The mirror is an important tool for barbers.
> (resource)

> The ancient Greeks usually receive credit for
> the creation of the modern mirror.
> (invention or innovation)

Group 1	Group 2	Group 3
1. Espresso	6. Rendition	11. LaserDisc
2. In	7. LED (light emitting diodes)	12. Such
3. Planck	8. LCD	13. Anomoly
4. Volt	9. Out	14. Ubiquitous
5. Watt	10. Cellular Phone	15. Roman Numerals

The world has changed very quickly in the past two decades. Information is abundant through electronic databases and the Internet. With the abundance of data, tools are needed to balances the positives and negatives of searching for information through computer systems. *The Imaginary Research Algorithm* was designed to bring the "active thinking" component back to research in an age of passively receiving instant answers. It provides a stimulating kick-start to research assignments whether small or big. Users of the Algorithm are presented with options that require thought and focus throughout its use. Lastly, *The Imaginary Research Algorithm* provides great options for sifting through data at various electronic databases or websites. This concludes your training in *The Imaginary Research Algorithm*. There is a third tier of resourceful words that can be found in the appendix A. Furthermore, there is a software companion component of the Algorithm (not included) that is updated more regularly.

Appendix
A

The Extended Search Grid, also known as the "Third Tier", provides additional words that assist in the research process.

Imaginary Research Algorithm: Extended Search Grid (Person)		
First Tier	Second Tier	Third Tier
Person (Is it a Person?)	Biography	Biography: Autobiography, Profile, Life Story
	Life	Life: Vita, Life History, Existence
	Career	Career: Livelihood, Vocation, Line of Business
	History	History: Chronicle, Record, Depiction, Portrayal
	Memoir	Memoir: Journal, Log, Account
	Occupation(s)	Occupation(s): Work
	Job(s)	Job(s): Employment
	Profession	Profession: Line of Work
	Time (of)	Time: Period (of)
	Existence (of)	Existence: Presence
	Biographical Data	Biographical Data: life data,
	Education	Education: Learning Experience(s), Literacy
	Portrait	Portrait: Artistic Depiction, Artwork, Art, Sketch, Image, Paintings
	Quotes	Quotes: Quotation(s), Excerpt(s), Citation(s)
	Timeline	Timeline: Chronology, Time Table, Schedule, Calendar
	Birth	Birth: Conception
	Death	Death: Departed, Deceased, Execution, Assassination, Disease
	Letters	Letters: Dispatches, Memos, Correspondences, Communications, Notes
	Accomplishments	Accomplishments: Attainment(s), Achievement(s)

Imaginary Research Algorithm: Extended Search Grid (Person)		
First Tier	Second Tier	Third Tier
Person (Is it a Person?)	Military Career	Military Career: Military Decisions, Military Actions, Military History, Military Commands, Defeats, Successes, Offensive(s), Raid(s), Triumph(s)
	Invention	Inventions: Contraption, Creation, Device, Gadget, Gizmo, Instrument
	Reign	Reign: Rule, Commands, Decisions, Exploits, Feats, Success(es), Failure(s), Political Decisions, Political History, Political Actions
	Teachings	Teachings: Beliefs, Opinions, Theory, Instruction(s), Tutelage, Philosophy, Principles, Guidance, Knowledge, Wisdom, Idealogy
	Art	Art: Photography, Photo(s), sketch(es), Painting(s), Sculpture(s)
	Documents	Documents: Writings, Essays, Compilation, Treatise, Account(s), Manifesto, Article(s)
	Feats	Feats: Achievements
	Books	Books: Essays, Compilation, Treatise, Account(s), Manifesto, Dissertation, Manuscript, Tome, Anthology
	Disposition	Disposition: Nature, Character
	Experiences	Experiences: Life Experiences
	Service	Service: Assistance, Military

Imaginary Research Algorithm: Extended Search Grid (Group of People)		
First Tier	Second Tier	Third Tier
Group of People (Is it a Group of People?)	Culture	Culture: Traditions, Ethnicities, Social Aspect, Mores, Civilization
	Population	Population: Populace, Inhabitant(s), Denizen(s), resident, citizen
	Accomplishments	Accomplishments: Achievements
	Feats	Feats: Breakthrough(s), Achievements, Accomplishments, Capabilities, Abilities
	Beliefs	Beliefs: Tradition, Mores, Faith
	Religion	Religion: Belief(s), Belief System
	Myths	Myths: Mythology, Legend(s), Fable, Tale
	War	War: Fighting, Battles, Warfare, Combat, Conflict, Combatants, Hostilities, Weapons, Campaign
	Architecture	Architecture: Artistry, Craftsmanship, Building Technique(s), Construction Style
	Engineering	Engineering: Building, Construction, Creating,
	Tools	Tools: Hardware, Instrument, Device, Apparatus, Equipment, Relic
	Art	Art: Style, Drawings, Paintings, Sketches, Sculpture, illustrations, Culture, Relic(s)
	Geographic Area	Geographic Area: location, site, position, map, chart, atlas
	Habitat	Habitat: Environment, Territory, Zone, Surroundings, Ecosystem

Imaginary Research Algorithm: Extended Search Grid (Group of People)		
First Tier	Second Tier	Third Tier
Group of People (Is it a Group of People?)	Customs:	Customs: Convention, Tradition, Ritual, Rites, Ceremony, Institution
	Resources	Resources: Assets, Natural Assets, Source, Natural Resource, Non-renewable, Renewable
	Politics:	Politics: Policies, Rule, Government
	Technology:	Technology: Relics, Machinery, Tools, Equipment, Know-How
	Language:	Language: Speech, Talking, Communication, Tongue
	Institution	Institution: Tradition, Ritual, Custom, Rites, Convention
	Ideals	Ideals: Belief, Values, Morals
	Attitudes	Attitudes: Disposition, Beliefs
	Antiquity	Antiquity: Ancient History

Imaginary Research Algorithm: Extended Search Grid (Place)

First Tier	Second Tier	Third Tier
Place (Is it a Place?)	History	History: Chronicles, Annals
	Climate	Climate: Atmosphere, Environment
	Features (geographical)	Features: Attribute, Quality, Element, Facet, Aspect, Highlight(s)
	Characteristics	Characteristics: Attribute, Quality, Element, Facet, Aspect, Highlight(s)
	Demographics	Demographics: Statistics
	Culture(s)	Culture(s): Demographics, Statistics, Ethnicities
	Economics	Economics: Commerce, Trade, Business, Barter, Exchange, Market, Financials
	Society (social Aspects)	Society: Social Classes, Civilization, Culture, Social Order
	Hydrology	Hydrology: Water Issues, Land rights, Importance of Water
	Story (of)	Story (of): Lore, Oral Traditions, Legends
	War	War: Battle (of), Charge, Offensive, Skirmish, Crusade, Campaign, Combat
	Battle	Battle: Attack, War, Campaign, Skirmish, Crusade, Combat
	Population (of)	Population (of): Number of, Inhabitants, Estimates
	Wildlife Habitats (of)	Wildlife Habitats (of): Environment of, Territory
	Ecology	Ecology: Flora and Fauna
	Biomes (of)	Biomes (of): Type of Environment
	study (of)	Study (of): Examine, Report, Investigate, Research, Analyze, Survey
	Resources (of)	Resources (of): Natural Resources, deposits, arable land, rivers
	Map (of)	Map (of): Chart, Atlas

Imaginary Research Algorithm: Extended Search Grid (Idea)		
First Tier	Second Tier	Third Tier
Idea (Is it an idea?)	Problems	Problems: Dilemna, Crisis, Difficulty, Predicament, Quandry, Drawback, Setback, Hindrance, Challenge, Concern, Debate
	Principle(s)	Principle(s): Rule, Code, Standard, Model, Law
	Effect(s)	Effect(s): Result, Outcome, Consequence, Meaning
	Importance	Importance: Significance, Value, Worth, Magnitude
	Issues	Issues: Topic, Problem, Concern, Subject Matter, Question, Query
	History	History: Accounts, Primary Source, Records
	Concern	Concern: Issue, Problematic
	Concept	Concept: Abstact, Abstraction, Thought(s), Supposition, Notion, Inkling, Conception, Impression
	Belief	Belief: Hypothesis, Thought(s)
	Impression	Impression: Notion, Thought(s)
	Notion	Notion: Inkling, Abstraction
	Knowledge	Knowledge: Information, Data, Experience, Wisdom, Intelligence
	Understanding	Understanding: Comprehension, Insight, Discernment, Awareness, Grasp, Clarity
	Perception	Perception: Observation, Opinion, Keen
	Hypothesis	Hypothesis: Guess, Educated Guess, Premise, Assumption, Conjecture, Speculation, Presumption, Assumption
	Theory	Theory: Proposition, Philosophy
	Thoughts	Thoughts: Hypothesis, Theory
	View	View: Position, Stance
	Point of View	Point of View: Outlook
	Viewpoint	Viewpoint: Attitude, Way of Life
	Interpretation	Interpretation: Version, Understanding, Explanation, Analysis
	Genre	Genre: Variety, Type, Kind

Imaginary Research Algorithm: Extended Search Grid (State, Condition or Quality)		
First Tier	Second Tier	Third Tier
State, Condition, or Quality (Is it a state, Condition, or Quality?)	Importance	Importance: Substance, Nature, Weight, Meaning, Significance, Foundation, Cornerstone, Magnitude, Elements, Core, Components
	Effect	Effect: Consequence, Outcome, Result End Result, End Product
	Characteristics	Characteristics: Quality, Feature, Trait
	Signs	Signs: Signal(s), Warning, Signpost, Symptom, Indicator(s), Notice, Notification, Indication, Cause
	Understanding	Understanding: Comprehension, Insight, Realization, Judgement, Grasp
	Issues	Issues: Concern, Problems, Topic, Subject
	Problems	Problems: Conflicts, Clashes, Divergence, Variance, Discord, Controversy, Dispute(s), Detriment
	Benefits	Benefits: Advantage, Help, Assistance, Aid
	Obstacle	Obstacle: Conflict, Detriment
	Summary	Summary: Synopsis, Outline, Summation, Abridgement, Digest
	Theory	Theory: Proposition, Explanation, Postulation
	Hypothesis	Hypothesis: Educated Guess
	Concerns	Concerns: Matter, Trouble(s)
	View	View: Viewpoint, Point of View
	Treatment	Treatment: Therapy, Medication, Care, Remedy, Healing, Preventative Treatment
	Study	Study: Examine, Scrutize, Analyze, Learn, Investigate
	Diagnosis	Diagnosis: Analysis, Findings, Judgment, Conclusion, Identification
	Disease	Disease: Ailment, Illness, Sickness, Condition, Malady
	Disorder	Disorder: Illness
	Role	Role: Function, Position, Task

First Tier	Second Tier	Third Tier
Imaginary Research Algorithm: Extended Search Grid (Activity)		
First Tier	Second Tier	Third Tier
Activity (Is it an Activity?)	History	History: Chronicle, Accounts
	Inventor	Inventor: Designer, Maker
	Creator	Creator: Originator, Architect, Origins
	Necessity	Necessity: Need, Requirement, Essential(s), Requisite
	Recreation	Recreation: Pasttime, Hobby, Sport, Amusement, Play, Playtime
	Requirements	Requirements: Essentials, Needs, Conditions
	Rewards	Rewards: Bonus, Prize, Gift, Perks
	Importance	Importance: Significance, Meaning, Weight, Consequence
	Perquisites	Perquisities: Rewards, Benefits, Fringe Benefits
	Benefits	Benefits: Gains, Advantage, Profit, Help
	Advantages	Advantages: Benefit, Gain, Improvents, Favor, Strength, Fortunate, Goodwill
	Disadvantages	Disadvantages: Inconvenience, Difficulty, Weakness, Weaken State, Drawback, Nuisance, Misfortune
	Strategies	Strategies: Tactic, Approach, Plan, Strategem
	Obstacles	Obstacles: Hardships, Barriers, Impediments, Obstructions, Blockage
	System	System: Arrangement, Organization, Structure, Technique, Routine, Procedure, Usage, Method
	Rules	Rules: Instructions, Orders, Directives, Laws
	Objectives	Objectives: Purpose, Intention, Aim, Goal, Object (of), Aspiration
	Variation	Variation: Modifications, Amendments, Change, Revision, Upgrade, Downgrade
	Effect	Effect: Result, Outcome, Consequence
	Technique(s)	Technique(s): Performance, Procedure, Usage, Method, Practice
	Tactic(s)	Tactic(s): Approach, Manuever, Way

Imaginary Research Algorithm: Extended Search Grid (Activity)		
First Tier	Second Tier	Third Tier
Activity (Is it an Activity?)	Method	Method: Way, Process, Means, Matter, Routine
	Approach	Approach: Procedure, Style, Practice, Methodology

Imaginary Research Algorithm: Extended Search Grid (Event)		
First Tier	Second Tier	Third Tier
Event (Is it an event?)	Cause	Cause: Reason, Root, Source, Origins, Foundation, Basis
	Theory	Theory: Argument, Proposition, Premise
	Conditions	Conditions: Circumstances, Environment, Setting, Situation
	Effect	Effect: Outcome, Result, Consequence
	Catalyst	Catalyst: Means
	Role	Role: Function, Job, Task
	Consequences	Consequences: Effects
	Outcome	Outcome: Conclusion, Results
	Knowledge	Knowledge: Realization, Comprehension, Understanding, Awareness, Know-How
	Understanding	Understanding: Knowledge, Comprehension, Awareness
	Impact	Impact: Influence, Impression, Effects, Reprecussions
	Views	Views: Perspectives, Observation, Analysis
	Hypothesis	Hypothesis: Educated Guess
	Issues	Issues: Problem, Topic, Concern, Subject, Matter
	Attitude (toward)	Attitude (toward): View, Standpoint, Viewpoint, Approach, Outlook
	Lessons	Lessons: Warning, Message, Moral
	History	History: Accounts, Primary Sources, Records, Relics
	Importance	Importance: Substance, Nature, Weight, Meaning, Significance, Elements, Foundation

Imaginary Research Algorithm: Extended Search Grid (Not Composed of Smaller Units)		
First Tier	Second Tier	Third Tier
Not Composed of Smaller Units	Element	Element: Matter, Material
	History	History: Discovery, Usage, Records
	Knowledge of	Knowledge: Information, Data, Statistics, Facts, Figures
	Use of	Use of: Exercise, Apply, Employ, Utilize, Operate, Treat, Expend, Exhaust, Conserve, Waste, Handling, Treatment, Depletion, Make use of
	Understanding of	Understanding of: Grasp, Take in, Digest, Comprehension of, Figure out
	Relationship (with)	Relationship (with): Bond, Chemical Bond, Link(s), Connection
	Benefits	Benefits: Assist, Advantage, Help, Promote(s), Gain
	Advantages	Advantages: Improvents, strength
	Disadvantages (of)	Disadvantages (of): Deficient, Deficiency, Loss, Detriment(s), Weakness
	Discovery	Discovery: Detection, Uncover, Retrieve, Pinpoint, Ascertain, Breakthough

Imaginary Research Algorithm: Extended Search Grid (Resource)		
First Tier	Second Tier	Third Tier
Resource (Is it a Resource?)	Benefit	Benefit: Assist, Advantage, Help, Promotes, Gains
	Importance	Importance: Significance, Meaning, Weight, Consequence, Worth, Magnitude, Import, Finds, Discovery, Usage, Trade, Commerce, Industry, Agriculture
	Advantage	Advantage: Improvement, Strength, Trade, Commerce
	Assistance	Assistance: Backing, Support
	Need	Need: Requirement
	Necessity	Necessity: Prerequisite
	Essential	Essential: Need
	History of	History of: Records of, Accounts of, Story of
	Usage of	Usage of: Practice, Handling, Application of, Management of
	Composition of	Composition of: Arrangement, Organization, Constitution, Structure, Makeup
	Location(s)	Location(s): Site
	Generation (of)	Generation (of): Production, Creation, Making
	Refinement	Refinement: Refining, Alteration, Modification, Enhancement, Enrichment
	Production	Production: Assembly, Fabrication, Construction, Manufacture, Creation, Making
	Discovery (of)	Discovery: Detection, Breakthrough, Uncover, Pinpoint, Retrieve
	Disadvantage	Disadvantage: Weakness, Loss, Detriment, Detrimental, Deficient, Deficiency
	Misuse	Misuse: Exploit, Abuse, Mistreatment, Harm, Harmful
	Example	Example: Instance, Illustration, Case, Model

Imaginary Research Algorithm: Extended Search Grid (Invention or Innovation)		
First Tier	Second Tier	Third Tier
Invention or Innovation (Is it an invention or Innovation?)	Inventor	Inventor: Designer, Initiator
	Creator	Creator: Architect, Author
	Maker	Maker: Originator
	Origin	Origin: Originate
	Application	Application: Usage, Relevance, Function, Purpose, Concentration, Treatment
	Necessity	Necessity: Requirement, Essential
	Need	Need: Basic(s), Prerequisite, Requisite
	Benefit	Benefit: Promote, Advantage, Gain, Profit, Help, Positive Effects
	Perquisite	Perquisite: Benefit
	Productivity	Productivity: Efficiency
	Advantage	Advantage: Assist, Assistance, Promote, Gain, Help, Profit
	History	History: Chronicle, Story (of), Description, Record(s), Account(s)
	Detriment	Detriment: Damage, Disadvantage, Loss, Harm, Harmful Effects, Negative Effects
	Obstacles	Obstacles: Barrier(s), Impediment(s), Roadblocks, Difficulty, Problem(s), Complication(s)
	Uses	Uses: Operate, Work, Employ, Utilize, Exercise, Apply, Assist, Help, Treatment, Treat
	Approach	Approach: Method, Handling, Mode
	Method	Method: Technique, Methodology, Process, System, Means, Routine
	Tactic	Tactic: Strategy, Device, Way
	Strategy	Strategy: Strategem, Plan, Approach

Imaginary Research Algorithm: Extended Search Grid (Natural Process)		
First Tier	Second Tier	Third Tier
Natural Process (Is it a natural process?)	Discovery	Discovery: Finding, Breakthrough, Unearth, Detection, Sighting
	Study (of)	Study (of): Examine, Analyze, Analysis, Investigate, Research, Inspect, Inspection, Inquiry, Survey
	Theories (on)	Theories (on): Hypothesize, Theorize, Explanation(s) of, Speculations (on), Conception(s) of
	Use (of)	Use (of): Apply, Utilize, Operate, Treat, Operation, Treatment, Manipulate, Manage, Manipulation, Management, Waste, Application, Handling, Conservation, Conserve, Exploit, Imitate, Replicate, Model, Synthesize
	Advancement (in)	Advancement (in): Evolution, Progess, Progression, Improvement, Advantage, Acquisition (of)
	Knowledge (of)	Knowledge (of): Facts, Data, Information, Expertise
	Understanding (of)	Understanding (of): Know-How, Expertise, Comprehension (of), Awareness (of), Intelligence
	Approach	Approach: Method, Methodology, System, Technique
	Diagram	Diagram: Map, Chart, Table Graph, Illustration, Representation, Model(s), Depiction, Demonstration, Interpretation

Imaginary Research Algorithm: Extended Search Grid (Synthetic Process)		
First Tier	Second Tier	Third Tier
Synthetic Process (Is it a Synthetic Process?)	Inventor	Inventor: Designer, Initiator
	Creator	Creator: Architect, Author
	Maker	Maker: Originator
	Origin	Origin: Originate
	Application	Application: Usage, Relevance, Function, Purpose, Concentration, Treatment
	Necessity	Necessity: Requirement, Essential
	Need	Need: Basic(s), Prerequisite, Requisite
	Benefit	Benefit: Promote, Advantage, Gain, Profit, Help, Positive Effects
	Perquisite	Perquisite: Benefit
	Productivity	Productivity: Efficiency
	Advantage	Advantage: Assist, Assistance, Promote, Gain, Help, Profit
	History	History: Chronicle, Story (of), Description, Record(s), Account(s)
	Detriment	Detriment: Damage, Disadvantage, Loss, Harm, Harmful Effects, Negative Effects
	Obstacles	Obstacles: Barrier(s), Impediment(s), Roadblocks, Difficulty, Problem(s), Complication(s)
	Uses	Uses: Operate, Work, Employ, Utilize, Exercise, Apply, Assist, Help, Treatment, Treat
	Approach	Approach: Method, Handling, Mode
	Method	Method: Technique, Methodology, Process, System, Means, Routine
	Tactic	Tactic: Strategy, Device, Way
	Strategy	Strategy: Strategem, Plan, Approach

Imaginary Research Algorithm: Extended Search Grid (Organism)		
First Tier	Second Tier	Third Tier
Organism (Is it an Organism?)	Home (of)	Home (of): Territory, Locale, Environment
	Habitat (of)	Habitat: Territory, Locale, Environment
	Rise (of)	Rise (of) : Growth (of), Ascent (of), Evolution (of), Surge, Spread, Arrival (of)
	History	History: Fossils, Records, Fossil Records, Accounts
	Type	Type: Kind, Sort, Taxonomy
	Body (of)	Body (of): Figure, Anatomy
	Life (of)	Life (of): Existence (of), Animate, Endure
	Unique Features	Unique Features: Distinction, Different Characteristic(s), Differentiator(s), Distinctive, Distinguish
	Extinction	Extinction: Nonexistent, Dead, Defunct
	Habits of	Habits of: Nature (of), Behavior, Routine
	Diet of	Diet of: Food, Nutrition, Sustenance, Nourishment, Edibles
	Discovery	Discovery: Finding, Sighting, Uncovering, Unearthing
	Life Span	Life Span: Life
	Diseases	Diseases: Disorder, Ailment, Sickness, Syndrome, Symptom(s), Genetic Issues, Genetic Problems
	Classification	Classification: Grouping, Taxonomy, Category, Categorization, Arrangement
	Species	Species: Taxonomy, Type, Sort, Kind
	Genus	Genus: Taxonomy

Imaginary Research Algorithm: Extended Search Grid (Organic)		
First Tier	Second Tier	Third Tier
Organic (Is it Organic?)	Role	Role: Operation, Function, Job, Task, Part, Responsible, Responsibility
	Characteristics	Characteristics: Features, Attribute, Trait, Quality, Distinctive
	Understanding	Understanding: Statistics, Facts, Figures, Synthesis, Analysis
	Knowledge	Knowledge: Comprehension, Realization, Information, Data
	Interactions	Interactions: Interface, Relation, Communication
	Relationship	Relationship: Association, Bond, Correlation, Connection, Link

Imaginary Research Algorithm: Extended Search Grid (Inorganic Compound)		
First Tier	Second Tier	Third Tier
Inorganic Compound (Is it an Inorganic Compound?)	Understanding	Understanding: Statistics, Facts, Figures, Synthesis, Realization, Analysis
	Formation	Formation: Making, Production, Construction, Development
	History	History: Accounts, Records, History of Usage
	Knowledge	Knowledge: Realization, Comprehension, Information, Data
	Interactions	Interactions: Interface, Relations, Activity, Active, Inert
	Relationship	Relationship: Association, Bond, Correlation, Connection, Link
	Chemistry	Chemistry: Blend, Mix, Merge
	Discovery	Discovery: Finding, Detecting
	Manufacture	Manufacture: Produce, Create, Construct, Concoct, Make

Imaginary Research Algorithm: Extended Search Grid (Mixture)		
First Tier	Second Tier	Third Tier
Mixture (Is it a Mixture?)	Understanding	Understanding: Analysis, Synthesis, Statistics, Facts, Figures, Hypotheses, Theories
	Formation	Formation: Development, Making, Production
	History	History: Accounts, Records, History of Use
	Knowledge	Knowledge: Comprehension, Realization, Information, Data, Synthesis, Analysis
	Interactions	Interactions: Interface, Relationship, Activity
	Chemistry	Chemistry: Blend, Mix, Merge
	Discovery	Discovery: Finding, Detecting
	Manufacture	Manufacture: Assembly, Concoct, Construct, Create, Make, Prepare
	Production	Production: Construction, Fabrication, Creation

Imaginary Research Algorithm: Extended Search Grid (Unknown)		
First Tier	Second Tier	Third Tier
Unknown	Example of	Example of: Instance, Model, Illustration
	History of	History of: Account, Record
	Excerpt	Excerpt: Passage, Selection, Quotation
	Portion	Portion: Segment, Piece
	Interpretation	Interpretation: Version, Construal, Explanation, Perception
	Summary	Summary: Summation
	Perspective on	Perspective on: Theories, Paradigm
	Understanding	Understanding: Knowledge, Insight, Theories, Analysis

Appendix
B

Imaginary Research Algorithm Glossary

Person: is a human or individual such as Hannibal, Alexander Hamilton, Ghengis Khan and Thomas Edison.

Group of People: is a collective of people with some type of common feature, trait, skill, objective, history, language, or physical setting(geography) such as Aztecs, Phoenicians, nomads, oncologists or civil engineers.

Imaginary Research Algorithm Glossary

Place: is a location whether current, historical, imaginary or mythical such as Ireland, Valhalla, Sicily or a tropical island.

Idea: is mental imagery or thoughts expressed that may or not be possible at the time to be acted upon. Something hypothetical. Something theoretical. Or something possibly replicable. Donkey Kong(video game), airplanes, tricycle, trains, pretzels, heart surgery, and space travel to Mars are examples of ideas whether former or current.

State, Condition or Quality: is a temporary or permanent characteristic or characterization such as fear, mummification, sympathy, antipathy, flu, disgust, dystopia and Heart Disease. Extended Example: Jake had the flu. The fear of thunder overcame the toddlers at daycare.

Activity: is a set of actions like dancing, fencing, playing, exercise, experiment, cook and hunt. Extended Example: The Hunt proved to be dangerous for the young lion.

Event: is a relative amount of time in which something occurs such as an act or activities such as World War 2, evaporation, volcanic eruption, supernova and the first moon landing.

Imaginary Research Algorithm Glossary

Not Composed of Smaller Units: Atoms are the building blocks of matter. This statement is dedicated to Elements located on the Periodic Table such as Helium, Hydrogen and Sulfur. Also, include subatomic particles like electrons.

Resource: is a usable thing whether it is a physical object, component, theory, hypothesis, or intangible idea, fiction, or non-fiction, as long as it can be used in some form or fashion such as treatises, balloons, imaginary numbers, cough syrups, air conditioners and soaps.

Invention or Innovation: is an idea whether accidental, inspirational, direct or indirect put into physical form, usually. Innovation is an improvement on an invention or means of doing things. Scuba gear, peanut butter, lightning rods, light bulbs and binoculars.

Natural Process: is a set of activities or events that occur in nature with a different result. Rust(rusting), rain, hurricane season, thunder, lightning and hibernation are examples of natural processes.

Synthetic Process: is a man-made set of activities. Is a human-directed set of acts. Man harnesses the laws of science to create something such as products from distillation, hydroelectric power, tailoring, and cooking.

Imaginary Research Algorithm Glossary

Organism: is a simple or complex set of parts that allow it to reproduce in some form or fashion such as E. Coli, green algae, palm trees, cheetahs, lizards and rabbits.

Organic: is a component of an organism that cannot naturally survive on its own. Organic is a portion of the composition, system, organ, tissue, cell, or organelle that has a relationship with carbon. Of a biological relationship. Examples are the cerebellem, white blood cells, heart, pituitary gland, book lungs, ribosomes and amino acids.

Inorganic Compound: is a substance consisting of varying chemical elements, lacking carbon. Not organically composed. Examples are magnesium phosphate, nitrogen dioxide, Potassium Chlorate and cobalt chloride.

Mixture: is a collection of different elements that maintain their own properties such as soil, english language, salsa and italian salad dressing.

Not Known: are words that you do not know or cannot describe.

Not a noun: Any word that is not a noun such as pronouns, verbs, adjectives, adverbs, prepositions, conjunctions and interjections.

Breinigsville, PA USA
06 November 2010
248810BV00002B/1/P